YEHUDI MENUHIN MUSIC GUIDES

Voice

YEHUDI MENUHIN MUSIC GUIDES

Also available
Violin and Viola by Yehudi Menuhin and William Primrose
Piano by Louis Kentner
Clarinet by Jack Brymer
Oboe by Leon Goossens and Edwin Roxburgh
Percussion by James Holland
Musicology, a practical guide by Denis Stevens
Cello by William Pleeth
Flute by James Galway
Horn by Barry Tuckwell

YEHUDI MENUHIN MUSIC GUIDES

Voice

edited by Sir Keith Falkner

MACDONALD & CO
LONDON & SYDNEY

First published in Great Britain in 1983 by
Macdonald & Co (Publishers) Ltd
London & Sydney

Maxwell House
74 Worship Street
London EC2A 2EN

The author and publishers wish to thank Victor Gollancz Ltd. for permission to
reproduce Winifred Radford's translation of Fauré's *Les Berceaux* (from a poem
by Sully Prudhomme), and the Royal College of Music for use of the jacket
photographs and the four on pp. 279ff. Grateful acknowledgment is also due to
the following for permission to reproduce musical passages: Bessel and Co., for
'Komnata Tesnaya'; Boosey and Hawkes Music Publishers Ltd., for excerpts on
pp. 55, 254–62 and 'Árva Vagyok' (originally published by Editio Musica,
Budapest), and for 'Before Life and After' (from *Winter Words*, copyright 1954
by Boosey and Co. Ltd.); Eschig, Paris, for 'Asturiana'; Novello and Co. Ltd.,
for excerpts on pp. 58 (from Purcell's *15 Songs and Airs*) and 59 (extracts from
vocal scores by courtesy); and Schott and Co. Ltd., for 'Trommel'.

ISBN Cased 0 356 09098 1
      Limp 0 356 09099 X

Filmset, printed and bound in Great Britain by
Hazell Watson & Viney Ltd, Aylesbury, Bucks

Contents

Part Three

THE SINGER'S WORLD

Introduction
by Yehudi Menuhin

This is a lively and attractive volume, as varied and colourful in its tones as one might expect from the masters of the many techniques here discussed. I must add, however, that there is one form of singing which I should like to include and it is something I, as a violinist, find indispensable – the singing voice as used by the instrumentalist, string player, pianist or conductor as he contemplates, studies, rehearses and reflects upon the piece in hand.

Reared as I was from earliest infancy in my father's vast repertoire of Chassidic song and my mother's love of Russian folksong, the human voice has always remained for me the ultimate reference, the supreme musical expression. I was enamoured of sopranos from my youth – Elizabeth Rethberg was my first, Marian Anderson followed and there have been many more since. I can remember hearing my sister Hephzibah always singing 'my' violin part as she practised sonatas at home. Hephzibah too lost her heart to several Italian tenors and I can recall among the first, a golden-voiced, never-glimpsed Neapolitan singing 'Guarda il mare, come e bello' on a record she owned in her early teens when we were living near Paris; and then there was Ezio Pinza, who often came to dinner in New York in the thirties.

We should remember that numerous conductors sing as they take the orchestra through its paces. Toscanini can be heard doing so on various recordings. I myself find, conducting in rehearsal, that the surest way of conveying my intention to my colleagues is to sing it and when I teach it is a totally natural impulse.

The singing voice has always remained the very source of musical expression and the 'shaping of a phrase' is impossible to achieve in its fullness unless one hears it not from the keyboard or the bowed string but silently in the heart's mind as song.

This is something which I feel the gypsies have always understood in their music and their violinists emulate the passionate, nostalgic voices of birds and other animals, employing incredible glissandi, often interrupted in the fashion of the Italian tenor's 'sanglot'; often with tremolandi in both hands (that is bowed and fingered).

It is imperative that player begin as listener. So many of our musical manipulators play as though they were deaf and watched some metronomic pendulum. Let them close their eyes and sing, count, listen. Traditionally the person most deeply attuned to the vital history and beliefs of tribe was the blind musician. Today the role is in danger of being taken over by the deaf.

I congratulate Sir Keith Falkner on his illuminating contributions to this book and thank most warmly all the distinguished contributors who provide us with insights into their very personal experiences and convictions.

May the human voice continue to stir us whether in the Negro spiritual, the operatic aria or the folksong. It is our defence against mechanical repetition, against the mindless, inhuman noise barrage, against electronic imitation and the ruthless, insensitive staccato of the machine gun. In the song may be heard suffering and joy transmuted, a living record of our humanity.

Editor's Preface

When Yehudi Menuhin invited me to collect and edit a number of texts from eminent singers and musicians to help young singers, I accepted with enthusiasm. The field is of course so vast – solo, choral, classical, folksong, opera, *Lieder* – that it would need a small library to cover it comprehensively. Yet I was convinced that a number of articles about different aspects of singing would not only be of value to teacher and pupil but would also interest the general reader.

This book is not a history of song, not a textbook on the physiology of the voice, least of all a singing 'method'. It is a symposium, an anthology compiled by artists I have long admired. I chose my contributors from those I knew from personal experience to be outstanding in their own branch of vocal music. Some of their articles are instructional, all are practical and all reflect professional experience and advice; the empirical knowledge of a score of world-famous singers and musicians. They don't always agree. How dull life would be if they did.

To encompass so wide a field within the narrow limits of a single volume raised a problem of priorities. The reader will therefore find much more about the art song, about the *Lied*, *mélodie*, *romans* and *canción*, than about opera – a comprehensive article on German *Lieder*, for instance, and nothing about the operas of Mozart and Wagner. Opera training is the field of the mature singer and a matter for special consideration between teacher and pupil. Not that opera has been disregarded – no one would invite Tito Gobbi and Thomas Allen to contribute to a book with nothing about opera in it.

I wish to thank Richard Tilney for his advice in the early stages of this book, Hugh Young for his expert help in revision, and above all my wife for her infinite patience and encouragement.

This book is designed to interest both those who sing for fun and those who wish to make singing their profession. (They may still find it fun.) The voice is the finest instrument of music in existence. Each one is unique in sound and quality. To sing alone or with others can give emotional and physical satisfaction and it is the healthiest of occupations or hobbies.

POINT

I have a song to sing, O! _____

ELSIE

Sing me your song, O! _____

Part One

The Singer and the Voice

*'The oldest, truest, most beautiful organ
of music is the human voice.'*

(Richard Wagner)

One
Ancestral Voices

Records of singing go back to the dawn of history. The Bible tells us that Moses and the children of Israel sang to the Lord when they saw their Egyptian pursuers drowned in the Red Sea (Exodus xv, 1), and that, scholars believe, was probably in the thirteenth century BC. By the time of King David singing was an established part of Jewish worship; some at least of the Psalms can be reliably dated from the tenth century BC.

Accounts of singing among the ancient Greeks are nearly as old. Music, both sung and instrumental, was an essential factor in Greek culture, bound up closely with the worship of the gods. Homer, whose epics are reckoned to date from the eighth century BC, speaks in the *Odyssey* (Book VIII, lines 72–100) of the 'tuneful bard' – 'Then came the muse, and roused the bard to sing' (Cowper's translation). Aeschylus describes how the Persians heard the Greeks singing in their ships before the battle of Salamis (480 BC). By the fourth century BC a class of professional singers was well established; Plato (427–347 BC) deplored the 'disorderly tastes of the professional musicians' and Aristotle (384–322 BC) wrote that in earlier days songs were sung by citizens (i.e. by amateurs) and warned students not to aspire to the standards practised in contests between professionals – 'those wonderful and elaborate performances which have now entered the competitions'.

Greek music was monophonic – without harmony or counterpoint – and was improvised by the singer, the melody and rhythm being shaped by the words of the poetry. Donald Jay Grout (*A History of Western Music*) speaks of the 'Greek idea of music as essentially one with the spoken word' – something that we still find further east, for if a Persian or a Pakistani offers to read you one of his poems, he will not recite it but sing or chant it. (The concept has persisted in the west, too. In his essay on folk song (Chapter 14) Douglas Kennedy writes of English folk singers who would say: 'I'll tell you a song but I won't sing it to you.')

Clearly there was more to Greek song than mere declamation, for Dionysius of Halicarnassus in the first century BC laid it down that 'music . . . insists that the words should be subordinate to the tune and not the tune to the words'. He tells us something else, too, about the music of ancient Greece: that the professional musicians were as ready to show off their vocal virtuosity as were the Italians in the heyday of *bel canto*, and that that virtuosity was not easily achieved. 'No rules can suffice,' he wrote, 'to make experts of those who are determined to dispense with study and practice. Only those who are prepared to undergo toil and hardship can decide whether such rules are trivial and useless or worthy of serious consideration.' Little is known of technical standards or of training methods. Something was evidently known about voice production in the Roman Empire, where Dionysius lived and worked, for the orator Quintilian (35–100 AD) wrote: 'The singer mellows all sounds, even the highest, by the modulation of his voice . . . we orators must not attempt to mellow our voice by coddling it.' However, technical facility was by then apparently in decline. Plutarch (46–120 AD) wrote that music had degenerated from its once high and noble estate, and '. . . our men of art . . . have brought into the theatre a sort of effeminate musical prattling, mere sound without substance'. (You can hear comparable things said about 'pop' singers today.) It did not mean that a beautiful voice was no longer enjoyed, but that vocal virtuosity was out of fashion. It was to remain so for a thousand years.

3

There is no reason to suppose that the practice of music was confined to the Greeks; indeed, it is fairly certain that much of their tradition came from further east. But Western European culture today stems from that of the Greeks, via the Romans – and, to the Romans, music was a Greek art. No trace remains of any pre-Roman Etruscan or Italian music, though it may well have existed; Etruscan carvings show that they had a form of horn as far back as the fifth century BC, but it was almost certainly used as a signal instrument and not for making music.

There was however one contemporary culture in which music, both vocal and instrumental, was of great importance, and that was the Jewish. We have a clear idea of what they sang at the services in their synagogues, though not of how they sang it. The psalms were sung in alternate verses, or half-verses, by a soloist and the congregation, or sometimes by two choruses in turn, and passages from the scriptures were chanted, certain set musical formulae being adapted to fit the texts. These usages were not only preserved in the synagogue services of the Jews but formed the model for the services of the first Christians. And it was through the Christian Church, almost exclusively, that western music was preserved and transmitted through the Dark Ages. Of secular music during the first millennium AD we know next to nothing; the Church discouraged music purely for entertainment.

There were none the less epoch-making developments in music during this first millennium, above all the introduction of a form of notation, beginning in the first part of the ninth century. But while musicologists can now reliably reconstruct some of the music that was sung, no one can tell us *how* it was sung. Isadore de Seville (570–636) wrote: 'The perfect voice is high, sweet and clear; it is high so as to be adequate in the upper range; it is clear so as to fill the ears amply; it is sweet so as to delight the spirits of the listeners.' Yet singers were not highly regarded: 'blind, ignorant beasts of habit', Boethius (475–524) called them, 'while the real musicians are the philosophers of music'.

(Even today other musicians are often condescending in their references to singers.)

The Middle Ages

In recent years scholars and performers have shown renewed interest in the mystery of medieval music. Thurston Dart in *Music of the Earlier Fifteenth Century* and Denis Stevens in his *History of Song* have in particular cleared the way for singers in the theory and practice of music of the Middle Ages, roughly between the years 900 and 1400. Problems of notation, pitch, time, speed have in the past often been guessed at, but both Dart and Stevens show that performance of much of the song literature can become a vital part of the repertoire.

There is no doubt that medieval listeners appreciated singing, for many wrote of good and bad qualities in no uncertain terms. Voice registers were recognized, chest, throat and head (see pp. 46–7), but much of vocal music handed down to us covers only an octave, occasionally a twelfth. However, singers began to decorate and embellish the vocal line – something that upset the conservative musicians and especially the Church, for it was felt that the 'discordant' descants that were being introduced disrupted the congregational nature of divine worship. Singers of the time, Thurston Dart tells us, 'like Chaucer's Prioress, seem to have adopted a strongly nasalized style of tone production, almost or wholly without vibrato'.

Of secular song before the Middle Ages we know little or nothing; not, to be sure, because there was none, but because it was not within the province of the monks who alone would have known how to write it down. The earliest recorded secular songs are those of the *Goliards* of the eleventh and twelfth centuries, peripatetic students and priests in lower orders. The texts of their songs were in Latin; but in twelfth and thirteenth-century France the *troubadours* in Provence and *trouvères* further north, many of them men of courtly standing, wrote in the vernacular,

5

composing music for their own verses and often, though not always, singing them themselves. Their art was emulated in Germany by the knightly *Minnesinger* and later by the more bourgeois *Meistersinger*, whose way of life is so brilliantly evoked in Wagner's opera; and in England and Scotland there were the minstrels and gleemen. These poet-composers travelled, composed and sang with lute or other instrument, and gave delight to many. Although there is a considerable corpus of their music available, much has been lost, since it was carried from ear to ear and not often written down. 'The appeal and personality of a fine solo voice,' writes Denis Stevens, 'was as great in those early centuries as at any other time and it is only when the songs are interpreted today by accomplished and sensitive artists that they take on some part of their former glory.'

The songs of the *troubadours* and *Minnesinger*, the songs of the gifted amateurs, were intended to be sung by a single voice, but in the churches, the sphere of the professional musicians, composed music was gradually replacing improvised, and with composition came polyphony.

The Renaissance

By the fourteenth century virtually all composed music was polyphonic, though still built commonly on plainchant and other traditional material, including popular songs. Nor was this polyphonic music confined to the churches. The oldest known six-part composition is the famous round 'Sumer is icumen in' (probably *c*. 1240). It had alternative words for singing in church, in Latin, and this was a common practice; the motets developed in Paris in the thirteenth century often used different words for different parts, and by playing the appropriate – or rather the inappropriate – parts on a lute or vielle they could be performed either as sacred or as secular works. Throughout the Middle Ages compositions grew in complexity, music was more and more subject to orders and principles; and then, with the Renaissance, the arts generally began to emerge from the prevailing obscurity.

Composers broke away from polyphony and developed greater freedom of expression through harmonic structure and solo singing with instruments. Baldassare Castiglione expressed the new idea in *Il Cortegiano* (1528, translated into English in 1561): 'Singing to the lute with the ditty, methink, is more pleasant than the rest, for it addeth to the words such a grace and strength that it is a great wonder.' In 1536 the first printed book of songs was published, with lute tablature, by a Spanish lutenist, Don Luis Milan, and in 1571 the first solo songs in English with string accompaniment appeared in *Songs of 3, 4 and 5 Voices* by Thomas Whythorne (1528–90).

Thus began the era of the 'English ayre', a song with choral or string accompaniment. The greatest of this galaxy of English song writers was John Dowland (1563–1626). Not only was he the finest lutenist of his time but, as Peter Warlock tells us, 'he chose for musical setting some of the most perfect lyrics that have ever been written in the English language . . . No one has left us a musical legacy of more intrinsic loveliness than John Dowland.' No one who has sung 'In darkness let me dwell', 'Shall I sue?', 'Lachrymae', 'Come away sweet love', 'Can she excuse my wrongs' can ever forget the joy and satisfaction in performance.

It is probable that Vincenzo Galilei (1520–91), father of the great astronomer, was the first to compose in the new style of dramatic recitative which was believed to be a renewal of the musical practice of the ancient Greeks. Galilei was one of the founders of the Florence Camerata, a group of composers, artists and poets in the late sixteenth century who wished to promote the 'new music'. In 1656 Blount was able to write: 'In Italy . . . opera . . . is not acted after the vulgar manner but performed by voyces in that way which the Italians term recitative, being likewise adorned with scenes by perspective and extraordinary advantages by musick.' As a result of the development of opera and oratorio, primarily in Italy, it became necessary to make a more scientific study of voice production to produce greater sonority, range and richness of tone.

The Baroque

The new style led in time to vocal pyrotechnics and displays of virtuosity which became more popular than the music itself. Voice training developed widely and certainly was at its most brilliant by the eighteenth century. The brilliance came chiefly from the *musici* (castrated singers), for it was discovered that such voices could in maturity develop tremendous intensity and agility. Farinelli (born Carlo Broschi (1705–82)) was probably the greatest of them all. 'His voice was heard,' we learn from Anthony N. G. Richards in *Ye Sette of Odd Volumes*, No. CVI, 'soft sometimes with the penetrating softness of running water, sometimes swelling into the irresistible volume and commanding tone of a trumpet, sometimes pouring out in endless cascades of notes delivered with unimaginable rapidity and ease, sometimes gently flowing in a quiet tune and always filling every corner of the room.'

Female voices were not in universal use in public until the decline of the *castrati* and annulment of the ecclesiastical law which forbade women to sing in church. Casanova in his memoirs tells of a female soprano, Theresa, who impersonated the *castrato* Bellino when he died and became famous throughout Europe as 'castrato-prima donna'. In Cesti's opera *Il pomo d'oro* (1667), D. J. Grout tells us, 'all parts were sung by men, with the quaint consequence that some of the male characters in the opera have higher voices than the female ones; a situation not uncommon in Italian seventeenth-century opera, even where there were women singers, for the composers favoured the woman's alto voice and commonly reserved the soprano roles for castrati.'

Virtuosity was all. Grout put it in a nutshell: 'The

importance of the aria was the glorification of the singer. The virtuoso singer was to the eighteenth century what the virtuoso pianist was to the nineteenth or the virtuoso conductor to the twentieth.' Methods of training were being published and P. F. Tosi's book, published in London in 1742 as *Observations on the Florid Song or Sentiments on the ancient and modern Singers*, explains the method of the Italian school and is rightly considered a classic.

During this period Henry Purcell (1659–95) and G. F. Handel (1685–1759) laid the foundations of fine English singing. Purcell was outstanding for his sensitive marriage of words and music. 'Music,' he wrote in the Prologue to his *History of Dioclesian*, 'is the exaltation of poetry.' If I had to choose four pieces that demonstrated Purcell's special virtues, they might be, for soprano, 'The Blessed Virgin's expostulation'; for contralto, 'Mad Bess'; for tenor, 'Sweeter than roses' and for bass, 'Ye twice ten hundred deities'. Handel's special brilliance lay in the emotional power inspired in his music by the text. Sir Charles Santley, the great English baritone who died in 1922, declared that training in the school of the Handel oratorio was the great reason why in England execution was much cleaner than in other places. Notable examples of Handel's particular talent for interpreting the emotion of the words he was setting are, from *Messiah*, 'I know that my Redeemer liveth', for soprano, and 'He was despised', for contralto; for tenor, 'Waft her, angels, to the skies' from *Jephtha*, and for bass, 'O ruddier than the cherry' from *Acis and Galatea*.

Romantic and post-Romantic

As humanitarian idealism spread in the nineteenth century, greater demand was made for dramatic tension, suspense and emotion in performance, and at the same time orchestral forces increased in number and potential power. Styles changed and vocal projection and stamina became more important. Both Beethoven (1770–1827) and Wagner

9

(1813–83) were accused of writing music impossible to sing. As ever, singers adapted technique to public demand. Agility and vocal display faded and lyrical and dramatic qualities took their place, so much so that when, in 1930, Sir Thomas Beecham asked me for my cadenza to 'The refiner's fire' aria in *Messiah* it caused mirth in the orchestra and consternation among the soloists. In fact, until very recent years, it was considered infra dig for a male singer to learn to trill.

Atonal and improvised music have asked further technical questions. Our young singers are answering them well. Older singers will feel for Sir Peter Pears when he says at the end of Chapter 13: 'If England is to become again a nest of singing birds, composers must fall in love again with the human voice', and I would add, 'return to seventeeth-century practice and learn to sing before they compose'.

Retrospect and prospect

It is clear that scientific knowledge of voice production was negligible until the nineteenth century, although much had been written down the ages about the anatomy of the voice. All had been by ear and imitation, and so, in the main, it is likely to continue. For although advances in medical research, notably the invention of the laryngoscope in 1854, have made it possible to observe the voice in action and recording and videotape help to correct technical faults, nothing can take the place of the teacher with a perfect ear, able to discern every quality and gradation of tone and placement.

We must for ever be thankful for the song schools in the religious communities before and after the Reformation, which provided the training for most professional musicians in Europe. Indeed, many of the seventeenth- and eighteenth-century composers – Purcell, Bach and Haydn among them – were trained as singers. There are still 35 choir schools in England providing excellent basic training for singers and instrumentalists. Several contributors to this book owe much to their early training therein. New College, Oxford, with its Choir School, celebrated its six hundredth anniversary in 1979. In addition to some twenty choristers there were at the school in that year 48 pianists, three organists, 37 string players, 41 woodwind, ten brass and three percussionists. Enough said.

Is training necessary? Many people believe that singing is a natural gift which needs little or no training. That is true if one only wants to sing at football matches. If one has the gift of a good voice it should surely be used to the best of one's ability. Norman Morris wrote in *The Guardian* (31 October 1963): 'It is nonsense to say that only the specially gifted should take music at school. Music is a discipline and cannot be taught any faster than any other language. Above all it is the discipline of learning to sing and play that makes the musician. Unfortunately there are far too many so-called musicians today whose discipline has been listening to music instead of making it.'

Too many students, like the world at large, demand bigger and quicker results. Too few are prepared to make haste slowly, and too often flit from teacher to teacher and attend so-called 'master classes' in the hope of finding a short cut to success. When I was at Cornell University, twenty odd years ago, a student called me one day to say: 'Prof, I'd like to take some of that vocal tuition of yours.' I noticed that as he entered the studio the rest of my class eyed him with admiration, almost with adoration; one whispered in my ear: 'Don't you know, he's in the top ten. He made over a hundred thousand bucks last year.' I was suitably impressed. When we were alone he told me that he wanted some of my 'vocal tuition' because his agent had told him that his next records must be more lyrical. 'Professor, can you teach me to sing more lyrical?' he said. I heard him yodel and sing a few bars without any idea of quality or control and was tempted to ask him if *he* would teach *me* how to earn $100,000 a year.

The Singer and the Voice

The great improvement in recording and television technique has been a boon to the general public and to music lovers. Yet it has robbed the human voice of much of its *natural* appeal and extrovert or photogenic aspects often take precedence over quality and virtuosity. A singer must be heard live, without mechanical aids, if one is to judge the calibre of his or her art. Yesterday the public taste was in 'live' opera, oratorio and concert and it was sufficient for a singer to have a beautiful voice and a repertoire of a dozen oratorios, operas and songs. Today, prospects are good for the young professional who can walk into performances and recording sessions at short notice, able to read music in many contrasting styles, medieval, oratorio, atonal, church, improvisation and 'pop'.

Broadly speaking, the professional singer, as we understand the term today, has existed for some four hundred years. Success has depended largely on the ability to please the public, for Dr Johnson's remark two hundred years ago is still true:

'We that live to please must please to live.'

Keith Falkner

Two
The Physiology of the Voice

Ardeshir S. Khambata, F.R.C.S. Born in 1935 in Bombay, India. Music, particularly vocal operatic music, has played an important part in his whole life. He studied singing in London while training as a surgeon. He practises as a Consultant in Harley Street and at the Dartford Group of Hospitals, Kent. He specializes in Ear, Nose and Throat as applied to the Voice. Opera and good food remain his consuming passions. He collects recordings of great singers from the earliest days of the gramophone to the present day.

The human voice is essentially a wind instrument – arguably the most beautiful of all wind instruments. Like all such instruments it requires two main mechanisms to sound it, one to provide the breath that activates it – in the case of the voice, the 'respiratory bellows' – and the other actually to produce the sound, as it were the reeds – the 'vocal cords'.

Good singing is governed by correct breathing; it cannot exist without it. The bellows mechanism is constituted not only by the lungs and the diaphragm but also by the muscles of the abdominal wall and the back. The singer must be able to fill the lungs rapidly and then empty them at a steady, controlled rate under the influence of the diaphragm and the muscles of the abdominal wall.

The breath thus released produces a sound when it activates the vocal cords. If I may stay with my simile of a wind instrument, the vocal cords can be likened to the reeds, the larynx to the mouthpiece; the resonators within

13

the head are the tube and the mouth, perhaps, the bell. Before dealing with the vocal cords, let me first describe the larynx.

The larynx

The larynx is the 'voice box' that forms a direct link between the lungs and windpipe and the mouth and nose. It is composed of a set of cartilages connected by a series of membranes and ligaments. At the top it is suspended from the hyoid bone, the U-shaped bone at the base of the tongue, by a tough resilient membrane, the thyro-hyoid membrane, and the paired thyro-hyoid muscles. At its lower end, where it continues downwards to the windpipe, it is tethered to the bony structure of the chest by groups of flat, strap-like muscles. It is the smooth interaction of these 'extrinsic muscles', suspending and anchoring the larynx, that maintain it in its normal position and prevent it from rising undesirably upwards. The 'intrinsic muscles' of the larynx are those that move the cartilages relative to each other.

The principal cartilages of the larynx are the thyroid, which may be described as shield-like and which produces the prominence of the 'Adam's apple'; immediately below it the cricoid, shaped like a signet ring with its broad area forming the posterior arch, and sitting on this the paired arytenoid cartilages, pyramidal in shape. The vocal ligaments, which constitute the vocal cords, are attached at the back of the vocal process of the arytenoid cartilages, and the muscles that, as we shall see, move the vocal cords apart and together are attached to their laterally placed muscular process.

The vocal cords

The vocal cords, then, are ligaments within the larynx, attached at the back to the arytenoid cartilages and at the front to the thyroid cartilage; their outer edges are bound by the muscle that runs between these cartilages, but their inner margins are free. They consist in the main of a meshwork of elastic tissue covered by epithelium (a fine membrane) but they have a few muscle fibres, constituting the vocalis muscle, which help to tighten the front part of the ligament. They are flat bands, triangular in section and pearly white in colour – whiter in the female than in the male. Above each of them is the vestibular fold or 'false vocal cord', with a small sac, the ventricle, between the two folds.

Vocal cords

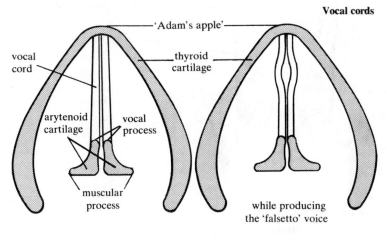

while producing the 'falsetto' voice

The average length of the vocal cord is from 17 mm to 25 mm in the male and from 12·5 mm to 17 mm in the female. The ratio of the length of the vocal cord to the diameter of the larynx from front to back is 1 to 1·5 in children, and remains unchanged in the female, but at puberty in the male it changes over a brief period to 1 to 1·3 as the vocal cords grow longer. This rapid change leads to a temporary loss of control of the voice, which tends to crack until it has completely broken and settled in its adult range, which may be as much as an octave lower. In the female, too, the inner edge is sharper, while in the male it is more rounded. It is these anatomical differences that govern the characteristic differences between the male and the female voice.

15

Unlike the reeds in other wind instruments, the vocal cords are mobile and alterable in shape. During breathing they lie flat against the sides of the larynx, the ventricles are closed and the false cords are withdrawn, so that air can pass freely through the larynx between the nasal passage and the lungs. During speech and singing the free margins of the vocal cords are moved towards each other

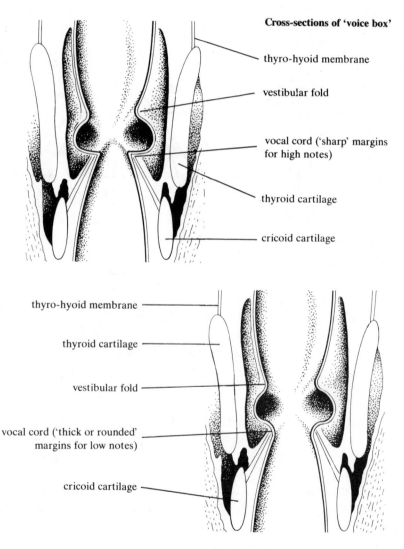

Cross-sections of 'voice box'

thyro-hyoid membrane

vestibular fold

vocal cord ('sharp' margins for high notes)

thyroid cartilage

cricoid cartilage

thyro-hyoid membrane

thyroid cartilage

vestibular fold

vocal cord ('thick or rounded' margins for low notes)

cricoid cartilage

until they nearly meet. The false cords also move outwards and the ventricles are filled with air, allowing the true vocal cords to vibrate freely. As the column of air is forced through the narrow elongated aperture between the vocal cords, the cords are made to vibrate. The vibration is particularly noticeable at their free inner margins. Studied in slow motion, with the aid of cineradiology, cinematography, stroboscopy etc., the free margins of the vocal cords are seen to roll upwards and outwards as they are forced apart by the stream of air. They can be seen to vibrate either along their whole length or in segments only, depending on the note being produced, and the vibrations have both a horizontal and a vertical component. The inner margins of the cords thus have an 'open phase' and a phase of 'closed contact', so that the air stream is cut up into a series of very rapid puffs – just as it is by the reed of a clarinet or oboe. The relative frequencies of these phases govern the pitch of the tone produced; the lower the tone, the longer the phase of closed contact. (See opposite.)

But these movements of the vocal cords do not result solely from the passage of breath between them. They are due also to rhythmic contraction and relaxation of the thyro-arytenoid muscles – the muscles that bind the outer edges of the vocal cords – independently of the air stream. These contractions cause the vocal cords to vibrate, the whole process being under cerebral control – initiated that is by the mind of the singer – and the breath is the agent that carries the sound. 'A high degree of self-vibration indicates the true singer; if this capacity is completely lacking, then there is . . . no singing voice' (Husler and Rodd-Marling, *Singing: the Physical Nature of the Vocal Organ*).

The loudness or volume of a tone depends largely on the pressure of the air under the vocal cords, called the 'subglottic pressure'; but it is also controlled by the contraction of the intrinsic tensor muscles of the larynx. This enables a well-schooled vocalist to sustain a note sung *forte* for as long as one sung *piano*.

Pitch

When the voice is producing its lowest tones the vocal cords are seen to be broad, with relatively low tension; the free edges are thickened and rounded and the whole length of the cords vibrates. As the pitch rises, a gradual lengthening of the vocal cord is observed and the vibrating edges become thinner and sharper. The lengthening and tension of the vocal cords is controlled by the thyro-arytenoid and crico-thyroid muscles. Increased subglottic pressure also tends to sharpen the pitch, something that can be corrected by a corresponding reduction in the tension of the cords. Nowhere is this more obvious than in the production of the *messa di voce*, the gradual *crescendo* and *diminuendo* on a held tone (see p. 64).

The amplitude of the vibrations diminishes as the pitch rises, and in the highest notes the arytenoid cartilages are held firmly together and only the membraneous part of the cords vibrates. In the production of the falsetto voice only the front segments of the cords appear to move.

The resonators

The sound produced in the larynx is by itself thin and weak; it is vastly modified by a series of resonators. More than anything else it is these resonators, and their skilful use by the singer, that govern the quality and timbre of the voice. The most important of them are the thoracic cavity and tracheo-bronchial tree; the pharynx, oral cavity and soft palate; the nose and the adjacent sinus cavities, the nasopharynx, the lips and the tongue. (See opposite.)

The capacity and shape of the pharynx can be altered by movements of the tongue and of the muscular walls of the pharynx itself. The natural tendency of the larynx to rise when singing up a scale and the contraction of the muscles of the soft palate and of those that form the posterior pillar of the fauces, all tend to reduce further the available size of the pharynx. The soft palate is naturally raised during

The main resonators

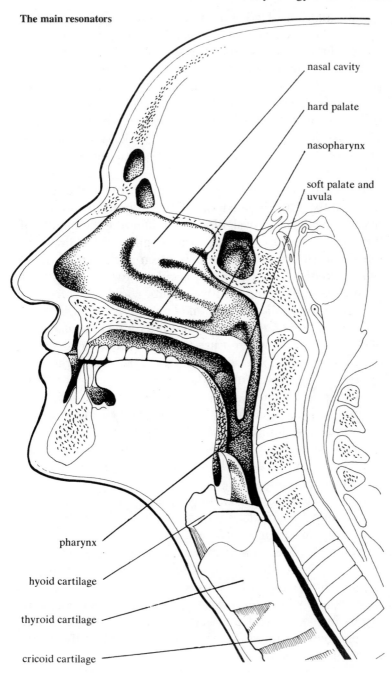

nasal cavity

hard palate

nasopharynx

soft palate and
uvula

pharynx

hyoid cartilage

thyroid cartilage

cricoid cartilage

the production of all pure vowel sounds; it can actually shut off the nasal cavity and nasopharynx. The nasal cavity is one of the main resonators in singing and must stay open and accessible to the larynx; consequently the correct positioning of the soft palate is of the greatest importance in singing. The characteristic sound of so many of the famous sopranos – Melba was possibly the most famous – who studied under Salvatore and Mathilde Marchesi probably owes a great deal to the correct positioning of the soft palate.

The hard palate forms the front, rigid part of the roof of the mouth. The dimensions of this important sounding board are particularly significant in affecting the quality of the voice. The ratio between the length and the depth of the dome of the hard palate is often a matter of racial characteristics, and doubtless accounts for the particular quality of sound produced by singers – and speakers, too – of different ethnic backgrounds.

The position of the tongue naturally alters the capacity of the oral cavity; when it lies flat, with the tip against the back of the lower incisor teeth, the capacity of the oral cavity is at its maximum. 'The tongue's best friend,' say some singing teachers, 'is the back of the lower incisors.' However, the tongue, together with the lips, must necessarily alter the shape of the oral cavity in order to produce different vowel sounds. When a vowel sound is correctly produced, the tongue will automatically maintain itself in the correct position.

The nasal cavity leads directly into the nasopharynx, and the hard palate forms its floor. It is one of the main resonators in singing; any anatomical defect such as a deflected nasal septum or chronic inflammatory processes will appreciably alter the quality of the voice. For many years singing teachers have spoken of 'sinus tone', and this term probably best describes the sensation experienced by singers in the mask of the face; contrary to the old belief, the paranasal sinuses do not appreciably alter the resonance of the voice.

The resonators described above are the supraglottal resonators, that is, those situated above the glottis. The lower resonators, below the larynx, are formed by the thoracic cavity and the tracheo-bronchial tree. All parts of the thoracic wall, and particularly the sternum, probably act as sounding boards.

That extinct breed of singers the *evirati*, *castrati* or *musici* were singularly well endowed in respect of the various resonators. F. Habock of Vienna tells us in his book *Die Gesangskunst der Kastraten* that the mouth and nasal cavities of the *castrati* were of abnormally large size, and so was the capacity of their chest and lungs.

The registers

Most singers recognize the existence of distinct registers in their voices. The characteristic sound of a tone in a particular register is governed by the changes called into play in the vocal cords and the resonators. The terms 'head' and 'chest' registers usually describe where the singer experiences the maximum sensation when singing a particular note, depending on its position in the scale. A distinct break is often heard as the voice progresses up and down a scale in most untrained – and unhappily in some trained – voices; it is due to the inability to alter mentally the tension within the larynx which is necessary at the junction of these registers. Rare and fortunate the singer in whom nature has already balanced and equalized three registers. Dame Nellie Melba wrote in her *The Melba Method* (1926): 'There are three registers in a woman's voice. The chest register should end on the E above middle C. I myself occasionally sing F in chest, but that is not usually right, and for heavy voices it is very dangerous. The medium (or middle) register consists of the octave from F above middle C. The head register must begin on F sharp above C on the third space.'

It must be remembered, however, that on the lyric stage many an eminent and distinguished artist often employs

the natural break in the registers for dramatic effect –
nowhere perhaps so strikingly as in the Italian *verismo*
school. The most easily accessible demonstration of the
technique is to be found in the recordings still available of
that most thrilling of contralto voices, that of Dame Clara
Butt.

Vibrato and tremolo

The vibrato is a healthy, natural and essential part of the
singing voice. It serves to give life, vibrancy and buoyancy
to the tone and helps the singer to move smoothly from
note to note in *legato* passages. It is not an attribute to be
cultivated; it will be manifest in itself when the voice is
correctly produced and the tone is alive and free. It consists
of a rapid and regular, though very slight, variation in pitch
above and below the mean pitch of the note.

During the vibration of the vocal cords in the production
of a tone an undulating upward and outward movement of
the free inner edges is observed. This causes a slight raising
of the pitch, and as the vocal cords return to their normal
position there is a slight lowering of the pitch. Thus when
a tone is sustained there is a regular and rapid fluctuation
of pitch either side of the mean pitch, creating a pulsation
responsible for flexible tone production. Oscillograph
studies show that, regardless of the loudness of the tone
produced, the 'vibrato cycle' occurs about six and a half
times a second. Changes in volume do not affect this
periodicity, but they can increase or decrease the amplitude of the fluctuation.

The muscular functions responsible for the movements
of the vocal cords in the production of the vibrato are not
under voluntary control. When the balance of them is
disturbed by extraneous voluntary muscular interference,
the vibrato function is replaced by a disagreeable, irregular
and uneven tremolo. Forcing the voice in an attempt to
increase the volume causes the registers to be pushed
beyond their natural limits and results in an uneven

variation of pitch and amplitude – the wobble. If the singer will refrain from pushing the voice upwards, restoring the registers to their natural limits, this undesirable defect will usually be eliminated.

The falsetto voice

All singing voices have an innate falsetto function that enables the singer to extend the range above its natural limits. The falsetto voice is characterized by a kernel or core to the tone, though it is usually of rather slight volume. As distinct from the tones produced in the head register, with which the singer feels the maximum sense of vibration in the cavities of the head, the falsetto is often described as being placed forwards against the upper incisor teeth. As we saw on page 15, during production of the falsetto the arytenoid cartilages are held firmly together and only the front segments of the vocal cords vibrate.

Though it is most readily heard in the male voice, the falsetto function is also present in the female, and when properly used is of inestimable value in the production of *pianissimo* effects on very high notes, particularly in placing the note prior to employing full voice.

Before the advent of the *castrati* the soprano parts in church music were sung by 'falsettists' – Spanish falsettists appear almost to have had a monopoly. Even the *castrati* were schooled to use the mechanism. Pietro Francesco Tosi writes (*Observations on a Florid Song*, 1742): 'A diligent master, knowing that a male soprano, without the Falsetto, is constrained to sing within the narrow compass of a few notes, ought not only to endeavour to help him to it, but also to leave no means untried, so as to unite the feigned and the natural voice . . . Many masters put their scholars to sing the contralto not knowing how to help them to the Falsetto, or to avoid the trouble of finding it.'

The falsetto function was developed and employed to great effect by tenors until the middle of the nineteenth century. The very high notes written into tenor parts by such composers as Bellini and Rossini were expected to be produced with a skilful admixture of falsetto technique. The modern counter-tenor voice is produced throughout its range in falsetto; the natural singing voice of most counter-tenors is baritone or bass. For long confined to alto parts in cathedral choirs and male voice glee parties, the male alto has made a striking return to popularity in recent years, very largely due to the outstanding skill and artistry of Alfred Deller, and contemporary composers now readily write solo parts for such voices; there is a notable one in Britten's *A Midsummer Night's Dream*.

The trill

Much research has been done on the mechanism of this most desirable yet all too elusive of vocal ornaments. The production of a full trill involves a shaking movement of the larynx. The larynx must be free of all muscular constraint and obstructive stiffness, something that entails a perfect balance in the various antagonistic muscles involved in its suspensory mechanism. The student of singing is frequently taught to practise on two separate alternating notes, gradually building up to the rapid and even sounding of them until the trill is achieved. The young Adelina Patti is said to have been puzzled on hearing her sister practising this and to have asked why they did not 'do it this way' – producing a perfectly tuned, even, sustained trill without preparation on the notes! It is a cause for regret that modern male singers do not cultivate the trill. There is certainly no anatomical reason why they should not be able to produce a fair trill, and trills are often called for by e.g. Handel and Bach. The great bass Pol Plançon and the baritone Mattia Battistini both had enviable trills.

It is a generally held belief that great singers are endowed with some special anatomical configurations in the larynx that could account for their pre-eminence. There is no evidence for this. When the larynx of the great tenor

Francesco Tamagno was examined at autopsy by a commission of doctors and scientists, they reported: 'The organ differs from that of a normal person only in that it exhibits an unusually large number of scars on the pharynx caused by catarrh.' What matters, according to Caruso, is 'a big chest, a big mouth, ninety per cent memory, ten per cent intelligence, lots of hard work and something in the heart'.

Three
What Every Singer Should Know about the Voice

Alfred Alexander, M.D.,
F.A.C.S., Hon. R.C.M., Hon.
R.N.C.M.
  Head of Ear, Nose and Throat
Department of St James's
Hospital until 1974. Subsequently
E.N.T. Consultant to the Home
Office. Author of *Operanatomy*.

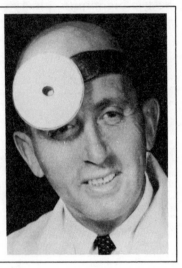

The 'singer' can be defined for our purposes as a person of adequate musicality, who is gifted with a voice of such power and beauty that competent judges can confidently recommend singing as a career. Approximately one person in 50,000 possesses such gifts, which means that in England and Wales, where there are yearly some 800,000 births, about sixteen first class voices are born every year. If the lifetime of a voice is thirty years, which is probably an over-estimation but a convenient measure as the thirty-year span is the unit of the generation, then five hundred or so great English and Welsh singers are active at any one time.

It is surprising how little we know about the physiological aspects of voice production. The only facts we know for certain are that the voice is produced by the vibration of the vocal cords and that the resulting sound (a so-called 'mixed' sound) is amplified by the resonators of the pharynx, mouth, nose and chest. We have no idea in what manner anatomical structures correlate to a big voice, nor do we know what gives the voice its carrying power and beauty. Our ignorance in so important a field may well be deplorable but, if one is scientifically honest, one can only say that the singer's sound qualities are due to some lucky shape of one resonance area or another: all the claims to the contrary made by many singing teachers are sheer humbug.

One sad fact that we *do* know is that beauty and power of the singing voice are transient, and that for reasons beyond our understanding they can fade without any sign of illness or disease.

Vocal performance itself is perfected by neuromuscular control which can be improved by persevering training, similar to the case of the athlete whose reflex activities are improved by diligent and assiduous effort. We know that vocal beauty depends on precision of sound, i.e. accurate intonation; on purity of sound; on vocal range; on openness and evenness of timbre throughout the reach, and on a vocal adaptability which permits technical and expressive qualities to emerge freely. Vocal technique is the method leading to the attainment of these aims.

Where do the best voices come from? Contrary to widely held beliefs, there is evidence that their incidence rate is the same all over the world. However, a voice must not only be there, it must also be *known* to be there, and be discovered for its musical function. This discovery rate varies enormously in different parts of the globe. Italy and Wales, for example, do not produce proportionately more good singers than other lands: but the high musical awareness, particularly of Italy, has made it rather unlikely for a really good voice to remain undetected.

The current wealth of fine Australian singers has been attributed erroneously to Australia's phonation, sunshine, dryness of climate, Italian immigration, etc. The true reason is that, in line with musical awareness, Australia's discovery rate has risen rapidly. Similarly, the fact that Britain now produces so many good singers is due to the country's greatly increased, as well as socially extended, musical activity.

The moment of consciousness of one's voice ('sonognosy') is a true turning point, influencing all future activities and emotions of the singer's life. Its timing varies. Some singers were already aware in their childhood of the ability to make a noise which was better than that of their school-fellows. Other fine voices (Kathleen Ferrier's, for example) were accidentally discovered in adult students of music who had opted for singing as a second subject. Once sonognosy has occurred, singers have to learn to live with their voice. Realizing that the voice behaves as if it were a Siamese twin, or a semi-independent living organism of its own, they develop the most intense commitment towards their twin. This devotion to the voice is for the non-singer very difficult to understand and forms a notorious peril in the relationship of singers with non-singers – even musicians!

The demands a voice makes on the singer are incessant and incisive. The voice claims precedence over all personal relationships. Every link of a singer with a person of the opposite sex is, from the outset, a *ménage à trois*, with the voice being number two. Apart from any other consideration, a singer will always wonder whether a prospective girl- or boy-friend is 'good for the voice' or not. No friend, no lover, not even a husband or wife exists, whom a singer would not abandon if that sacrifice were persistently demanded by their voice; no food, drink or habit that a singer would not willingly give up for it. If the voice demands 'eat cheese only' the singer will eat nothing else, and if the demand is 'don't eat cheese', the singer will not touch it.

Most voices – though not all – make it clear that smoking is undesirable and, in fact, very few singers smoke. Dietetic fads are common among them, but these are generally harmless and often helpful as they may express instinctively felt needs. Not surprisingly, though, any one item a singer's voice craves may be anathema to another.

In contrast to instrumentalists or conductors, singers conform neither in their educational nor in their social background to a standard pattern. Some well-known singers could hardly scrape together a couple of passes at 'O' level, whereas others hold university degrees in highly complex subjects. Their physique, as well as their physical fitness, differs enormously: singers have represented their countries at the Olympic Games, while others may be unable to walk more than a few steps without discomfort.

Whether singing is a desirable career is open to doubt. Whichever way the career goes, the strain is enormous. The exposure in singing, unparalleled in the performing arts, is so taxing that it can cause the breakdown of the requisite moral fibre – and of a career – with the voice in perfect order. The waiting for opportunities, the endless chain of forgotten promises and disappointed hopes, the paraphernalia of the auditions and the attendant periods of suspense can be heartbreaking. Singers are now even forced to audition for agents who may know little about music or voices – an iniquity no other profession has to bear. If the career is successful, a potentially critical audience has to be faced afresh on every occasion. To mitigate the tension *before* a performance by the use of alcohol or other drugs is an expedient which has never helped in the long run and caused many a disaster. Afterwards, the beginner and established performer alike have to brave the critics, well aware that the untutored public only too readily accords the personal opinions of musical journalists the weight of judicial verdicts. The critics' views of what singing should or should not sound like are often rather queer, but the performer is never in a position to answer back to them.

The voice always presents problems and the fear of losing it is never far from a singer's mind. Every morning the singer steps into the bathroom to test the 'twin'. If the voice feels well, all is well, but if the twin is out of sorts, the singer is at once upset and worried. Singers are generally reputed to react hypochondriacally to minor physical troubles, but this accusation is unjustified. The attitude of non-singers to coughs and colds is governed by the fact that such indispositions do not place their capacity to earn their living in jeopardy, but for a singer such ailments are never trifling: work, career, and livelihood seem immediately endangered, and this naturally causes anxiety and apprehension. Even the actor's position is, in this respect, significantly different from the singer's; some loss of resonance or clarity of voice is of surprisingly little importance to the actor.

The purely technical aspects of singing are comparatively readily acquired, and it has been claimed that singing's basic technical requirements contain nothing that a competent instructor could not teach, and a gifted pupil could not learn, in one afternoon's session. However, a singer can hear his or her own voice only in a somewhat distorted way, and needs critical assessment of the sound produced, with constructive suggestions for the mechanics of its improvement. He has therefore, more often than not, to embark on the choice of the right teacher. This is complicated by the fact that even very experienced teachers are able to help only in certain cases and not in others, which explains why the very same teacher can be rightly referred to as 'brilliant' by one pupil and 'hopeless' by another.

A great number of textbooks on singing exist but most of them contain a good deal of nonsense. Many are written by teachers with charlatan ideas, who paint gloomy pictures of the danger of having one's voice 'ruined' by rival methods. This danger is, fortunately, non-existent: no one can ruin someone else's voice, though persistent attempts to force a pupil to measures which do not suit him could have a bad effect and cause prolonged difficulties. Nor, for that matter, can one ruin one's own voice by singing music that, in the opinion of whoever it may be, is not suitable for a certain voice. The only thing which could damage a vocal cord is the strenuous and violent forcing of a voice which does not respond willingly.

The person trained to inspect the mechanism of singing is the laryngologist, though his crucial gadget, the laryngeal mirror, was invented by a singing teacher and not by a doctor. His main asset is that by seeing with his own eyes that all is well, he can convincingly reassure a singer tormented by doubts about the state of his cords. An understanding laryngologist can be helpful with minor problems; he can become a trusted friend, and the link thus established is for some singers more necessary than for others. For serious voice problems, though, he can be found pretty useless.

Supplementary to his technical needs are the singer's artistic needs, which must be met by a person with the training and capability of a conductor, though he may be called *répétiteur* or coach. There is also the intelligibility problem: critics and public blame singers when they cannot understand them, and accuse them of bad enunciation or pronunciation. They fail to realize that for physical reasons a listener unfamiliar with the libretto cannot possibly understand more than a small proportion of the text; good pronunciation of foreign languages does not necessarily help, particularly when an orchestra complicates the issue. On the other hand, people who know the text intimately are not reliable either because they do believe that they understand every word. In this dilemma the singer has to follow his own instinct and, realizing that one cannot achieve the impossible, try to impart to his sound the correct colouring for the overtones of the respective languages.

The professional outlook for singers is not good, although no other profession is taken more seriously by those engaged in it. The individual effort made is often enormous, and even passionate over-ambition not at all uncommon: but the present abundance of gifted and competent singers has greatly worsened their career prospects, and it is becoming increasingly evident that apart

31

from all the art and musicianship a stroke of good fortune as well is needed for a decisive success. Only one among two or three thousand singers achieves international recognition. The second most favourable outcome, a national reputation, is gained by one in three or four hundred. For many young singers, chorus-work is a good experience, but the would-be soloist often finds this eventually unsatisfactory and frustrating. Ancillary activities such as the teaching of singing or music can give satisfaction, but there can be no doubt that many singing careers, begun with high hopes, come to a disappointing end.

However, against these risks must be set the wonderful feeling of giving, by means of one's voice, such intense delight to others. And even more important than that, perhaps, is the singer's own 'transcendental ecstasy': an incomparably glorious sensation (when all goes well!) of physically sensing one's own beautiful sound, and experiencing in this a fulfilment and a happiness which amply compensate for all the anguish and humiliations which had to be endured.

Four

The Secret World of the Singer

Dr Macdonald Critchley, C.B.E.,
M.D., F.R.C.P., Hon. F.A.C.P.
Emeritus President of the
World Federation of Neurology
and an honorary Consultant
Physician at the National
Hospital for Nervous Diseases,
Queen Square, London. He has
taught, practised and lectured
throughout the world, and is co-
editor of *Music and the Brain*.

While listening to music, some sensitive sophisticates are
capable of perceptual extremes especially when the stimu-
lus is massive. Victor Gollancz touched upon this matter
when he wrote that there are various pleasures to be had
from listening to music, and he proceeded to specify the
intellectual and the sensuous. He went on to write: 'But
there are moments, and not only in listening to the works
of the few supreme masters, when it is no longer a question
of mere pleasure or even of happiness; it is a question of
joy inexpressible.'

It is precisely this 'joy inexpressible' which I have
recently referred to with the term ecstasy.*

Ordinarily 'ecstasy' is something which pertains to the
disciplines of both theology and psychology, but it also
applies to musical appreciation. What is meant is a sense
of merger of self with external reality, reality having in
itself, seemingly, a peculiarly personal significance,

* See *Music and the Brain* ed. Critchley and Henson, 1977.

linked perhaps with the illusion of self-oblivion. There is something well-nigh ineffable or transcendental about these experiences, but they may be identified as including what is technically called depersonalization. One seems to be outside oneself, looking on, listening perhaps. This state is indeed implied in the etymology of the word 'ecstasy'. There may be an obliteration of the actual environment, a loss of time sense, a subjective shrinkage or less often an augmentation of self. Malibran, a soprano celebrated in the early nineteenth century, daughter of the famous singing teacher Manuel Garcia, used to describe her voice as something separate from herself – almost as an enemy. A psychologist would read into such a remark evidence of a depersonalization coupled with a malefic type of dissociation.

Then too there is the mysterious, yet by no means uncommon, experience of synaesthesia, whereby musical sounds evoke an imagery of colour. This phenomenon of *audition colorée* may be vague or vivid, stationary or mobile, associated perhaps with kaleidoscopic shapes and forms. Many of the great masters have been so endowed – Beethoven, Scriabin, Rimsky-Korsakov, Liszt. Indeed it is possible that most musicians are synaethetics but take it for granted, even perhaps in the belief that everybody else is similarly privileged. The colours evoked may vary according to the character of the music, the key, the individual instruments or the composition as a whole. In Chapter 17, *The Italian Singer*, Tito Gobbi writes of deliberately 'colouring the voice': in the first scene in *Rigoletto* he feels his voice is yellow, later at different times dark purple and a foggy grey.

To what extent are instrumentalists and singers capable of, or susceptible to, such synaesthetic feelings and such states of ecstasy? This question is difficult to answer with confidence. An orchestral conductor may be so, while at work, but only to a limited degree, because above all he must never lose control of the actions of those under his direction. He must be an ever watchful commander of the situation, like a tennis champion, or a pilot performing aerobatics.

The listener, on the other hand, is in a fortunate state of passive inactivity, a receptive vessel. A professional music critic is a little different, for he has to be in a permanent state of vigilant appraisal. The musical executive is still less susceptible because of the technical demands imposed upon him by composer and conductor. Technology transcends aesthetic passivity.

Where does the singer belong? In his *Psychology of Music* C. E. Seashore observed that a fascinating problem was raised by the question as to whether or not it was necessary for the singer actually to feel the emotions which he portrays. The author pronounced that a 'yes' or a 'no' answer had lost its meaning, and he successfully evaded tackling the question.

In general, the singer – like the instrumentalist – is also the slave to technique rather than to enchantment. But there are many grades of both song and singer, and these diversities of circumstances lead to diversities of performance.

What prompts an individual at any particular moment to give voice? In solitude, song probably reflects some mild feeling – tone, mood or affect – given of course a modicum of vocal proficiency. It may reflect contentment, mental vacuum, a talisman which wards off the task of thinking. Here belongs the solitary whistler. Among manual workers singing, ululating, intoning or some other kind of vocalization may accompany and perhaps facilitate hard physical exertion – co-ordinating the efforts of a team in the case of shanties in the days of sail. Soldiers used to be encouraged to sing on the march.

The niche occupied by the solitary singer differs from the more usual state of affairs in which there are others in earshot. At times the audience may comprise merely one other person, not necessarily attentive, as when a mother croons a lullaby. The serenade may also belong here.

More commonly the audience is large, even though all

who are present may be participants rather than listeners, as in the choirs of the Welsh valleys. Here it matters little whether or not other onlookers and listeners are present. In this category belong the ecclesiastical choristers, members of Bach choral societies, and the singers participating in *Messiah* or *Elijah*. Without doubt in such circumstances, expertise is linked with a shared aesthetic pleasure. The Welsh term *hwyl* exemplifies this state.

To adopt an *argumentum ad absurdum* we can assert that when a number of persons break into song, musical ability may be irrelevant. In hilarious assemblies, in vaudeville audience-participation, the louder the noise the greater the applause. This may perhaps represent the basest possible level of ecstasy, but an experience outside the world of the professional singer.

When it comes to the concert or operatic singer, constant awareness is paramount regarding voice-control, the ordinances of the composer, the conductor's beat, accurate co-ordination with the performance of fellow-singers. The singer cannot afford to relax the dictates of virtuosity and technique.

Nonetheless, some elements of the listeners' ecstatic-synaesthetic feelings may invade the world of the singer. Thus most accomplished singers are temporarily oblivious of the passage of time. Many, too, lose awareness of the audience before them. This is not always so, for some sensitive singers make great efforts to transmit to their hearers something of the emotions which they are feeling. This represents a heightened sense of sharing as between executant and recipient. At times the emotional as opposed to the technical faculties reach great intensities. Especially so when a climate of religious exaltation is concerned. Although an unlikely event in Gregorian chants or in the cathedrals of the Eastern orthodox church, it may however be conspicuous among revivalists, and also in the *chazzanim* of the synagogue. Here, the earlier cantorial display-singing with its tonal embroidery has given way to fewer embellishments, trills and such ornaments, to become disciplined by a hard apprenticeship as a *meshorer*. But nevertheless the *chazzan* is always an advocate, the defending counsel of his fellow-worshippers. To quote Nathan Ausubel 'he tries hard – sometimes even too strenuously – to evoke by means of his singing all the multitudinous moods and nuances of liturgical piety. These run through the entire emotional spectrum of pathos, contrition, repentance, compassion, God's anger, lamentation, despair, tenderness, humility, fidelity, sweet reasonableness, exhortation, laudation, invocation, thanksgiving, adoration, and many other tonalities of faith, self-revelation, and petition'.

Here then is ecstasy both experienced and transmitted by a singer.

The operatic singer is in a different category, but some professional artistes in their work at times experience to a lesser degree something of this 'joy inexpressible'. An example may be quoted in the case of Giuditta Negri, better known as Pasta, a soprano famous in the early nineteenth century. According to a critic who attended her performance of Paisiello's *Nina*, '. . . not only did this enchantress hold her listeners spellbound; she was herself so seized and carried away that she collapsed before the end. She was recalled, and duly appeared; but what a sight! Too weak to walk alone, supported by helping hands, more carried than walking, tears streaming down her pale cheeks, every muscle of her expressive face in movement, and reflecting as touchingly as her singing, the depth of her emotions! The appearance rose to the highest conceivable pitch – and she fainted!'

It must be confessed that the pure gold of her exaltation seems to have been tainted by the dross of hysteria in this case.

De Musset appears to have taken it for granted that the great singer is the servant of the feelings. Referring to Pauline Viardot he said that 'before expressing something, she feels it. She does not listen to her voice but to the heart'.

It has been said of Adelina Patti that she knew the extent to which emotions would exhaust and injure the voice, and she sang accordingly. Later, the same view was held by Melba.

If then some controlled degree of emotivity has been felt by singers belonging to the golden age of music and the grand operatic era, the same cannot, in all probability, be said of the earlier exponents in the seventeenth and eighteenth centuries. This was the heyday of *Bel Canto*, when *castrati* and falsettists were in vogue. The *martellato*, trill, turn, *appoggiatura*, *canto figurato* and fantastic volume-control marked the acme of cold technical brilliance. However much the listeners may have been enraptured, the singer probably concentrated entirely upon his vocal gymnastics.

So far we have been dealing with the harmonic music of the West. What is the situation as regards the purely mensural type of music of the East with its lack of musical notation? Although in the Islamic world, as also in India, instruments are employed, greater store is set upon song, with its complicated *igā* or rhythm, its quarter-tone decorations, and its repetitiousness. In the *Arabian Nights* we read that 'to some people music is meat, and to others medicine'. Indeed the Persian philosopher and mystic Al-Ghazāli (d. AD 1111) discussed the state of heightened auditory and visual power engendered by listening to music. In his treatise *Music and Ecstasy* Al-Ghazāli set out seven reasons for maintaining that singing is more potent than the Qur'ān in producing pure ecstasy.

How far does the Islamic singer share these transcendental states produced by his complicated art? Possibly to a very considerable extent, more so perhaps than his occidental counterpart. Whoever has heard the singing of Um Khaltoum, the Melba of the Islamic world, would find it hard not to believe that she was as entranced in her own way as were her appreciative audience.

Passing from one extreme to another, we must face the question whether 'joy inexpressible' ever comes within the experience of the contemporary 'pop' singer. In the first place, what constitutes the line of severance between the noble and the ignoble in the world of song? Perhaps this is to be found in the 'microphone-in-hand' technique of the performer who is unable to liberate himself from the shackles of an electric life-line. And yet without doubt the modern scene is one where the pop singer, alone or one of a group, is capable of rousing a most abandoned spectacle of frenzy in his audience. How far is he, too, sensuously involved? The picture is one of mass hysteria wherein the singer may find himself prisoner as well as instigator. Hysteria represents the basest example of emotional upsurge, for which the word ecstasy is far from appropriate. As to the artiste himself, the frenetic state may all too often be complicated by chemical corruption in the way of alcohol, pot, and various other psychedelic drugs. The pattern conforms more with the Voodoo orgies of the Caribbean.

The subject is potentially an ugly one but it cannot be overlooked or brushed aside in any serious attempt to explore the psychology of musical expression and perception.

Part Two

Becoming a Singer

*'Since singing is so good a thing,
I wish all men would learn to sing.'*

(William Byrd)

Five
Training: the Singer as Technician

Singing for pleasure requires only the desire.
Singing for other people's pleasure demands certain standards of excellence.
Singing for professional standards requires an excellence comparable to the best singers of the day.

Sergius Kagen, *On Studying Singing*

We must applaud those who desire to sing for pleasure and those who sing to give pleasure to other people, but we must not encourage those without the right equipment to become professional. The choir member may get just as much satisfaction as the prima donna – possibly more, for the professional is not often satisfied with a performance. Those who sing in church or chapel or choral society obtain healthy enjoyment without serious training. It is remarkable what fine tone and effect can be produced from a body of untrained voices.

But the soloist is another matter. An untrained voice is obvious, and should be developed by a sound teacher. Dr Alexander's advice (Chapter 3) may at first sight be a little frightening to a young singer, but it must be said that the unsuccessful singer is one of the saddest things in the profession. (They tell a story at the Royal College of Music of a student who persevered for 55½ terms (eighteen years) and yet failed to get her diploma; in those days, of course, the main qualification for entry was the ability to pay the fees.) What follows is addressed primarily to the student or would-be professional; but most of it is just as vital for the amateur if he or she wants to sing for other people's pleasure.

Requirements

Professional advice should be sought before any young singer embarks on the slow and arduous training for a professional career. Very few young singers have any idea of the sonority of their voice and often imagine, perhaps through hearing it amplified, that they have a dramatic soprano when the voice is really suitable only for the drawing room or small hall. What are the requirements? Rossini said: 'Three. First – voice; second – voice; third – voice.' Santley was more specific: 'The first great requirement is a sonorous voice; (second) enunciation to make the sense understood; . . . (third) modulation to adapt the voice to the expression of different sentiments and passions.'

Singers have always had two basic things to consider: the physical and the aesthetic. They do not change. Alterations in training are only necessary in the application of technique to current fashions; the principles of fine singing are constant. Indeed, they are obvious; but they are not often present together in one person. The *voice* must have volume, intensity, wide and pleasing quality throughout its range. The *breath* must be in complete control, unnoticed but in constant support. The *attack* must be clear and clean. *Enunciation* should be eloquent, *intonation* impeccable, *rhythm* vital at all speeds and in all moods. *Interpretation* should be natural, faithful to composer and poet, revealing a lively intelligence and personality. *Deportment* should be upright, giving the impression of an artist absorbed in his work.

The sooner you begin, the better. The boy or girl can acquire basic technique – breathing, ear training and musicianship – before the voice is ready for grown-up training; indeed, probably long before the question of a career as a singer has ever been considered. Every aspect of singing is controlled by mind and ear and becomes intuitive in singers who begin the ABC of singing early in life. Few who only begin training at nineteen or twenty get beyond an elementary standard of musicianship. And musicianship is essential today, no less for the choir member than for the would-be professional.

The ideal is perhaps realized at the Thomaskirche Choir School in Leipzig, where Bach was Cantor from 1723 to 1750. There a choirboy rests his voice when it breaks, while continuing his music studies, and rejoins the choir after two years as alto, tenor or bass.

Study

'For the first three years,' wrote Sir Henry Wood in *The Gentle Art of Singing*, 'singing students should be trained to make their voices like a beautiful even instrument. There are registers in every musical instrument, but they must not show. There are muscles, reeds, but they must never be perceptible in an artist . . . No singing student can pretend to have any technique until he has acquired the habit of singing every tone in his voice, throughout a wide compass at all breath pressures, with any vowel cavern arranged and without the slightest change in quality.'

No British musician ever worked harder or did more for public performance of music in this century than Sir Henry Wood. In addition to a full season of choral and orchestral concerts, he rehearsed and conducted every day and night of the ten-week season of Promenade concerts. Yet he had time to teach singing to a large number of would-be professionals and to be a landscape painter and carpenter of distinction.

Sir Henry sketched out an ideal timetable for young singers which not many can emulate. It left no time to be wasted from 7.00 a.m. on Monday morning to bedtime on Sunday evening: early rising, breathing and physical exercises, vocal exercises, piano practice, theory work, frequent walks, transposing songs, listening to concerts, reading prose and poetry, languages and memorizing, morning noon and night until Sunday afternoon. On Sunday evenings he suggested that one might be permitted to visit friends, if any!

How good it would be if we could all carry out such a programme. Yet it is a great help to get one's teacher to devise a broad scheme to develop every aspect of training, musicianship and health. Not only does it take care of the subsidiary aspects but it ensures that the voice is not over-used, as it sometimes tends to be, and is able to stay unblemished in quality and gradually develop stamina and resilience.

First steps

A singer beginning to sing is like a child learning to walk. Progress must be slow and thoughtful; each note must be listened to carefully, not only by the teacher but also by the pupil. One of the first things to learn is to be able to judge the quality of sound being produced. Later this faculty becomes instinctive; mind and ear will anticipate and find the desired quality. Tape and cassette recordings help to correct technical faults, as Roy Henderson tells us on page 78, but judgment of quality and placement must rest entirely with teacher and pupil.

Quality: open throat

Beautiful tone implies easy and smooth production of sound, free from discordant qualities and built on the pure universal vowels written in the International Phonetic Alphabet as a, e, i, o, u. (These are not of course the same sounds represented by those letters in English; see Pierre Bernac's article, page 125.) It is usual to find the best natural notes in a voice and to develop and match them to all vowels throughout the voice. The sensation of the ideal position of the throat and tongue to produce the best quality is most commonly described as *open throat*. Some call it a 'yawning sensation', a 'sensation of space at the back of the tongue'; German teachers speak of 'hot potatoes' in the throat. Elisabeth Schumann called it the 'bottomless pit'. It is thus that a basic singing quality is developed to give instrumental tone, which is often lacking in young singers. When the student can maintain this basic quality over an octave or so, he or she may be allowed to learn a song.

Registers

It is commonly accepted that there are three registers in the human voice:

chest

medium

and head

The blending of the registers is of course of vital importance between teacher and pupil. The areas concerned for all voices are chest to medium, often called *il ponticello* (the little bridge)

and medium to head

A good singer will appear to have only one register, since all three will have been well joined. In addition, both men and women may add several notes to the top of the voice by the use of falsetto, provided it is good enough and blends easily.

At the same time, the ability to move from one note to another smoothly, clearly and in tune will develop. This will be done in short scale passages, triads, diatonic and chromatic scales and arpeggios as facility and accuracy improve.

During this early part of training the teacher will be assessing the voice by its quality and timbre, for it is a mistake to classify a voice by its compass or range alone. The four main types of voice, soprano, alto, tenor and bass, may be subdivided, as shown in the table overleaf. Not all voices are easy to classify. Some sit easily into type and placement but a few, the unlucky ones, may be difficult to place; only time and care can prove. It has been known for professional singers to change category in midstream, so to speak; occasionally baritone to tenor, like two famous Wagnerians, Lauritz Melchior and Set Svanholm, but more often mezzo-soprano to dramatic soprano. These changes are generally due to physical maturity or newly developed head voice or falsetto.

Breath control

Breath control is the basis of all good singing, the ability to take breath quickly, to hold it and control its emission, so that attack is clean, *legato* passages are smooth and *staccato* crisp, *aspirato* agile and the *messa di voce* well controlled (see next chapter). The lungs, as we learn from A. S. Khambata's article (Chapter 2), are the bellows of the voice and are controlled mainly by the diaphragm, the muscular dome that divides the thorax from the abdomen. For the lungs to be charged for singing the diaphragm contracts, the stomach is drawn in, air is inhaled through

Becoming a Singer

SOPRANO

Coloratura or *leggero:* light and agile, with high range

Dramatic: big, and capable of a wide range of dynamics throughout its compass

Lyric: less volume but a warm quality

MEZZO-SOPRANO

A warm voice, often rich and lyrical

CONTRALTO

A noticeably deep chest voice, usually less agile

COUNTER-TENOR or MALE SOPRANO

A voice capable of great flexibility and delicacy, with considerable variations in compass and range. It generally loses intensity below middle C (see Chapter 2)

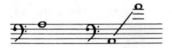

TENOR

Robust: large and sonorous

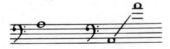

Lyric: less volume, with a warm quality

BARITONE

Capable of brilliance in high notes

BASS-BARITONE

A lyrical, mobile voice, with less depth than Bass

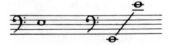

BASS

A dark voice with rich low notes

nose or throat and the ribs expand. Raising the shoulders and constriction of the lower ribs prevent full and easy expansion and are to be avoided.

The teacher will establish sound breathing methods: control of intake of breath, holding and easy emission. Here, by way of illustration, are four short elementary exercises:

1. Take in a breath slowly and fully through the nose and mouth together, *hold it* for a few seconds, then release it. It will give you a feeling of leaning on your breath.
2. Inhale as before. Hold the breath for two seconds and release it as though whispering the word 'who' on to the back of the hand, sustaining it gently and steadily for ten seconds. You will be aware that you are controlling the emission of breath with the diaphragm.
3. Inhale, hold and intone a note steadily for ten seconds.
4. Put your hand on your diaphragm. Inhale, hold the breath for two seconds and then give a series of short attacks on 'ah' sounds. You will feel the actions of the muscle controlling release and holding of the breath.

The motive power, the beginning and end of all singing, depends on sound breath control. It is vital that teacher and pupil have complete understanding on the matter. As study continues you will gradually develop the ability 'to conserve, hold, save and retake breath with perfect ease', so that you will be able to sing the four-bar phrases in Schubert's 'An die Musik' and the two-bar phrases in 'Pie Jesu' in Fauré's *Requiem*, or florid passage work such as Handel's 'O had I Jubal's lyre' at the correct tempo with facility and with power in reserve.

Attack

The attack has been variously described by great teachers. It needs a certain amount of courage and mental and aural preparation; it is not unlike the first brush of paint to an artist. Manuel Garcia called it 'the neat articulation of the glottis that gives a precise and clean start to the sound . . . (with) the object, that sounds should be free from slurring up to a note or noise of breathing.' Julian Gardner says: 'The sensation at the moment of launching is as if the larynx were gently tapped by a tiny hammer.' Ida Franca teaches that the attack is completed in two distinct phases, the 'preparatory effort' and the 'flutelike attack above the breath' (*l'attacco flautato sopra il fiato*).

Voices and people are sensitive and individual. Description of sensations of tone production can be a tricky business. That is why it is so important to have a sympathetic and sensitive teacher with a lively sense of imagination.

After the fundamentals, breath control and open throat, are established, teacher and pupil will proceed to sustained sounds, agility and the execution of ornaments. Most teachers have a preference for a book of studies for the purpose; perhaps the most famous is the *Practical Method* by N. Vaccai (1790–1848), published for high and low voices.

Six
Training: the Singer as Musician

The eloquence we expect to hear in the declamation of a fine actor should be just as evident in singing. There are two elements in it. *Vocal expression* is built on vowels. *Verbal expression* is built on consonants, and it is well to establish the wide difference as soon as possible.

Vocal expression is linked to the words of a song, but is to an extent independent of them. It is so easy to sing a phrase thinking of the start and finish and to neglect the content. What you do with the content can make the difference between mediocrity and excellence. So much of day-to-day singing is laudable for its efficiency but lacking the magic spark which spells vocal expression. I recently heard one of my contributors broadcast a contemporary Hungarian song and I was amazed that she could communicate so much – note by note – to the listener and give so much pleasure within the content of a phrase. As the voice develops in training, so will the ability to match its colour and volume to the emotional content of the song.

Words are more complicated. How can one possibly know if a person is singing well, however musical the sound they produce, if one cannot tell what they are singing about? Do we often stop to think what is implied when we hear someone say: 'Her diction is so good'? Good diction certainly includes the ability to make the words understandable, but that is only a small part of it. Diction is made up of *articulation, pronunciation, intonation, declamation* and *punctuation*. When you hear an eloquent singer you can bet your life all these components are present.

Articulation that is clear implies that the words are heard and clearly understood. Here, consonants are the chief problem. On no account should they interfere with the instrumental tone. The shorter they are, and the longer the vowels, the more intelligible and effective will the articulation become. 'Consonants must be spat out at lip level, they have no connexion with the rising flow of breath and tone,' said Elisabeth Schumann. We should always remember that articulation in singing must be more distinct, or exaggerated, than in normal speech.

Some 'microphone' singers have a habit of sustaining certain consonants as a humming finish to a word – sha*ll*, co*m*e, woma*n*, so*ng*, love*r* (American 'r'). This is intended to make the words more distinct and is accepted when the volume, and sometimes the quality, of the voice is controlled by mechanical means. It is only acceptable in normal 'live' singing in exceptional circumstances. In the final phrase of Graham Peel's 'In summertime on Bredon', for example, the hum on the final crotchet helps to convey the resignation of the singer and is a matter of tone colour:

Pronunciation is the manner of pronouncing words. It goes without saying that students should learn to pronounce any foreign language they sing in not just correctly, well enough to pass a basic oral examination, but idiomatically; there is more to singing in a foreign language than merely knowing the rules. Pronunciation of sung English, paradoxically, may be the hardest of all, because vowel sounds in spoken English are so complex and so many syllables are normally spoken with a neutral 'uh' sound. When words are sung instead of spoken, there can be a danger that the singer's diction will sound affected.

Intonation in enunciation is more subtle than mere pitch and can be described as the modulation of the voice in articulation, so that one could say of a singer 'Her intonation is gentle and sweet' or 'His intonation is forceful and direct'.

Declamation means correct articulation of the words in a manner suitable or matched to their meaning.

Punctuation is the use of accents, breaths or commas to make a better understanding or sense of the words. For example, the sentence 'This song is a little gem, if ever there was one' may be punctuated or inflected in many different ways. It once caused a famous BBC announcer much agitation and rehearsal just before going on the air.

Recitative

There is no doubt that a student can soon be in vital contact with his listeners when he has mastered the various types of recitative, to which all these aspects of diction are basic. Recitative is 'speech in song' and without it one might just as well sing *vocalises* or 'songs without words'. There are, roughly speaking, three kinds of recitative: dry, accompanied and dramatic.

Dry recitative (*recitativo secco*) requires the ability to get rid of unimportant words quickly and clearly, exactly as in speech, while reserving a singing tone and vocal colour and accent for the important syllables of a phrase. Examples abound in Bach, Handel and Mozart. Patter songs – there are none better than Gilbert and Sullivan's – call for much the same technique.

Accompanied recitative (*recitativo accompagnato* or *arioso*) is sung smoothly and steadily so that good ensemble may be maintained with orchestra or other instrument. The consonants will be short and crisp but the vowels as long as possible, ensuring clear articulation and good instrumental tone. 'For behold darkness shall cover the earth', from Handel's *Messiah*, and 'Mein Jesus schweigt zu falschem Lugen stille', from Bach's *St. Matthew Passion*, are fine examples of accompanied recitative in its most eloquent form, a beauty in which Handel and Bach particularly excelled.

Dramatic recitative (*recitativo drammatico*) is much more exaggerated in emphasis and colour. It can be a mixture of dry and accompanied recitative, subject to the content of words and music. 'I rage, I melt, I burn', from *Acis and Galatea* by Handel, and 'Seid ihr nun fertig', sung by Beckmesser in Act I of Wagner's *Die Meistersinger von Nurnberg*, are typical.

'Singing with the ear'

The finished singer, it has been said, sings more with the ear than with the mouth. It is vital to a singer to have a natural ability to hear and reproduce sounds. With a keen ear and well placed voice, well tempered intonation should present no problem; it is intuitive. If a pupil normally sings in tune it should not be difficult to train the ear to avoid pitfalls and lapses. Intervals and diatonic and chromatic scales are used to assist accurate intonation. It is a good habit to hear a note before it is sung.

Bad intonation may be due to defective hearing. It may also be due to ill health, tiredness or faulty placement of the voice and resonances. A forced voice will tend to go off pitch because of unsteady breath control. It is surprising how many otherwise accomplished performers fall down on elementary points of intonation. It is common among young sopranos in florid scale passages, with inexact semitones and whole tones, thirds and the fifth and leading note. For example, the first phrases of 'Dove sono' and 'Porgi amor' in Figaro, of 'Celeste Aida' in *Aida*, are seldom exact in pitch, nor are the runs in Mozart's 'Exsultate, jubilate'.

Sometimes harmonic progressions need special care. I well remember, at the Proms, Sir Henry Wood raising his left eyebrow to me as we approached the G and A in the final cadence in Vaughan Williams's 'Bright is the ring of words':

Perfect pitch, the ability to recognize notes and keys and to reproduce them, can be a great asset. As the great teacher Nadia Boulanger has demonstrated, the gift is not entirely God given. It may be acquired by steady application, and should be the objective of ear training classes.

Listening is an important part of a singer's training. It is possible to learn as much from a poor performance as from a good one. The ability to criticize bad singing and appreciate – and sometimes imitate – good needs a keen and intelligent ear. Taste and individuality must be acquired.

Reading, too, is important – appreciation of the sound and rhythm of words in poetry and prose. Reading aloud and declaiming poetry help to develop a sense of expression, to say nothing of broadening the mind. Who was it who said: 'No tears are shed in performance; they have all been shed in rehearsal'? – meaning that an artist must be moved, or emotionally involved, by words – and music – in private if he is to convince in public.

Musical paper work is desirable, harmony and counterpoint, but it has little relation to the singer's need. Many great singers have known little of the theory of music but

55

have possessed the ability to listen, assess, reproduce and remember arias and roles with remarkable ease. I recall a case in point. Tudor Davies (the original Hugh in the first public performance of Vaughan Williams's *Hugh the Drover*) asked me to help him learn and memorize *La Bohème*. We went through the work twice and the third time he sang Rodolfo from memory with few mistakes of notes or time. It is this ability which is so much more valuable to a singer than the skill in analysing form and harmony, desirable though that may be.

Musicianship

The other day an international singer said in a television interview: 'Singers used not to be intelligent, today they must be musicians as well.' What did he mean by that? A good musician's concern is chiefly for the music and less for the vocal and dramatic aspects. Some years ago, at Glyndebourne, Jani Strasser told a well-known singer and teacher: 'You'll never be a singer, you're too good a musician.' Today things have changed, and singers cannot approach the professional market without exceptional musicianship. The development of atonal and abstract music makes it a *sine qua non* for young singers to have conscious singing of intervals and good sight reading at their fingertips. It is of great value to be able to 'pick notes out of the sky' and read atonal music, and many can do so nowadays. But it is also desirable to be steeped in early music and the classics, and it is vitally important in these days to begin basic musicianship studies, ear and eye, mind and memory, as early as possible.

Rhythm

A strong sense of time, or basic pulse, is essential for all performances, fast or slow. It should be firmly in mind with singer and accompanist before the music begins and should remain in mind throughout. That does not mean that one should sing like a ticking clock or a metronome, but with momentum and at the same time a sense of *rubato*. Changes of time should only occur when the composer says so. Elasticity of time, *tempo rubato*, is another matter. It is part of the interpretation within the basic speed. It is easy to forget the basic tempo and let emotion and *rubato* run amok. Music cannot be vital as the composer intended unless expressive *rubato* is in parenthesis within the paragraph or song. All great conductors have a strong rhythmic sense and so should singers.

Young singers tend to rely too much, perhaps, on expressive vocalization and declamation, forgetting that it is the motive power that holds music together. It is not always the singer who is to blame. It may be the accompanist – a 'follower', too kind to the singer, helping him to enjoy all his foibles, or a 'pianist', riding roughshod through entrances, cadences, climaxes, breaths and punctuation, thinking only of the printed notes and deaf to the singer's attempts at punctuation. In Chapter 27 Gerald Moore tells us how it is done by a master.

But, to be fair, it is generally the singer who is to blame for lack of rhythmic vitality. Technically it is again a matter of breath control and basic pulse, which must be properly organized so that the singer breathes (full breaths, half breaths, snatch breaths) at the right places without disturbing the rhythm. How much easier it would be if vocal music was printed as we sing it, with notes in a phrase slightly shortened where we must breathe or punctuate. For although rhythm will not sag if we cut short an ending, it certainly will if we are late for the next beat or pulse.

Snatch breaths

The ability to take these quick 'revivers' is vital. They are not an attempt to fill the lungs but to get just enough air to reach the next possible breathing space, like running across a stream on stepping stones. Care must be taken to see that they are inaudible – especially close to a microphone – by keeping mouth and throat open. They are essential in a song like Purcell's 'I attempt from love's sickness to fly':

O *full breath* V = *snatch breath*

suggested phrasing

Long phrasing

A 'long line' is the hallmark of all good singers. To manage long phrases in one breath should be the objective, as it is for the woodwinds; think of the oboe and flute *obbligati* to Bach's arias or the clarinet in Messiaen's *Quatuor pour le fin du temps*. There are many classic arias which extend to several lines without a visible breathing space. If they are impossible, then snatch breaths must be so organized that rhythm remains vital. These examples, ('Esurientes' from Bach's *Magnificat* and 'Beglückte Heerde' from the same composer's Cantata No. 105) illustrate the need for impeccable control: the first for long phrasing,

the second for snatch breaths:

- fe, die Welt ist euch ein Him-mel reich _____

Interpretation

Interpretation in song is the re-creation of words and music plus the singer's personality and intelligence. If a talented singer gets inside his work there is no need for additional presentation or distortion of the music. If he is untalented, nothing will make it effective. 'The simplicity of nature and strength of sentiment should be your guide more than anything else. Whoever strays from these generally falls into absurd incongruities that keep one in the class of mediocrity,' wrote Gluck in 1782. Interpretation is a matter of understanding and personality; a sense of style and magnetism. What you are, what you know, think, imagine, hear, read; all have an influence.

Listening to a fine singer can help by inspiration, not by imitation. By all means find out all you can about text and music but it is the personal rubber stamp on a performance which marks it as ordinary or magical.

Tone colour

'I always think of painting with my imagination when I am singing,' writes Tito Gobbi in Chapter 17. 'There is a splendid palette of shades and colours to choose from.' No one who heard him sing could forget the immense range of tone colour and characterization in his singing. Tone colour comes from the adjustment of the cheeks, mouth, soft palate, throat muscles and resonant cavities, so that the vowels take on a quality depicting the emotion involved. All voices have an individual tone colour or timbre. By concentrating on words or the character you are expressing, varied colours are at your command. For example, your facial muscles for 'With joy the impatient husbandman drives forth his lusty team', in Haydn's *The Seasons*, will be working high, wide and handsome. But for Beethoven's 'In questa tomba oscura' your tone must be low, dark and sombre. To this end it is not uncommon for a singer to massage his cheeks and lips in the artistes' room before a concert to ensure utmost flexibility.

The singer is faced with many types of auditoria – 'dead' concert halls, echoing churches, carpet-clad drawing-rooms, recording studios. The ideal is the hall with just enough warmth or echo to give satisfaction to the performer, for if he is uncomfortable how can he give of his best? The teacher will explain that one must sing naturally in every situation and never try to fill a 'dead' hall. It is quality that fires the resonance, not weight.

It is sad that two of the finest halls for sound in Europe no longer exist, both destroyed by fire: St Andrew's Hall in Glasgow and the old Philharmonic Hall in Liverpool. Yet we must be grateful for the admirable acoustic properties of the Snape Maltings Hall near Aldeburgh, for it shows what can be achieved by modern architects when advised by sensitive musicians.

Styles in singing

Bel Canto was not a phrase in common use until after the publication of Vaccai's *Dodici Ariette per Camera per l'Insegnamento del Bel Canto Italiano* in 1838, yet it is often used now to describe the style of singing in the 'golden age' of the seventeenth and eighteenth centuries. It includes several styles of vocalization: *canto spianato* (smooth), *canto fiorito* (florid) and *canto declamato* (declamatory).

Canto spianato, or *legato* singing, means moving from one note to another as smoothly as possible. Phrasing that is even, expressive and well sustained is often described by musicians as 'a long line' and is the objective of all good singers. It calls for perfect intonation, steadiness and beauty of tone, crisp and expressive articulation, swelled sounds, embellishments where necessary, *portamento* (carrying or sliding the tone quickly from note to note) and *rubato* (rhythmic give and take). Examples: songs of –

Atmosphere	'King David' (Herbert Howells)
	'Feldeinsamkeit' (Brahms)
Reminiscence	'Der Doppelgänger' (Schubert)
	'O wusst ich doch den Weg zurück'
	(Brahms)
Contemplation	'Auf ein altes Bild' (Wolf)
	'By a bierside' (Armstrong Gibbs)
Dedication	'The roadside fire' (Vaughan
	Williams)
	'An die Musik' (Schubert)
Smooth line	Most of the Italian *Arie Antiche* and
	probably three quarters of all singing.

Canto fiorito, florid singing, requires the ability to negotiate rapid passage work, ornaments, roulades, cadenzas, arpeggios, trills, with light tone and perfect intonation. It is used chiefly by light or coloratura sopranos. Examples:

'Lo! here the gentle lark' (Bishop)
'Martern aller Arten' (Mozart)
'O luce di quest'anima' (Donizetti)

Canto declamato needs dramatic expression, rhythmic strength, incisive utterance, colourful illustration. Beauty of tone and agility are of less importance although they may be required. Examples:

'Archibald Douglas' (Loewe)
'Ride to Rome' (Britten)
'Ethiopia saluting the colours' (Charles Wood)
'Song of the flea' (Moussorgsky)
'The Erl King' (Schubert)
'Young Dietrich' (Henschel)

To obtain proficiency in all styles one needs command not only of *legato*, agility and intonation but also of *marcato*, *portamento*, *staccato* and *aspirato*. One should also develop the intuitive sense of tone colour expressing all emotions that I mentioned above (page 60).

Marcato. Each note accented without separation or stopping the breath. A slight impulse is noticed in the diaphragm. It is indicated by dots or stress marks with a phrase mark above, ⌢⌢⌢⌢⌢⌢⌢ or > > > > > > > thus:

Portamento. The ability to glide the voice through all tones between two notes. Upward *portamento* is generally more graceful than downward. Discretion is needed in either case if it is to be expressive or elegant. It is printed

or

Staccato. Each note separate or detached from the next. Its effect varies according to the amount of accent needed. It is similar in action to a fresh attack on each note. No breath is to be taken between notes and long phrasing is just as important as in *legato*. It is indicated by separate dots over each note.

Aspirato. Breath is allowed to escape before each note, giving the effect of 'ha' or 'ho'. It is often described as the 'intrusive "h" '. It should be used sparingly and for special effects, as in repeated notes in seventeenth and eighteenth-century music. It is deplored in a normal *legato* line; to change the passage work into a laughing chorus in Bach's B minor Mass makes a travesty of the music.

Messa di voce. The swelled tone is one of the most expressive embellishments in music. It is a long note begun quietly, increased to full voice and returning to its original volume. It should not be attempted until a singer has developed the ability to hold, increase and decrease volume at will:

A singer should be able to command all types of vocalization and apply them with intelligence and common sense.

Languages

It is desirable but not essential that one should speak a language fluently before singing it; a phonetic accuracy plus a knowledge of the meaning of every word and of the character and mood is sufficient to make a beginning. Indeed, singers often pay more attention to clear articulation in a foreign language than in their own. When one is able to perform in English with eloquence it is likely that the same distinction can be achieved with foreign repertoire. It is not only a question of clear articulation but the modulation, inflexion and punctuation of poetry that is so important. The point is discussed by Pierre Bernac in Chapter 15 and by Rosemary Hardy in Chapter 22.

There is no doubt that if a poem is translated and a colloquial text is substituted, the magic is gone. Italian, with its wealth of rhymes, often defies translation; there can be no convincing English equivalent of:

Ridente la *calma*   Nè *resti* un *segno*
Nell'*alma* sid*esti*,   Di *sdegno* e timor.

Not all the lyrics set by Schubert are great poetry, but the colour of the words, the German vowels and consonants, have everything to do with the songs' magic. When we get to Wolf, with his 'poetic supremacy', and Schoenberg with his *Sprechgesang*, the would-be translator finds that virtually every syllable has to be matched in sound, stress and sense.

In the translation of recitative there is another, even more basic, problem. Addison wrote in 1711 (and it is perhaps even more true today than it was then):

The recitative music in every language should be as different as the tone or accent of each language: for otherwise what may properly express a passion in one language will not do it in another . . . Thus the notes of interrogation, or admiration in the Italian musick (if one may so call them) which resemble their accents in discourse on such occasions, are not unlike the ordinary tones of an English voice when we are angry; insomuch that I have often seen our audiences extremely mistaken as to what has been doing on the stage, and expecting to see the hero knock down his messenger when he has only been asking him a question, or fancy that he quarrels with his friend when he only bids him 'Good Morrow'.

Of course there are exceptions. Translated versions of many famous arias and songs have been accepted by English audiences through common usage. In settings of a sacred text – notably the Bach *Passions* – the language of the Bible is so well known and loved that there is a special reason for using English instead of German. Sometimes, too, a foreign composer sets a well known English poem translated into his own language (Schubert's 'An Silvia' – 'Who is Silvia?' – is an obvious example). When the original fits easily into the music, it may even be preferable to substitute it.

The teacher

Great singers may make fine teachers but it is not always so. Teaching and singing have little in common unless the teacher has the ability to impart knowledge. It is the personality of a teacher – and little of his method – that older singers remember about their teachers.

The objective must be to inspire and develop the student's ear, mind and voice by guidance, correction and demonstration. 'No teacher will be successful unless he teaches his pupil to teach himself,' wrote Arthur Cranmer in *The Art of Singing*. Basic musicianship can be taught in class – the younger the better – but voice training must be personal and individual, for each voice is unique and there can be no 'cut and dried' method.

Since the voice, unlike other instruments, is invisible, the teacher requires (a) a sound knowledge of the mechanism of the voice, (b) a sound knowledge of the registers and their marriage and (c) above all, a perfect ear to assess every sound for quality and placement.

A good working knowledge of the repertoire – including exercises and studies – is another important facet of the teacher's skill. It does not follow that all good teaching songs are necessarily right for all voices. Transposition is helpful but not always desirable. Many songs transpose well but only if the *tessitura*, the average pitch position, is right. A study of Schubert's songs *written* for low voice shows how easily they 'sit' in the voice. Many others transposed to suit a bass voice do not lie easily at all because the *tessitura* is uncomfortable, e.g. 'Auf dem Wasser zu singen' and 'Der Neugierige'. The graphs on pages 68–9 show the *tessitura* of a few famous arias for particular types of voice.

Health

It is, of course, vital that singers should be healthy inside and out. This was recognized as far back as Aristotle, who said: 'Lack of sleep makes the voice rougher; drinking makes the voice lower and more cracked than the normal voice of the sober' (Philip A. Duey, *Bel Canto in its Golden Age*).

In medieval times it was considered that physical robustness was essential and could be found in walking, rubbing down with oil, sexual abstinence, easy digestion and the simple life. Leeks, garlic, eels, firm fleshed fish, egg yolk have all been thought to produce smoothness and clarity to the larynx. Apples, figs, nuts and cold drinks were considered harmful. Spirits were considered bad, but sweet wines good for young voices and dry, astringent wines for older voices.

In the sixteenth century it was said that the best time for singing was four to five hours after eating. 'When the stomach is full the windpipe and the voice do not possess the necessary purity and clarity' (Duey). Much the same holds good today, though, as Dr Alexander says in Chapter 3: 'Any one item a singer's voice craves may be anathema to another.' In my time oysters and stout were considered sustaining and easy to digest and I have no doubt that wine is good for the voice and spirits bad, especially for young voices.

Smoking in moderation can do you no harm. In excess it can affect purity and clarity of the voice. If it irritates the mucous membranes one should certainly desist. Caruso was fond of a cigar and Plunket Greene said he would prefer to give up singing than smoking. A room full of stale smoke and air should always be avoided.

Some singers are very susceptible to colds and sore throats. Many develop from cold and damp feet or standing about in cold or draughty places after singing. Like an athlete, one should take special care to keep warm until back to normal.

Your voice is with you for life. You cannot fit new strings or new reeds to it. Therefore nurture it. There is no need to coddle it, but never misuse it or flog it when tired.

Otherwise, be rational and sensible. Take plenty of fresh air and exercise. Walking is excellent and golf is considered the ideal exercise by many singers. The Penguin book *Physical Fitness* offers a daily alternative for city dwellers.

Keith Falkner

Becoming a Singer

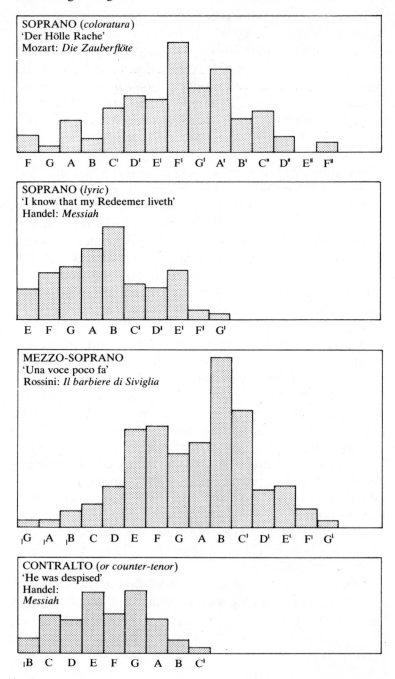

SOPRANO (*coloratura*)
'Der Hölle Rache'
Mozart: *Die Zauberflöte*

F G A B C' D' E' F' G' A' B' C" D" E" F"

SOPRANO (*lyric*)
'I know that my Redeemer liveth'
Handel: *Messiah*

E F G A B C' D' E' F' G'

MEZZO-SOPRANO
'Una voce poco fa'
Rossini: *Il barbiere di Siviglia*

ᵢG ᵢA ᵢB C D E F G A B C' D' E' F' G'

CONTRALTO (*or counter-tenor*)
'He was despised'
Handel:
Messiah

ᵢB C D E F G A B C'

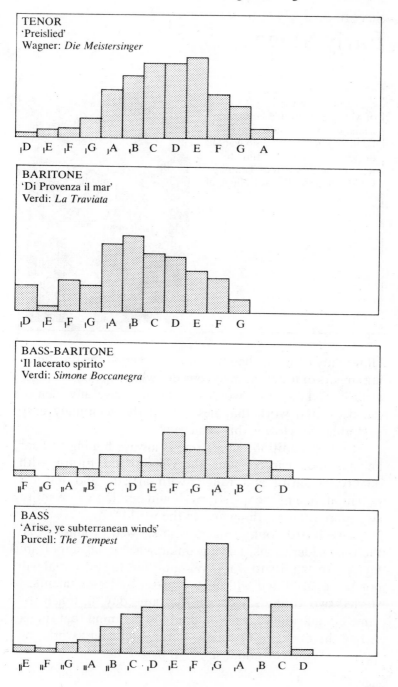

TENOR
'Preislied'
Wagner: *Die Meistersinger*

‚D ‚E ‚F ‚G ‚A ‚B C D E F G A

BARITONE
'Di Provenza il mar'
Verdi: *La Traviata*

‚D ‚E ‚F ‚G ‚A ‚B C D E F G

BASS-BARITONE
'Il lacerato spirito'
Verdi: *Simone Boccanegra*

ıF ıG ıA ıB ‚C ‚D ‚E ‚F ‚G ‚A ‚B C D

BASS
'Arise, ye subterranean winds'
Purcell: *The Tempest*

ıE ıF ıG ıA ‚B ‚C ‚D ‚E ‚F ‚G ‚A ‚B C D

Seven
Early Stages

Meriel St Clair, F.R.C.M.
A Scholar of the Royal College of Music and studied later with Elena Gerhardt and Claire Croiza. After the '39–'46 war she decided to devote her time to teaching at Southlands Training College and the Royal College of Music.

How many people, when listening to some of the outstanding singers of today, stop to consider what their early stages were like? Few, even would-be singers, have any idea of the dedicated work that lies behind the seemingly easy performance. How is this achieved?

At a first audition, where one is always hoping to hear an outstanding instrument, the voice of the future, with quality, quantity and range, with artistic and musical potential, one of the questions should be: 'Do you want to sing more than anything else in the world?'

I have heard young singers who showed promise in all these considerations, leaving unknown one all-important factor – the ability to work. Without this, the potential will not be realized and will be overtaken by lesser talents. I started two young singers on the same day, in much the same circumstances, with no doubt in my mind that singer A had the outstanding talent; but by consistent work and dedicated concentration, singer B passed her by.

70

The early stages should be a time of endless enjoyment both for the student and the teacher, for there is nothing more exciting than to hear a young voice develop, and to watch the unique quality which belongs to each personality being realized, so that it becomes the magic gift of communication which makes a performance memorable. There can be many reasons, both psychological and physical, for withholding this unique offering. Only when the mind is free can the imagination be released, and for this the singer must have confidence in both her vocal and musical security.

One young singer came to me with a most beautiful, natural voice but totally preoccupied with the sound she made and with a dormant mind. She sang nothing but slow songs and assured me that she had neither imagination nor a sense of humour. In time when her mind was awakened her assurances proved to be far from the truth and her singing was full of sensitivity and life.

I do not think that it is possible to generalize on the age at which study should begin, for it depends on the individual. There are some voices that mature quickly at a young age and suddenly stop, while others develop slowly and steadily and need time to reach maturity.

Much will depend upon whether there is a really good teacher within reach, since, I believe, the early lessons are all-important. A voice can be easily damaged and to unlearn is much harder than to learn. Faults are frequently due to the over-eager school-teacher who puts the good musician to sustain a line where the choir is weakest, regardless of the natural compass and quality of the young voice. Quite recently, a fourteen-year-old schoolgirl was sent to me for an opinion of her voice. She offered for her audition high soprano, mezzo and contralto arias.

At nineteen, most voices should be ready for serious study. Ideally, the voice should be free from bad habits and the student sufficiently mature to see the point of doing the basic study that is so essential in the early stages.

Later, both voice and personality become more set and change becomes harder. It is true that there is much music for which the younger voice must wait, but one hopes that financial needs will not dictate the course of study. Discussing this with a now very successful soprano who began at seventeen, I asked her if she thought it would have been better to wait. She replied that her only alternative would have been to go into a factory near her isolated home, instead of which she had grown up in a musical atmosphere.

From the beginning, it is the teacher who must listen, to get to know the voice, in order to discover the inherent quality that makes it different from all others. Just as no two people are alike, so no two voices are alike; therefore the training must be unique. Only when the individual quality is recognized can the voice be satisfactorily developed. This takes time and patience for both teacher and student; it cannot be hurried. The teacher's aim should be to bring out the student's own interpretation, never imposing her own; to try to encourage the love of music, the enjoyment in the making of it, and the sharing of that enjoyment with the audience.

It is the teacher who should remember from lesson to lesson what the student should do next so that the course of study is without gaps. Vocal technique has already been discussed in detail in a previous chapter, but in the early lessons the main task will be to place the middle of the voice securely, from which both ends can develop until the voice is even throughout its compass.

Learning to sing through consonants without disturbing the *legato* line, while still maintaining clear diction, is an all-important study. The organs of articulation must be so fast-moving and flexible that there is no delay between one word and the next, while the flow of breath is continuous. To this end, the Italian language, with its emphasis on vowel sounds, is helpful in itself, and the *Arie Antiche* lend themselves to early training. Handel, with his long, sustained lines, Purcell, Mozart and the less demanding songs of Schubert are also invaluable.

Few students seem to know how to study and from the first the teacher must be a guide. Young singers do not seem to realize that it is only the regularity and concentration of their practice that will form secure vocal habits on which they can rely with confidence when their minds are given over to interpretation or characterization. Fear of one bar can ruin an entire performance; the singer is waiting in trepidation for it to come and then giving thanks that it is over. But to correct the bar when studying, it is not necessary to sing the song from beginning to end, as so many young singers tend to do. Of course, at first the practice should be little and often, but gradually lengthening in time, so that ultimately the voice can sustain all the demands that will be put on it, be it in opera, oratorio, recital or recording session.

I believe the power of concentration is one of the most valuable assets a singer can have, both in study and performance; it can be trained, it can be developed, it is the secret of memorizing – it is the foundation of the really committed singer.

I like to encourage my singers to stand when they practice their singing, but sit in an armchair when they learn; a habit that is invaluable should they ever become busy professionals when their plane and train journeys can be used in this way.

There is so much to learn!

The approach to a song should be the study of melody, line, phrasing, dynamics, harmony and accompaniment, the student all the time trying to discover the composer's intentions.

Once it has been seen how the composer has treated the poem (and comparison of settings of the same poem by different composers can be an enlightening experience), it should be studied and memorized independently to gain a true understanding of the words, their stress and significance. So many young singers fail to appreciate that singing is a union of words and music; they rely on the tune to supply the words and have little conception of their real meaning. Only when words and music are memorized can the imagination be released, and only when there is vocal security can the most imaginative ideas be communicated to the audience.

Deportment and movement is a study in itself, and one which, in the early stages, many singers find difficult. The development of the voice must go hand in hand with projection of the personality, for singing involves the whole being. The audience must see as well as hear, therefore the singer must be totally immersed in the interpretation, mentally and physically, from head to toe to fingertips: only then will the interpretation come to life.

It is then that the imagination, that most magic gift, can communicate with an audience, and ensure a response that makes the performance unforgettable.

Eight
The Post-graduate

Roy Henderson, C.B.E.,
F.R.A.M.
A student and professor of the
Royal Academy of Music. His
career began in dramatic fashion
in April 1925 when he sang the
baritone role in Delius *Mass of
Life*, at very short notice, from
memory, in the old Queens Hall
– in place of Percy Heming.
Kathleen Ferrier asked him for
lessons after singing with him in
Elijah. He was chorus master of
the Nottingham Philharmonic
Choir under Hamilton Harty;
and John Christie once remarked
'No need to ask if he can act, he's
a cricketer.'

The post-graduate singer is usually from the best of our
music colleges. The development and management of the
voice, with artistic expression in many languages and
styles, is a lifelong study, and at the end of the course the
student is only at the threshold of knowledge.

The basis of all good singing is technique, and technique
requires constant practice of scales, so often forgotten
during one's career. A singer's technique must be so good
that it can be forgotten when actually singing. The singer
must play on his instrument as any other musician does,
with the same musicianship and care for rhythm and
phrasing but with the addition of words which often
determine the rise, fall and point of a phrase. It was the
words that inspired the composer. Study them first, recite
them to see where the natural stresses fall, then look at the
music. Singers bear the responsibility of bringing to life
the work of the poet and composer, which they should
regard as a privilege. When a passage is marked *pianissimo*,

75

it is not enough simply to sing it softly: sing it in such a physical, mental or emotional mood that you cannot sing it any other way. Does it express bodily weakness, the stillness of the night, the lover's whisper, a breathless excitement? The context will tell you.

No technique is perfect. Even intonation is often uncertain, sometimes unknown to the singer. An oscilloscope with a microphone attached will reveal on the screen the slightest variation of pitch on any tuned note, and the singer soon gets the feeling of singing in tune by watching the picture. It is usually a matter of keeping the focus of the voice the same throughout the compass. Too much vibrato, a wobble, and the picture looks like a rough sea. A smooth vocal line can be taught ten times more quickly with the help of the oscilloscope. A dot on the screen becomes a perpendicular line when singing. If there are gaps of sound between words (syllabic singing, or barking), the line goes up and down like a Yo-Yo. The object is to keep the line as steady as possible, with the merest flick for consonants; in other words, to blow through the consonants continuously. We don't always hear what we are doing, but when we can see it on a screen it is easier to correct.

Repeat the composer's tempo. Conductors nowadays seldom ask: 'Is this a comfortable tempo for you?' Many think *pace* is more important than rhythm. It is the age of speed – but that does not apply to music written years ago. Rhythm can be strict or elastic, according to the type of music sung; but obey instructions. How many singers in 'Von ewiger Liebe' drag out the last words? Brahms wanted the accompanying quavers to keep moving to the singer's climax on *bestehn*, with a *molto ritardando* three bars before the end – and a *diminuendo* to *piano* as the despairing youth falls into the tender arms of the girl.

The hallmark of interpretation is sincerity. Joy, sorrow, love, hate, worship and contempt, the singer must feel them all sincerely. You cannot move an audience without being moved yourself. Sincerity, a vivid imagination and the ability to sing the words as though they were your very own and said for the first time, are the chief ingredients of interpretation. Imagination which can blot out the audience and see a lover, a child, a stream, a landscape or whatever one is singing about, or to; imagination which feels the hot tear falling down the cheek in 'Die Mainacht', smells the scent of lime flowers in 'Ich atmet einen linden Duft', tastes with a castor-oil face (ask your grandfather what that is) the 'tea and stuff' in 'Captain Stratton's Fancy' and hears with serene joy the bell in 'Die junge Nonne'. There is a story behind each song; sometimes it is clear or well known, but often singers must make their own. What is the story behind 'Verborgenheit' or 'Allerseelen'? When tenors sing 'Every valley' from *Messiah*, what is in their minds? Most would say: 'I just sing it.' But that is no interpretation. Could it not be that when the Lord comes we must change our values? Humility will be a virtue, the high and mighty laid low, the crooked in mind and body healed and rough diamonds like Peter made saints? That is one idea, there could be others, but there must be a meaning behind each obscure sentence. And remember, you cannot interpret anything with your eyes on crotchets and quavers. You do not *know* any music until you can sing it from memory. I often ask a student: 'Where was your mind when I stopped you singing?' Mental concentration, which blots out all inward thought when it should be outward, all outward thought that should be inward – that is the beginning of concentration.

Acting, vital in opera, is far more subtle on the concert platform. First, the actor must learn to stand still – movement which means nothing is distracting and often irritating. A man's facial expression is more clear if he is clean shaven. All expressions you might need should be practised before a mirror. Stand with one foot forward, so that weight can be transferred to either foot with the body erect. The forward balance is used for pleading, invitation, attraction and so on, the backward for reception, dislike, fear, surprise etc. The Erl King leans forward to seduce the child; the child, terrified, is on the backward balance, while the father is on two feet trying to reassure the boy. The balance only changes for emotional disturbances. The difference between 'Du bist die Ruh' and 'Meine Ruh ist hin' is in the absolute stillness of the former and the slow movement of the head from one side to the other to represent restlessness in the latter. A whole book could be written about what and what not to do, and exact timing of any movement to the music. A video-tape I find invaluable, as is sound recording – on tape or cassette – to correct faults.

Singers often need advice on dress, deportment, attitude to an audience and behaviour backstage. Men are lucky, with the choice of full evening dress, dinner jacket and morning coat. As soon as you can, go to the best tailor possible. A well cut dress suit lasts a lifetime if you don't lose your figure. Women must choose not only the best dressmaker possible, but suitable colours. A blonde can wear light colours, but if you are overweight keep them dark. A hair style to suit your personality and the shape of your head and face is most important.

The way you behave, both on the stage and in the artistes' room, is bound to make an impression, on both the audience and your fellow musicians. If you are singing with a small choral society, for instance, remember that it is the choir's great day, and turn to applaud its members at the end of the concert. In the artistes' room, be civil and considerate; others may not share your sense of humour. And never – do I need to say this? – never blow your own trumpet. If nobody else blows it for you, it isn't worth blowing.

A book could be written on choice of programmes. Types of concerts vary from the popular to the orchestral and the highest form of the singer's art, the recital. Whatever the concert, don't sing trash.

A recital programme differs according to the personality and preference of the singer; a song or song-cycle that suits A may be out of the question for B. As a good general rule, think of your programme as you would a good dinner.

Choose the meat course first and then the others around it. Hors d'oeuvre could be a group of seventeenth and eighteenth-century songs, English or Italian. Start with a slow song which has some bars of accompaniment before you come in. A slow *legato* will give you the feel of the hall, which differs according to the size of the audience. Durante's 'Vergin tutto amor', Stradella's 'Pietà Signore', Purcell's 'Music for awhile', or, if it is a French group, Lully's 'Bois épais', all are good first songs. Vary the group in tempo and mood. 'Danza danza, fanciulla gentile' by Durante is a good finish for an Italian group. About four, or at most five, songs is enough to start with. The second group should be short; a Mozart concert aria or three Mozart or Haydn songs make an excellent light fish course. The meat course could be a song cycle, but if it is longer than twenty minutes omit the fish. Beethoven's *An die ferne Geliebte*, Schumann's *Frauenliebe und Leben*, Brahms's *Vier ernst Gesänge* are typical. A group of songs by a major composer, Schubert, Brahms, Wolf etc, would also do. A good variety is needed. Here is a Schubert group for a male voice:

'An Silvia'
'An die Leier'
'Der Doppelgänger'
'Fischerweise'
'Gruppe aus dem Tartarus'

and here is a group of Wolf songs for female voice:

'Gebet'
'Auf einer Wanderung'
'Das verlassene Mägdlein'
'Du denkst mit einem Fädchen'
'Herr, was trägt der Boden hier'
'Er ist's'

Be careful that the change of mood from one song to another is matched by a sufficient change of key.

After the interval, for dessert, which should be interesting but not too heavy, perhaps a French, Spanish or English group or *short* song-cycle. If you want to attract the press, try to find an out of the way group or preferably a first performance. If you want to please the audience, Poulenc's *La Bestiaire* or *Fiançailles pour rire* (but your French accent must be good) or Britten's *Charm of Lullabies*, or a group of Spanish songs, or Strauss, would fit the bill.

The coffee and liqueur is a time for pleasantry, a group of folk songs or English songs. Add a little humour if you have any. The total number of songs in the programme should be between eighteen and twenty-two – and I emphasize, don't overdo it.

Of course the above is a conventional recital of singable songs. I have avoided *avant-garde* music, perhaps because I am an old fogy who believes that the young singer should be brought up on the music of composers who really understood the human voice.

In my day the way to get press notices was through a recital. One could count on six to a dozen papers being present for part if not all the time. Nowadays the quickest way to fame is to win one of the major competitions at home or abroad. The first stage is vital, and you must knock the jury for six, choosing your best items and making an immediate impression to separate you from the mob. It is so easy to be left out of the few that make it to the next stage.

Nine
The Young Professional Singer

John McCarthy
Chorus Master at the Royal
Opera House Covent Garden,
Music Director of the Ambrosian
Singers, Opera Chorus and
Consort and of the Carmelite
Priory. He has acted as Choral
Director to all the great
conductors. Has had five
nominations for the U.S.A.
'*Grammy*' award and conducted
three winning L.P.s for the
'Grand Prix du Disque'.

Introducing the young professional singer into the prospects and difficulties to be encountered in the professional world of singing would require a volume in itself, but here are some basic facts. Upon completion of his or her college training, the young singer is faced with the prospect of making a career in one of several fields. Let us review the possibilities. He ('he' here includes 'she') can aspire to become a great operatic soloist, or to be a superb oratorio singer; to be an expert in performing modern classical music; to star in musical comedy or in cabaret, or to make a name on television, films or radio. For any of these he must have the vocal technique to survive the taxing efforts called for to stay the course. In the meantime, whilst awaiting the delights of international acclaim, the artist may need to supplement solo engagements in some way so as to earn a living, preferably in some field where he can also extend his musical experience. As Sir Alan Herbert put it so well in his autobiography (Heinemann 1970) 'Till you have got a foothold in the foothills of Parnassus, arrange to win some bread lower down . . . a freelance is not free from anxiety but he has some fun.'

The best of these supplementary occupations is probably the session world, by which I mean work in recording studios, generally as part of an established group such as the Ambrosian Opera Chorus, Ambrosian Singers etc, taking part in anything from opera to 'pop'. Recruitment into the session world is made through auditions with an Equity-approved choral manager, who is not an agent and takes no commission from the singer. Recommendation by a professor or other singing teacher aids the speed with which the application for an audition is dealt.

Many foreign film and recording companies, besides the famous British firms, do their recording in studios in and around London. The amount of work afforded depends on the singer's ability to switch from one kind of music to another, from classical to pop, from pop to plainchant. He should be capable of tackling any type of singing required of him. In any of these fields, however, it must be stressed that expert sight-reading is called for, since rehearsal time is at a premium, and an approximate sense of pitch, if not absolute pitch, is essential. A good solo technique is not enough, since the best professional choruses depend on blend and the general technique of working as a team. Every session is a production, and there can be no 'prima donnas' in a chorus.

Sessions work is a unique form of employment, peculiar to London, which not only enables the singer to earn money but also affords him the opportunity of hearing the great soloists of the world in action and of observing how they overcome the difficulties of arias and recitatives. In addition the singer will work under the foremost conductors, thus learning how the excitement of a performance is generated. Yet another bonus is the experience of learning idiomatic pronunciation of foreign languages, as expert coaches are brought in to supervise this aspect of the performance. Many famous soloists have gained early and valuable experience in the session world; Heather Harper, Dame Janet Baker, Helen Watts, Robert Tear, John Shirley-Quirke and many others started in this manner and so built up their reputation as soloists of international repute. In this way they avoided the danger of over-exploitation at an early stage of development.

Gramophone recordings provide the most prolific source of earnings, with 'pop' sessions much more highly paid than so-called classical sessions. One must not underestimate the requirements of technique and musicianship in this field. Some 'pop' music has close harmonies involving extremely accurate intonation, and complex rhythms demanding great concentration and brilliant ensemble singing, more than in the most difficult madrigals or modern classical compositions. The singer must also adapt himself by learning microphone technique. Too many of our august musical training establishments refuse to recognize the existence of this form of musical employment, and the student has no instruction in the special skills involved. Consequently very few 'trained' singers can turn their hand to this style of music, having assumed (wrongly) that 'anyone can sing that sort of thing'. Their colleagues in the orchestral world generally fare much better, since the real 'heavy rhythm boys' are specialists in 'pop' only, and the string players in particular have more sustained and 'straight' parts to play – with no words to sing, moreover. One can frequently see members of our leading symphony orchestras using these sessions as a sideline.

Opera recordings are usually made in the summer months, between June and September, when most of the world's opera houses are on holiday, thus releasing the opera stars for recording. England's main film studios are at Pinewood and Elstree, but most of the sound tracks are made at large sound studios which have projection facilities, such as Anvil, C.T.S. at Wembley, Olympic at Barnes and a number of smaller studios. Post-synchronization is a useful source of work; this is the dubbing over the voice of some actor or actress whose singing didn't match up to what the producer had in mind, done on to a loop of film which repeats the track until the singer achieves the required result, phrase by phrase.

There is, of course, a variety of fields outside the recording studio at which the young artist can aim. Opera companies employ a considerable number of singers for their permanent chorus. Stamina and good technique are essential in this sphere, because the average opera chorister has a powerful voice, and anyone surrounded by strong voices tends to sing more loudly than nature intended, with disastrous results, particularly to a young voice. The advantage of this type of employment for anyone intending to make a career in opera, lies in being able to work on stage nightly with the world's greatest soloists – something of incalculable value to the young artist. Talented young singers who do not feel adequate to tackle the strenuous demands of the chorus can audition for small character parts which can eventually lead to greater roles.

Male singers may enjoy singing in cathedral choirs. (The editor of this volume himself sang for five years at Westminster Abbey and St Paul's Cathedral while establishing his career.) Vacancies in cathedral and other church choirs are advertised in the *Musical Times* and in church magazines of various sorts of all denominations. The stipend is not large, but can be a useful anchor for a regular income; extras in the shape of weddings and so forth add considerably to the singer's earnings. The time required is not too exacting, so that the singer can do 'session work' without too much difficulty. Work with a church choir can be a very satisfying adjunct to the professional singer, enabling him to enjoy the wonderful heritage of the inspired music of all the great composers from all ages.

Musicals are for the young, good-looking singer who can move reasonably well. This, of course, includes the Christmas pantomime season. Musicals are well paid, enjoyable, tremendous experience and an 'open sesame' to recordings, television and radio. Summer seasons are a very pleasant way of spending the summer – usually not too arduous, pleasant surroundings, and once you know the show all you have to do is the nightly performances. The pay is not so good when you have to find 'digs' and keep a place in town, but it's worth trying for one season at least. All musicals and vacancies for U.K. summer seasons and pantomimes are always well advertised in *The Stage*.

In the winter, ship's cruises are a wonderful way to escape our cold weather by doing cabaret. They are usually well paid, with first-class accommodation and food – almost a holiday, with the opportunity of making interesting new acquaintances. In some cases you can bring the family along. Details of your act should be well circulated to the Entertainments Sections of the various shipping lines.

Television can be profitable and interesting. Here again, as in films, the more versatile the singer, the greater the possibilities, not only in television operas and musicals but in plays, background music and even comedy shows. Television jingles, those catchy little songs that accompany the commercials, are most rewarding financially, but probably the most difficult field to break into. They are within the domain of the choral manager, but are also cast by individual advertising agencies. There are studio fees and the 'residuals' (or repeat fees) for every block of ten showings in each area of transmission. For some jingles which use the same music for different presentations during a year or more, the singer could receive over £500 for just an hour's work. The casting department of all leading advertising agencies should be supplied with your details; for 'in vision' work you should send a good photograph of yourself, since if the face 'fits' the product you could be chosen regardless of voice.

Sound radio has a permanent chorus of singers, the BBC Singers, regularly employed as BBC staff, who perform a variety of classical music of all periods. The BBC also employs *ad hoc* singers to augment the regular chorus when extra resources are needed and to sing in their regional choruses. For work as a soloist on sound radio auditions are held; if successful the singer is placed on a Solo Panel from which producers may select artists suitable for their particular programmes. The short cut to this list is of course from opera and stage musicals, which all the main producers of the BBC go to see to assess the available talent.

Concerts, festivals and recitals unfortunately afford very little employment to the professional chorus singer, but for the soloist they can be quite rewarding, aesthetically and even financially. Since the soloists are usually provided by a booking agency, the singer should apply to be accepted by one of these, or have a good personal agent.

I have myself suffered thousands of aspiring candidates for all the different media, and I must advise all singers to examine the situation carefully. It is most important to present for audition the right piece for the occasion – it is no use singing a number from 'Hair' for an opera audition or 'Caro nome' for a rock musical. This may sound ludicrous, but the realities are almost as bad. Too often a singer turns up with one party piece instead of a selection of appropriate songs, well contrasted and thoroughly prepared (for nerves can dry up the most experienced artist). Unless you bring your own accompanist, you should make sure that the copies you provide are clearly written, in the right key, and without too many difficult repeats and hieroglyphics.

The most important thing of all is that, no matter what sphere of the profession you finally select, you should enjoy the music you perform. For a true artist the pursuit of perfection will far outweigh any idea of doing a job of work, and each individual must decide where his own greatest pleasure and rewards are to be found.

Ten
The Life of a Singer Today

Dame Janet Baker
   Fellow of the Royal Society of Arts, Holder of the Hamburg Shakespeare Prize, the Copenhagen Sonning Prize, seven honorary degrees, member of the Munster Musical Trust and Artistic Co-Director of the King's Lynn Festival. One of the most beloved international singers of this generation.

The days have long since gone when famous performers travelled across continents in luxurious trains, over seas in large floating hotels, arriving refreshed in mind, voice and body for the next engagement. Outer circumstances have changed because of the pressures of life: it is now lived at an amazing speed. One of the most common remarks made to me is 'You aren't doing too much, are you?'. Everything about a career is geared to doing precisely this; even the season, which used to stop after Easter and start again in September, has been greatly extended owing to the many festivals which take place during the summer, and which fill in the precious weeks which were used for rest and study. As soon as the individual raises his hand and says 'No more' the harder everyone tries to persuade him to take 'Just one more concert'. It's like dieting, no one really likes you to do it on the night of their dinner-party!

   Because of fast methods of travel, we can take on a far greater number of engagements than ever before. The resulting mental, physical and vocal strain perhaps mean shorter working lives. The opportunity to do more work means that we also meet large numbers of colleagues, from whom we learn and with whom we feel close contact. The profession appears smaller, just as better communications in radio, television and the telephone have made the world feel smaller. We all affect each other and work much more as members of a team than singers of former years. The development of communications has meant that our repertoires are enormous compared with those of a hundred years ago. We can't tour the world with a few operatic roles and a couple of recital programmes.

The symphony orchestra, the piano, the techniques of instrumental playing have also changed; they all make a louder noise! Schubert's accompaniment of 'Erlkönig' written for the fortepiano, a much softer and more gentle instrument than today's Steinway, must have been far easier for the singer to ride. The composers of the *bel canto* era realized very clearly that the public came to hear the singer's voice and wrote so that this was always possible without any sense of strain. Nowadays we are regarded as extra orchestral wind instruments and much of our life is spent in struggling to be heard across the pit or in the concert hall. An accompanying dynamic is always relative; a purely orchestral *forte* must surely be a very different sound from a *forte* used by the same forces when supporting a single voice. It is possible for eighty people to play a most wonderful pianissimo under the voice; I have actually experienced this! Unfortunately, it is all too rare for the singer to be able to obey scrupulously the dynamic markings of a vocal line; all that is necessary to change this situation is a conductor with enough courage to continually remind the orchestra that it *is* accompanying. Continually is the operative word, because the players forget, naturally; but it can be done.

Whatever the differences in outward circumstances, two things remain constant for the singer of today, the paramount necessity for an excellent technique and the development of an inner spiritual process which enables us to say something of value through the medium of the voice.

It has always been the most difficult thing in the world for a singer just to move from one note to the next. It takes a lifetime to remember to breathe out air and to join one note to another without a gap in-between. This is the process called *Bel Canto* or 'beautiful singing'. The distance caused by inserting a consonant between two consecutive notes, even if they are only a semitone apart, is enormous! The voice has particular trouble in joining up sound, more than most instruments and the body has equal difficulty in breathing deeply enough to support it because the vital, smooth passage of air is the first thing affected by nerves.

Any change of emotion is immediately reflected in our breathing pattern. We all know this. Just think how our breath alters when we are frightened; the heart begins to pound and the breath rate accelerates; this is exactly what happens to a singer when he walks out to face the public and it is the very moment he needs equilibrium most in order to produce an even sound. What a cruelty!

Some singers, very few, seem to need no teacher, they have absolutely natural voices which look after themselves. Most of us have to try and find a teacher; the good ones are rare indeed. We all try as best we can, to produce our own individual sound easily. Since we are individuals, no two singers produce their voices in the same way and so it is easy to understand why teaching of voice production is a well-night impossible task. We get hints from the teacher but we have only the feel inside our own throats to tell us whether or not what we are being asked to do is safe for us. In other words, if it hurts it's wrong!

If we actually succeed in bringing the voice under reasonable control, the real task can begin; to interpret the music placed in our care. Performers are middle-men; we stand between the composer and the audience serving as a bridge to bring the two together. What gives us the right to seize a great piece of music and decide to perform it? Whenever I play through a piece, new to me, I expect an immediate, strong reaction, a physical response which makes me say 'This is marvellous; I must learn it.' In other words, I must love it; this is the first requirement because if I do not feel this at the outset, I haven't a hope of persuading an audience to feel the same way.

Suppose the work speaks of a situation or an emotion which is right outside my own direct experience? I must then rely on imaginative ability, something without which no singer can survive. I must draw upon this facility to carry me through, say, the Mahler 'Kindertotenlieder', which speak of the pain felt by a parent on the death of children. I may not have lost children, but as a human being I know what 'loss' means. We have all lost something or someone; the memory of this feeling must serve me now, intensified, as indeed it is, by the music itself. Schubert had a great love of Nature. I know what it means to me to walk through a country lane on a summer's day, so it is easy to transfer that feeling into his songs; the hard thing is to feel the world's beauty as deeply as Schubert did.

Performers are privileged people; our close contact with the minds of men like Bach, Mozart and Beethoven suggests to us that although we can never hope to inhabit their world of creative genius, we can, by trying to interpret their thoughts and discover their meaning, develop our own minds; by recapturing the emotion they felt, make ourselves more sensitive. We can't know what it is really like to live and feel at such intensity but it is our most sacred duty to try to reproduce it even though it is a pale reflection.

This sacred duty applies to all the performing arts; we are re-creators and to develop our hearts and minds for such a purpose means that every single moment of our lives must be used to feed the inner person. Each human being we meet has something to teach us if we listen; each situation we meet during a day has something valuable to tell us if we are open-hearted enough to learn. At the end of a day we are not the same as the person who woke that morning. Life changes us, if we will allow it to do so. Every experience should be stored away in our imagination, like food, to be drawn upon when we are confronted by a new challenge in our music. This is a transmuting process and, in digesting each situation which comes to us, it is also a transforming one. We stand in front of an audience and all we have to give is ourselves; we must strive to become more and more sensitive so that we can reflect more truly the great music which is placed in our hands; it is an enormous responsibility.

The singer's life is rather like that of an athlete. We have to keep ourselves in first-rate physical condition. This means eating properly, which also means not too much weight; we need to be, ideally, five or six pounds over the correct weight for our height. This is a visual age and audiences find it difficult to accept us playing roles for which we are physically wrong. It is a fallacy that singers must be fat. Singers must be fit, superbly so. The body we are given has a certain weight for perfect health; this body will carry the voice we are given too: if a singer is grossly overweight and suddenly slims drastically, of course the voice will suffer; but a healthy body will carry its own voice perfectly well. I know singers with enormous voices and very small bodies; they are doing fine!

We need to make time for thought, preparation, study and rest. We overuse our vocal cords, both by singing and by talking; singers should talk as little as possible, certainly on performing days. Another vital lesson is to learn early in life how much singing the voice can safely cope with. We find ourselves taking on too much work and suffering the consequences before we are able to judge the limit properly. It is a real danger, especially in the opera house, to sing too much and to sing unsuitable roles. Only the individual can really tell how much work is safe; most of us sing too much; the actual number of engagements in a year must be at least doubled because of rehearsals which are just as demanding vocally as the performances themselves.

Everyone should have one or two trusted, unbiased, knowledgeable friends, colleagues or teacher, who have his/her welfare at heart and know the voice and its capabilities.

We are lucky in that concert seasons are organized at least one year if not more, ahead, so we can plan our studies. It is very important to memorize in plenty of time, even more important to give the words and music a chance to 'settle' into the depths of the mind. I think about an operatic role for at least a year and by the time I get to production rehearsals the person I am to play is someone I know very well indeed. The character must have this extra dimension which is only achieved by living within the heart and mind of the player. It is exactly the same with the *Lieder* repertoire. As one sings a great Schubert *Lied* it changes and grows even from performance to performance and this fact of our working lives is an exciting one; we never give the same performance twice and no singer ever sings like any other.

The singer today as in any age must be a completely dedicated person (not to the pursuit of fame and fortune, although both are nice!) First, to being a good servant of music, the composer and the public. Our first concern is those three things and if our motives are right the dangers and pitfalls waiting for those who work in the limelight can never overwhelm us. We are such vulnerable people; the voice is affected by many factors outside our control; travel-fatigue, hotel life and its attendant lack of peace, quiet and the sort of food we need and the odd hours we need to eat it; above all, public judgment. Because our voice is also our being in the deepest sense, criticism of our work is a judgment of both nature and character. To damage the confidence of any performer, young or old, is an action very easily achieved, far too lightly taken. The critic fondly claims no one really takes him seriously; those who employ singers certainly do. I used to think critics a necessary part of working life; I no longer think so; critical journalism may be useful to those members of an audience who have to read the paper in order to find out whether or not they have enjoyed a concert the night before, but one man's opinion, often one who is not an expert in the art of singing, cannot have any value or interest for the performer.

We do need highly expert advice from those whose job it is to guard the standards of performance, conductors, coaches, teachers, accompanists, and composers too. I know from my own experience and from what other singers tell me that much of the fear we suffer in performance comes from knowing that a journalist will write about us the following day. The difference in the theatre between a first night and a second is unbelievable just because of reviews.

Not very long ago I realized I had had quite enough of that sort of mental pressure and decided not to read anything at all which was written about me, ecstatic, lukewarm or bad. This decision has given me a most wonderful sense of freedom and has actually helped me to be very much more calm in the moments of performance; I wish I had taken it years ago. What I am able to do is concentrate on the moments of performance in a much deeper way; it is the moment which matters, only the 'now' of one bar leading into the next; it doesn't concern me what the critics say about my performance – I shall never know; neither does it concern me what the public think. My mind is filled with only one thing, a caring for the music and that this music should be allowed to flow through me unaffected by personal concerns of success or failure.

I have indeed to stand there looking the audience smack between the eyes; it's a difficult thing to do. There's such a lot going on out there; people are restless, they are gazing around, talking to each other in the middle of a song even leaving the hall altogether; inevitably I think it must be because the performance is so hateful, they can't stand it another minute! Everything seems to conspire against a perfect concentration on the job in hand. All these distractions have over the years become less important to me; it is not my business if some people don't want to listen; it is not for me to wonder if I am reaching anyone out there; all I have to do is get on with my work, to enter the world the composer has made for me, oblivious of everything else. If a heart is touched in the process, that is wonderful but that is a mystery between God, the composer and the individual concerned; it should not concern me. I have known people come round to the green-room in tears after a concert and I have been told that at the very same concert others have been reading and doing crossword puzzles! If we allow ourselves to be affected by either the tears or the indifference we are absolutely lost.

The only thing we have is the actual moment of performance, that timeless eternity when we strive to make ourselves mirrors to reflect as truly as we can the great works placed in our hands. Our vital concern is to make sure the glass is polished brightly; and how shall we make sure? By love. Love for God Who gave us a gift to use; love for our profession, our music, the message we deliver; love for our audiences, especially them; it is for them we suffer and somehow summon up enough courage to perform at all.

Eleven
The Amateur

David McKenna, C.B.E.,
F.R.C.M.

General Manager of the
Southern Region of British Rail
and later full-time Member of
the British Railways Board. He
was brought up with music never
far away, for his mother was an
excellent pianist and his father,
Reginald McKenna – Liberal,
Chancellor of the Exchequer –
maintained a benign interest in
the art. He is Honorary Secretary
and a Vice-President of the
Royal College of Music. He is
also a Vice-President of the Bach
Choir of which he was an active
member for over forty years.

I am one of those who believe that one's enjoyment of
music as a listener is enormously enhanced if one has had
the opportunity of participating in the making of music, on
however modest a scale. And one of the simplest and most
natural ways of participation is by singing.

The initial requirements are small; a voice of some kind,
an ear which can distinguish one note from another, and
that subtle co-ordinating mechanism which enables the
voice to produce a sound at a pitch which the ear dictates.
Either you have these requirements or you do not, and if
you have them, they provide a foundation for a superstructure of musical enjoyment of immense range. Development
of that superstructure, by training and practice, is entirely
a matter of personal taste and aspiration. There is seldom
a lack of opportunity.

It is as well to start young; nursery rhymes and Christmas
carols are an excellent beginning.

I was fortunate in that, at the age of seven, I went to a

singing class, presided over by a remarkable old lady whose, first requirement at each session was to ensure that every child was properly dressed, that is to say, equipped with a kind of gardener's apron, in the pouch of which was a couple of pencils, pencil sharpener, india-rubber, ruler, manuscript book, and such other booklets or pieces of music as were being studied. This itself was an exercise in rehearsal discipline never to be forgotten.

She taught us tonic sol-fa, that is, to give names to the notes of the diatonic scale, irrespective of the actual key. After a very short while we were able to put the appropiate names to the notes of well-known tunes. Good King Wenceslas, which every child knows, became 'doh, doh, doh, re, doh, doh, sol; la, sol, la, ti, doh, doh'. But she did not regard tonic sol-fa as an end in itself; it was essentially a means to another end. For, as soon as we had mastered the names of the notes in the scale and could recognize their position, we were made to 'translate' them into the staff notation, first in the key of C, then working outwards, one sharp, one flat; two sharps, two flats, and so on. It did not take long to spot that B♭ – G was doh-la in the key of B♭, a concept that seemed easier to absorb than a major sixth.

We were taught our 'time' simultaneously in the sol-fa and staff notations, but more emphasis was placed on the latter. We did weekly homework consisting of written translation of tunes from tonic sol-fa to staff, and vice versa, and we did dictation in class; first we took down a given tune in tonic sol-fa, and then we translated it into staff notation in a nominated key. After a while we would skip the intermediate tonic sol-fa stage, and take down our dictation straight on to the stave.

At that stage of life we did not move rapidly around the keys in the course of our instruction, but confined ourselves to the simplest modulations, to the dominant or sub-dominant. But we emerged with a good basic grounding in the elements of musical grammar and notation. The succession of notes on the stave meant sounds which we could reproduce vocally with confidence and accuracy, with the one proviso that the notes moved within the framework of a diatonic scale. Fortunately this proviso applies to the greater part of the music with which the amateur is likely to become involved.

I have described but one route towards an ability to read the simpler kinds of music at sight, with accuracy. There are other methods. But I would regard this ability as by far the most important and rewarding skill for the amateur singer to acquire.

With such a grounding, the door is wide open to an enormous range of music making. In my own case it started at school, where I insisted on singing alto in Chapel because it was more fun sustaining an inner part rather than just singing the tune. Then we had active music making in the home, reading through collections of songs and arias, gathering together some like-minded friends and singing rounds, madrigals, Bach chorales, and choruses from *Messiah*.

Just as the amateur violinist may seek his ultimate satisfaction in playing chamber music or in an orchestra, so the amateur singer may likewise find the ultimate satisfaction in joining a choir. There is no part of the country where a choir of some sort is not available; usually there is a choice, both of size and of proficiency. Being an enthusiastic singer, and working in London, I was fortunate to join two, a small choir specializing in madrigals and smaller scale sacred works, and a large choir with a long tradition of performance of the major choral works from Bach onwards. The discipline of regular rehearsal was properly strict, but the satisfaction of preparing for public concerts under the guidance of very distinguished musicians has been refreshing in the extreme, and an uplifting antidote to the exigencies of a normal working life. Alas, two evenings a week in the end became too time consuming, and the small choir was dropped; but membership of the large one continued, and became a way of life rather than a passing recreation. It led, incidentally, to all kinds of unexpected musical experiences, such as recording and touring abroad.

The sure passport to these musical delights is a reasonable natural voice and an acquired ability to read music. Is some vocal training necessary? My answer is that such training is desirable, but not so important as a thorough grounding in the basic elements of music. Many choral conductors themselves give some instruction to their choirs in the elements of voice production, in the technique of breathing and in the clear enunciation of words. This kind of training is always of value.

In conclusion, I would say to the amateur, join a choir; consciously set out to learn to read simpler music with accuracy – you will always be helped with the more difficult; have a few lessons so as to learn something of breathing and voice production. Then go on making music regularly for the rest of your life.

Twelve
Frustrated Professional or Contented Amateur

Philippa Thomson, A.R.C.M.
P.A. to Sir John Tooley at the Royal Opera House Covent Garden. She has been successively student, Secretary of the Student Association and P.A. to the Director of the Royal College of Music. From 1974 to 1980 she was Secretary of the Bach Choir.

How much more satisfying it is to be a happy amateur with countless opportunities to make music than to be a struggling professional soloist. It is even better to be in the position of a paid musical administrator, having experienced the gradual frustration of training as a professional singer without achieving fame and fortune.

With musical parents and many musical childhood friends it was no surprise to anyone when I was awarded a music scholarship at school. I received every encouragement to develop my talent with solo singing lessons at a comparatively early age which naturally led to solo performances at school concerts and music festivals.

Entrance to the Royal College of Music proved no problem, but not being considered for an Entrance Scholarship was perhaps the first indication that my talent was less than I had been led to believe.

Becoming a Singer

Being a large fish in a small school pond was an unrealistic sort of life. It was lovely while it lasted, but once at College it became patently obvious to me that most of my fellow-students had also been large fishes somewhere and many of them had talent not only comparable to my own but often far superior.

Subconsciously, I blamed the fact that the progress of my development was slower than that of most of my fellows on the unfamiliarity of London and the long periods of unorganized time in which I was left to my own devices, time which was supposed to be used for private study and practice. The determination to make the fullest use of these free study periods did not come naturally and I found myself becoming bored and restless. The offer to be Secretary of the Students' Association at College came as a welcome relief from the frustration of lonely practice for hours on end.

Through the Association there were endless outlets to develop the administrative leanings that I had found inherent in me at school and I found myself completely immersed in quite a different aspect of College life from that of a first-study singer.

No Students' Association in a non-residential college has an easy task in organizing social activities, but music, the all-absorbing pastime, provides a natural social life for students who are prepared to give a great part of themselves to their music-making. We felt that as an Association we were there to help them to meet one another and to make music outside the normal curriculum. We organized parties, debates, theatre outings and sport, but easier by far was the concert promotion. Many choral, orchestral and chamber concerts were promoted both inside and outside the College and there was no shortage of willing volunteers to take part, whereas many had to be coaxed away from their studies to attend non-musical functions.

Through these concerts many student composers were able to give the first-performances of their compositions and it is very gratifying to look back to such events and to notice how many of the names of those student composers and conductors are now well-known in the profession. Occasionally we were privileged to have guest artists, already well-known, who would give their services either as soloists or section leaders in the orchestra. These gestures of goodwill gave great encouragement to the students and helped to generate a larger audience than that to which student concerts were accustomed.

The contacts I made whilst Secretary of the Students' Association were to prove invaluable to me later in my career. At the end of three years at the College it was quite obvious that I was not destined to become a soloist. I was holder of a teacher diploma in singing, but not being a pianist felt severely handicapped when it came to giving private lessons. It was no use pretending that I was a dedicated singer, for if I had been I am sure that I would have felt the need to sing and to keep singing despite all odds, just as a painter needs to paint and a dancer to dance. I enjoyed my college career enormously but not for the reasons that I had imagined when I embarked upon it.

It was curious how, having achieved secretarial skills after leaving the Royal College of Music, and quickly settling into the routine of office work, I seized every opportunity for music-making in the evenings and week-ends.

A professional church choir, an amateur choral society and solo concerts in old people's homes and clubs filled my time. I was the singer in a group consisting of piano, voice viola/violin and clarinet and we gave a number of concerts in schools over a couple of years. We charged expenses only and derived enormous pleasure from playing to audiences who came essentially to enjoy rather than to criticize. Once we were even the budget artists of the season in a local music club.

It was with a feeling of mixed excitement and apprehension that I returned to the Royal College of Music as Secretary to the Director only eighteen months since I had ceased to be a student. Very few of those who are fortunate enough to have studied music ever have the opportunity of joining the administrative side of the profession. Seldom can they experience the supreme satisfaction that can be gained from singing in concerts that one has organized, or watch the gradual progress from studentship to professionalism of many musicians.

As the Secretary of a large amateur choir I never cease to be fascinated to see how a body of merchant bankers, doctors, company executives, students and housewives, to name but a few, can join forces with such dedication and enthusiasm that their social lives are planned round their musical activities.

Very stimulating also is the experience of engaging famous musicians for performances without feeling any rivalry towards them and only a sense of pride at taking part in the same concert from the ranks of the sopranos.

To be an administrator in music having set out on the path of a performer can be regarded by some to be an admission of defeat. It is far more important to face up to one's limitations and to make the most of them, than to struggle against the tide of frustrations and insecurity, not to mention the bitterness that can be engendered through constant rejection.

How fortunate we are that amateurs and professionals are able to join forces to perform works which would otherwise not be heard. Long may this co-operation continue.

Part Three

The Singer's World

Thirteen
Text and Voice in English Song

Sir Peter Pears, C.B.E., F.R.C.M. Educated at Lancing, Oxford and the Royal College of Music. His collaboration with Benjamin Britten has been of world-wide importance. Together they started the Aldeburgh Festival in 1948. Britten wrote twelve principal operatic roles for Pears besides song cycles and other works such as the *War Requiem*. Pictured here with Benjamin Britten, he is the Founder and Director of the Britten-Pears School for Advanced Singers. Their recitals together showed technique, texture and intelligence unsurpassed in our time.

It is surprising perhaps at first to learn that in the greater part of the earliest English music which has survived, the language set is not our own but Latin. Musically the Church functioned only in Latin, and the Church was the largest employer of musicians. Though surely music was always sung in court for profit and at home for pleasure, the singers in daily practice used the open vowels and Italianate consonants of ecclesiastical Latin. When they came to cope with the buzzings and hissings of the English language they probably met the same sorts of problems that we have to meet today, and for four hundred years and more we have welcomed the Italians who can teach us to loosen our jaws and 'open' our throats, and at the same time to keep the flexibility which our diphthongs and triphthongs demand.

Today the vogue for early music has put students on the alert for new songs from the fifteenth century and earlier. Ensemble songs are fairly numerous and with the emergence into the spotlight of the counter-tenor there are plenty of groups capable of singing them. The first great period for the solo song remains the age of Shakespeare. It was then that the relationship between poet and musician was most close. In the case of Campion and Rosseter it could hardly have been closer; they must have created their songs together and the result was uniquely beautiful.

Yet Campion complains that 'there are some who admit only French or Italian ayres, as if every country had not his proper Ayre which the people thereof naturally usurpe in their Musicke'. And at the same time John Dowland (1568–1626), one of the very greatest song writers, lashes out at 'people who shroude themselves under the title of Musicians . . . simple cantors, or vocal-singers who though they seem excellent in their blind division-making, are merely ignorant even in the first elements of Musicke . . .' Here perhaps is an early sign of a tension which has persisted through the centuries between singers and composers, between voice fanciers and musicians, between those to whom the text is of vital importance and those who accept it only as a peg for the voice.

Henry Lawes, whom Milton admired so much for his word-setting, wrote in 1669:

I acknowledge the Italians the greatest Masters of Musick but yet not all. I confesse the Italian Language may have some advantage by being better smooth'd and *vowell'd* for Music, which I found by many songs which I set to Italian words; and our English seems a little over-clogg'd with consonants; that that's much the composer's fault who by judicious setting and right tuning the words may make it smooth enough . . . I never lov'd to set or sing words which I do not understand; and where I cannot, I desir'd help of others who were able to interpret.

Lawes was the leader of the song writers between Dowland and Purcell, much printed, but those printed songs (decorated in performance as they undoubtedly were) were not elaborate enough for the Restoration generation. The Italian and French influences were both very strong, but Purcell made his masterly way through them both. Dryden gave him a few beautiful lyrics, all too small a proportion of his great output. Most of Purcell's texts are at the same time modish and conventional.

The eighteenth century was the century of reason and since the classical Italian taste was the yardstick in all the arts, the song-poets and, more specially, librettists were fully aware of the inadequacy of English as a sweet stream of honey for singers' throats, and they did their best to challenge the foreigner in this field. A prime instance is the ravishing text which Pope or Congreve produced in the opera *Semele*, set by Handel.

> Where'er you walk, cool gales shall fan the glade.
> Trees where you sit shall crowd into a shade.
> Where'er you tread, the blushing flow'rs shall rise
> And all things flourish where'er you turn your eyes.

The poet could hardly have produced a more smooth and flowing set of verses for the singer. Rough consonants are used to the minimum, and strongly contrasting vowel sounds are separated by soft-sounding consonants (s, sh). The first three words, vital words in a classic aria which will be heard many times over, are here made entirely of changing vowel sounds; indeed it is difficult to say how many different vowels are sounded in those first three words. They are all at the least diphthongs and the first is a triphthong, and together they make a gently undulating shape for Handel to adorn with one of his most beautiful and simple melodies. Of the 35 words which make up these four lines, 29 are monosyllables; a proportion only possible in the English language.

' 'Tis almost needless to speak anything' wrote John Dryden (1691) in the preface to one of his operas 'of that noble language in which this Musical *Drama* was first invented and perform'd.' He went on:

All who are conversant in the Italian, cannot but observe, that it is the softest, the sweetest, the most harmonious, not only of any modern Tongue, but even beyond any of the Learned. It seems indeed to have been invented for the sake of Poetry and Musick; the Vowels are so abounding in all Words, especially in the Terminations of them, that excepting some few Monosyllables, the whole Language ends in them. Then the Pronunciation is so Manly, and so Sonorous, that their very Speaking has more of Musick in it than Dutch Poetry, and Song. . . .

The English has yet more natural Disadvantages than the French; our original Teutonick consisting most in Monosyllables, and those incumbered with Consonants, cannot possibly be freed from those Inconveniences. The rest of our Words, which are deriv'd from the Latin chiefly, and the French, with some small Sprinklings of Greek, Italian and Spanish, are some Relief in Poetry, and help us to soften our uncouth Numbers; which together with our English Genius, incomparably beyond the trifling of the French, in all the nobler Parts of Verse, will justly give us the Preheminence. But, on the other hand the Effeminacy of our Pronunciation (a Defect common to us, and to the Danes,) and our Scarcity of Female Rhimes, have left the Advantage of Musical Composition for Songs, though not for Recitative, to our Neighbours.

The struggle to make English as mellifluous as Italian occupied the poets and composers over a whole century of opera. The most successful of the English operas which were based on Italian models, in this case Metastasio, was Arne's *Artaxerxes*, which lasted the whole of the later eighteenth century and into the nineteenth. All the vocal devices of the great Italian school of singing are called for in this grand opera. It was the same composer who produced a number of the most beautiful little songs in our language. There is nothing better in English music than his Shakespeare settings.

As the quality of the composers declined on the way to and in the nineteenth century, the writing for the voice became hackneyed. In Handel's time the quality of the texts which were available fell away sadly. Dryden, Congreve and Gay (*Acis and Galatea*) gave way to the banality of Morell and the unknown librettist of *Solomon* and *Susanna*. Their attempts to Italianize English sometimes work, and an occasional lead in an aria draws a marvellous response from Handel. 'Angels, ever bright and fair' is a gift for a soprano, so is 'Waft her, angels, to the skies' for a tenor. 'Chastity, thou cherub bright,' begins a beautiful air – the words pleased Handel and he never failed in musical ideas.

It is in the recitative (where Dryden thought the English language was well equipped to succeed, with its strong monosyllables and bunches of consonants) that the formality of eighteenth-century utterance stops the movement and clogs the sense. Nahum Tate with his

'Thus on the fatal bank of Nile
weeps the deceitful crocodile'

got a much stronger music from Purcell, than Handel in *Susanna* could give to

'Tis thus the crocodile his grief displays
Sheds the false tear and while he weeps betrays'

(– two lines which perfectly display the English traps for Italian singers). When this language is extended over pages, scenes, whole acts, it is inevitable that audiences (even eighteenth-century ones) feel confused and bored, and the singers are frustrated. So some of Handel's masterpieces are neglected. *Theodora, Susanna, Jephtha* remain rarities; and the one oratorio with the indisputably great text from the Bible, *Messiah*, reigns supreme and hackneyed. For English singers the new vogue for national airs was on the whole a healthy influence.

The nineteenth century in England may not be regarded as our most splendid time, musically, but *das Land ohne Musick* was most certainly a misnomer, for the country was thick with choral societies and the drawing rooms resounded with songs. Unfortunately the poets who provided the texts for such composers as we possessed (Balfe, McFarren, etc.) could not rise above the banal for the most part, though the Tennyson-Balfe 'Come into the garden, Maud' was a notable exception. Tennyson indeed should have appeared as the shining light for song composers of the period. Maybe he did, but the fact is that when in the 1880s a noble volume of *Songs from the published writings of Alfred Lord Tennyson* appeared, humbly dedicated to the Queen, no great English songs found their way into it. The best in the book, in spite of the presence of Sullivan, Parry, Stanford and Cowen ('the Schubert of our time') are the foreign contributions. Franz Liszt caught something of 'Go not, happy day', and Charles Gounod of 'Ring out, wild bells', a marvellous poem for a splendid song. 'Now sleeps the crimson petal', however, had to wait another twenty-five years for its definitive setting.

No poet has been more delicately aware of the beauties and musical qualities of the English language than Tennyson. What could not Schubert have done with 'Sweet and Low'? Still Barnby's glee is beautiful and we must be thankful for it. It is a sad pity that when Tennyson had the task of producing for Arthur Sullivan a cycle of poems which could have been (in theory) another *Schöne Müllerin*, the composer was quite incapable of giving his best. The words were very adequate even if the story was not very exciting, and Sullivan could write some beautiful songs, but not alas! on this occasion.

Tennyson was best served on the larger scale by Arthur Somervell, whose *Maud* songs do have an intensity and sufficient invention to make an outstanding cycle which strongly reflects the Laureate's fine and passionate text.

Arthur Somervell was among the first of the composers who pounced on the new treasury for song-writers, A. E. Housman's slim volume *A Shropshire Lad*. Somervell's song-cycles are still in the eighteenth-century tradition, fine but a little academic. He was followed in the twentieth century by a host of Housman setters. Vaughan Williams, George Butterworth, John Ireland, E. J. Moeran, Herbert Howells and C. W. Orr are the first that come to mind, but there are many more. The strong atmosphere and bitter feeling of most of the *Shropshire Lad*'s songs are a long way from the ninety-ish lyrics of Ernest Dowson set in large numbers by Cyril Scott. While Dowson looks for the smooth sequences of Verlaine and Swinburne, which can perhaps be seen as liquid Mediterranean sounds for singing, Housman is terse, intense and notably monosyllabic and un-Italian:

'Is my team ploughing that I was used to drive,
And hear the harness jingle when I was man alive.'

and

'Look not in my eyes for fear
They mirror true the sight I see.'

It is not easy to write a free and easy-flowing melody over these rocks, even if you want to, and in any case melody was going out of fashion. The folksong movement restored something of what we had seemed to be losing, but no one except Percy Grainger seems to have spotted that the importance in folksong singing lies in the singer's freedom to sing it *his* way, decorations, free rhythm and all, which went far beyond and against the earlier collectors like Cecil Sharp.

Peter Warlock produced a large number of lively and melancholy songs on Elizabethan and earlier texts, using his contemporaries on only a few occasions (notably in the matter of beer with Belloc). The delicate fancy and musical colouring of Walter de la Mare's work attracted many composers in the years between the wars. 'Silver', for instance, was set over and over again, notably by C. Armstrong Gibbs, whose setting of 'Five Eyes' too was immensely popular. Indeed de la Mare helped to fill the large gap which lay between the nostalgic irony of Housman and Thomas Hardy's uncompromising pessimism, the latter poet being for years the almost exclusive concern of Gerald Finzi. Finzi's extrovert settings have been frequently sung but it is his more restrained songs which are most characteristic of both composer and poet. Over an almost improvisatory piano-part, he lifts the chunky words with a modest and sincere lyricism, which lacks the harshness of Ireland's settings.

When Benjamin Britten was studying at the Royal
College of Music, the setting of words to music accepted
as desirable was on the principle of one syllable to one
note, with very few exceptions. His teachers John Ireland
and Frank Bridge, who had both written fine and successful
songs, did not depart from this convention. Ireland in
particular held his vocal line very close to the movement
of the words. For instance

'My true love hath my heart and I have his,
By just exchange one for another given'

is on the one hand far away from the naive tune which the
nineteenth century would have clothed the words in. On
the other, it is in no way folk-y or pentatonic. It is a close-
fitting line for the words, well tailored if not very free. In
all Ireland's settings of Housman too, the strongly dissonant nature of the accompaniment prevents the vocal line
from soaring, though undeniably it produces a strong
intensity.

Britten found this convention adequate for some purposes, but not for all, and when Auden liberated his literary
horizon, he felt free to set words in whatever musical
method he thought suitable. So in the first song of *On this
Island*, 'Let the florid music praise', the words were taken
at their face value and we were given a highly original
burst of energetic melismata in the shape of a recitative
and aria. Several of the other songs in the set also look
away from his teachers; it was to the younger generation
an exciting and bold step, and led to a great deal of much
livelier vocal writing, indeed still does. The next three or
four years were spent in setting the French of Rimbaud
and the Italian of Michelangelo, in an effort to 'Medi-
terraneanize' English music and lead it away from folksong
and modes on to a broader track.

In both the *Donne Sonnets* and *Canticle No. 1* the traces
of Mediterranean lyricism are clearly visible and greatly
welcome. The *Donne Sonnets*, had they been thought of in
syllabic terms, would hardly have taken wing at all, so

intense are the texts, but difficult as they still are, a positive
warmth glows strongly in 'She whom I loved' and 'Death,
be not proud'. The Italian line is not too far off. In *Winter
Words* (1954) the treatment of the text is less free, more
sparked off by key-words and fanned by musical figuration.
The storm, the train, the wagtail, the table, the hymn tune
and the violin are there in the piano part. The music of
'Before Life and After' is reproduced below. In this
song Britten, as if to show that he had nothing against the
syllable-to-note method of setting poems used by his
teachers, produces one of his most impressive songs, with
a sure sense of the registers of the tenor voice, an object
lesson in the art of composing a song. This cycle could be
compared with Michael Tippett's *The Heart's Assurance*,
where there is little detailed illustration of the text and a
more general mood is developed from a purely musical
idea.

Britten *Before Life and After* ("*Winter Words*")

tes-ti-mon-ies tell Be-fore the birth of

con-scious-ness,___ When all went well.

None suf-fered sick - ness, love, or loss, None knew re-

-gret, starved hope, or heart-burn-ings;___ None

bright - ness dimmed, and dark pre-vailed,

No sense was stung. But the di-

-sease of feel-ing germed,___And pri-mal right-ness took the

tinct of wrong; Ere ne - science shall be re-af-firmed___

In the last twenty years many songs have been composed and published, some too difficult to be performed by any but specially gifted singers, and there remains the problem of finding songs which are a pleasure to perform and to listen to, without being far beyond the skill and range of the average trained singer. If England is to become again a nest of singing birds, composers must fall in love again with the human voice.

Fourteen
Singing a Folksong

Douglas Kennedy, O.B.E., M.B.E.
Comes of a long line of folk
singers. In 1925 he succeeded
Cecil Sharp as Director of the
E.F.D.S. (English Folksong and
Dance Society). In 1926 he
established – with Maud Karpeles
– the International Folk Music
Council. Later he helped to
develop the American C.D.S.
and visited U.S.A. annually for
teaching and lecture tours. He
was President of the Folklore
Society in 1964/5, and is well-
known for his work at Cecil Sharp
House. Now he and his wife – a
professional musician – spend
their spare time sailing in Suffolk.

Not so long ago it was thought that a folk musical
inheritance was the portion of only certain peoples – of
Scots, Irish, Welsh, but not of the English. Certain classical
music had a distinctive national flavour on account of the
folk themes available to the composer. Today, we know
that every nation possesses a stock of its own ethnic
melody.

In England it was not until the founding of the Folk
Song Society in 1898, coinciding with a wave of song
collecting by the pioneers Lucy Broadwood, Cecil Sharp,
Percy Grainger, Ralph Vaughan Williams and others, that
the English themselves accepted the facts of their own
music heritage. Much earlier in history, literature had been
enriched by the publication of the poems and stories
enshrined in popular balladry, but little attention had then
been paid to their music. The new revelation focused
attention on a rich vein of beautiful melody.

Being Scots and a family of dedicated singers, my father

117

and all his brothers and sisters turned to these newly published English versions with astonishment at the rich variety of the find and delight at the simple beauty of the melodies. But they discovered that these were not so easy to interpret by the trained singer with a consciously developed vocal technique. My sister and I who were not trained singers were at this time sitting literally at the feet of Cecil Sharp learning these English versions which he sang to us as he directed the class from the piano. In spite of our Scots background and our own family versions of many of the Scots folksongs these English folksongs from Somerset and other counties were a complete revelation and indeed became fundamental to our musical experience. And we were not the only ones. There must have been countless others, who like us, have continued to enjoy this rich and varied English song vocabulary. One brave girl I know kept herself alive and sane with her rich store of folksong. She had been taken prisoner by the Nazis while helping refugees to escape from Austria and was kept for years in solitary confinement. She survived by singing every folksong embedded in her memory and that meant both words and music, for instinctively, like native traditional singers, she could not recollect the one without the other.

Style and Technique

Admittedly there is a difference between singing or saying a song to yourself and proclaiming it in public. Such performance demands a controlled technique. The difficulty with folksong for the trained singer is that its simple directness calls for an unselfconscious approach and apparently artless presentation. Several professional singers sought Cecil Sharp's aid on this point and he found difficulty in giving it. Once you try to be unselfconscious of your performance you fall into other traps. If you consciously avoid over-expression then the life will go out of your voice. For a time there was indeed an apparent epidemic among concert singers of dead-pan folk singing.

Another device was to try to imitate the exact method of some more successful performer. The danger here was to fail to distinguish between mere personal mannerisms and elements of essential technique. Rather than start off with the idea of performance I would recommend singing just to yourself one of the narrative song stories, or ballads which are all the better for being almost spoken. Songs of a lyrical or declamatory nature do require controlled vocalization even when singing to yourself and whatever choice of song, I would recommend the singer to say or 'tell' the song over and over again. The expression 'I'll tell you the song but I won't sing it to you' is one often used by the older traditional singers apologetic about their uncertain voices.

Telling the story

The singers who sang to Sharp almost invariably sang unaccompanied by any instrument and so had the freedom to 'tell their songs'. Their method made the melody more difficult for the collector to note, each verse often having its own variable of the tune. Although Sharp was first and last under the spell of the loveliness of the melodies when it came to their singing, he insisted it was to the story that the singer had to give tongue. And we remember that the minstrels in Sir Walter Scott's experience were as skilled at reciting their ballads as chanting them. In my own limited experience I found the best way to the impersonal technique, that also demands the listeners' attention, was to tell the song-story over and over again letting the melody come more into the picture by degrees.

The Icelandic folk singer Engel Lund was wont to say that she had to live with a folksong for two years before she could trust herself to sing it in public. Harry Plunket Greene, a great concert singer of my youth, also believed in constant repetition but he never altered his fundamental technique just for a folksong, and who would question his method after hearing him sing 'Poor old horse'?

Accompaniment

The early collectors published their songs with piano accompaniment to help the student, conditioned to the tempered scale, into the less familiar world of modal music. When Sharp and Maud Karpeles in 1920 introduced us to their newly found English folksongs from the Southern Appalachian mountains they sang unaccompanied. But they also had a professional concert singer to illustrate other of their songs in the old way with accompaniment and with Sharp at the piano. While the audience relished the homely performance of the two collectors many clearly preferred the orthodox and admittedly more polished accompanied singing. Today the folksong scene is very different. Audiences are now accustomed to a much wider range of musical vocal sounds.

Learning by Ear – Variants

For the concert singer in training, who learns much of his repertoire from musical scores, there is much to be said for learning a folk song from the live performance of another singer. This is after all the age-old method of oral transmission. The hearer is aware of much more than the notes of the melody and even how these follow the flow and sense of the words. There are emotive overtones and undertones and other imponderables not easy or even possible to translate into musical notation. As a child I learned my Scots songs not by consciously listening to the singing of my elders, but just hearing them when I was around. They had heard their versions no doubt more consciously from their famous father David Kennedy, the internationally known singer of Scots songs, who had picked up his versions from his not so widely recognized father, well known locally in his native Perth as 'Auld Supertonic'. Had the individual versions of all four generations been recorded they would have shown that while the songs were indeed the same, each version was identifiable by the small evolutionary variations in the transmission. For any type of singer the best introduction to his native song is to hear an example sung by one with the idiom not just in his head but in his blood and bones.

Tapes and Cassettes

Today we can make a short cut to examples of singing by using tapes and cassettes. My son Peter Kennedy, maintaining our family tradition, has travelled widely in the United Kingdom recording surviving folk singers and using the modern electronic methods that were then just becoming available. The fruits of his labours over the years are reflected in his volume of the *Folk Songs of Britain and Ireland*, published by Cassells in London and Schirmer in New York. At his Centre for Oral Traditions at Portishead near Bristol, established originally as part of Dartington College of Arts, one can obtain cassettes illustrating songs in Scots, Gaelic, Irish, Welsh, Manx and Cornish as well as Norman French from the Channel Islands and in English from many parts of Ireland and the United Kingdom.

To illustrate some of the various styles of singing folksongs I would suggest a particular cassette (Folktracks PSA-60-136) containing, among other items, brief selections or 'quotations' from different English singers. These include an example of the ballad 'Barbara Allan' with selected singers from South Wales and several English counties – only a verse or two from each one. For comparison of method there is the well known 'Seeds of Love' sung unaccompanied by a modern folk singer, then with piano accompaniment by a concert singer – just a short example from each, and the whole song recorded from a Somerset folk singer much as it was sung to Cecil Sharp in 1903 when he first became interested in folk music. Another song from Somerset, 'Hares on the Mountains', illustrates several styles including that of a very fine traditional singer from Virginia, USA. A good example of concert platform interpretation with piano is given by an

American artist singing 'Black is the Colour of my True Love's Hair', collected by Cecil Sharp in North Carolina in 1916, this to be compared with other singers using for accompaniment the guitar and the harmonium. A very modern arrangement by an up to date folk group is the song 'A Blacksmith Courted Me' which Dr Vaughan Williams noted in 1904, setting its tune to Valiant's speech in *Pilgrim's Progress* to make the well known hymn 'He who would valiant be'. An interesting example is 'The Riddle Song' or the 'Devil's Nine Questions' or 'Captain Wedderburn's Courtship', which is the Scots version. One well known English version of 'The Riddle' is 'I will give my Love an Apple without any Core', with Vaughan Williams's piano setting. To the singer looking for live folksong material for the first time and prepared to use the cassette recordings as a possible guide and source, I would certainly suggest using the cassettes available at the Centre for Oral Traditions, but for many, the more general source of information is to be found in the Sound section of the Vaughan Williams Memorial Library at Cecil Sharp House in London, the headquarters of the English Folk Song and Dance Society.

Printed Scores

An alternative is to choose a folk song from the page of a printed collection made by one of the early collectors, say Sharp, Vaughan Williams, Percy Grainger etc. Do not ignore the piano setting, for that often reflects the collector's own attitude to that song, but seek to absorb the combined text and melody. Perhaps drop the study for a spell and come back to it later. Having lived with it unconsciously it may well have taken root. Only after that has happened is it fair to give tongue to it in public.

Rhythm

My last words of guidance must be on rhythm, for it is

this vital element that weds melody and word-poetry. Over-emphasis or an even metre may kill the life of the song at birth. In this a folksong is no different from other *Lieder* or indeed from any other form of music.

Fifteen
Singing in French

Pierre Bernac
   Born in Paris 1899 and died in
1980. He was a master of the
subtle and difficult art of the song
recital. He was unrivalled as an
interpreter of the French
mélodie. With Francis Poulenc as
pianist he toured Europe and the
U.S.A. for 25 years and over 80
of Poulenc's songs were written
for their recitals together. On
retiring from the concert
platform Bernac devoted himself
to teaching. His integrity,
humour and warmth of
personality made him as great a
teacher as singer.

There is sometimes a prejudice among singers and voice
teachers against singing in French. They think that the
French language is unfavourable for voice production.
This is wrong because they have a false idea of the
language. On the contrary, it is particularly favourable for
the production of a perfect *legato*, since it is entirely based
on pure vowel sounds, and vowel sounds are the musical
sounds. Consequently, if one wishes to sing correctly in
any language, the primary consideration is a precise
awareness of its different vowel sounds, and I should like
first of all to try to clarify this question.

   After many years of teaching foreign singers (mostly
English speaking) to sing in French, I have come to the
conclusion that the quickest and best way is to use the
International Phonetic Alphabet. I trust that many young
singers already know this alphabet, in which a phonetic
symbol corresponds to each sound. It only takes a few
minutes to learn it, though it is not easy to indicate the

precise shading and colour of the different vowel sounds without the advantage of live demonstration. The chart below gives for each sound a number, a phonetic symbol and examples of words using the same sound with different spellings. The examples are given in French, German and English. Although the equivalents may not always be exact, they are near enough to be used as a basis.

		French	German	English
1	i	midi, il, lit	Liebe, bitte	Peter
	ɪ	(*short*)		
2	e	été, aimer, et, nez, j'ai	gehen, lesen, See, schwer	safe (*as spoken in Scotland*)
3	ɛ	mère, mer, belle lait, mais	wenn, helfen Bächlein	when
4	a	la table, art	alle	cup (*in the south of England and in N. America*) cap (*in the north of England*)
5	ɑ	âme, passe	Vater, Bahn	hard (*spoken with a British north-country accent*)
6	ɔ	mort, comme, sonne	Sonne, dort	pot, sorry
7	o	mot, eau, au, dos	wohl, Sohn, Rose	bowl, soldier
8	u	ou, doux, sous	du, Schuh	shoe
	ʋ	(*short*)		
9	y	dur, nu, lune	grün, über, süss	no English equivalent; round the lips as for 'oo' and try to say 'ee'
	ɣ	(*short*)		
10	ø	deux, feu, peu	schön, König	no English equivalent; round the lips as for 'oo' and try to say 'eh'
11	œ	le, je, fleur, coeur	können, Götter	nearest British English equivalent is the
	ə	lune		second syllable in 'butter', but with the lips more rounded.

To these eleven sounds, one must in French add four nasal sounds:

12	ɑ̃	enfant, lent, quand, tr<u>em</u>ble
13	õ	bon, mon, non, t<u>om</u>be
14	ɛ̃	fin, pain, vin, bain, <u>sim</u>ple, ri<u>en</u>
15	œ̃	un, h<u>um</u>ble, parf<u>um</u>

When the right production has been established these nasal sounds are not unfavourable for the voice. It is not a question of singing into the nose or through the nose, but simply of exaggerating to a slight degree the nasal resonance of certain vowels. Singers who are not French often have a tendency to overdo this resonance. The sounds should be rich and full, and carefully blended with the pure vowel sound revealed by the phonetic symbols, the numbers 5, 7, 3 and 11 with a tilde above them indicating that they should have a nasal resonance. One must also be aware that, in a nasal sound followed by a consonant, one must never sound the 'n' or 'm'. They are simply a matter of spelling to indicate a nasal vowel. (But the letters 'a', 'i' and 'o', when followed by a double 'nn' or 'mm', are not nasal.)

There is much more, of course, to say about the vowel sounds and also about the consonants, but that would overrun the limits of this short chapter. But I must warn that the so-called uvular 'r' which is generally used in spoken French (and which night-club and folk-singers use in their popular songs) should never be used in serious music; it makes the diction quite vulgar. The 'r' should always be rolled with the tip of the tongue, as in Italian or in sung German, even after a vowel sound.

'S' is always hard (unvoiced) at the beginning of a word, but soft (like 'z') between two vowels; double 'ss' is always hard. English speaking singers must be careful about 't', 'p' and 'k' (hard 'c') – too often, they have a tendency to surround them with air, as if they were followed by an aspirate 'h': 'A c'hup of t'hea'. This is 't'hotally imp'hossible' in any other language.

I can recommend some books on French pronunciation: in French, Pierre Fouché, *Traité de prononciation française*

(Klinsieck, Paris) and Ph. Martinon, *Comment on prononce le français* (Larousse, Paris), and in English T. Grubb, *Singing in French* (G. Schirmer, New York) and my own book, *The Interpretation of French Song* (Gollancz, London and Norton, New York).

It is a fundamental rule in French, more so indeed than in any other language, to obtain a proper line, a proper *legato. One must fill the entire length of each note with the vowel sound.* In other words, in French one has to carry the vowel sound unaltered right through the duration of the musical sound, without anticipating the following consonant. The consonant should never be placed at the end of the note one is singing, but at the beginning of the next note. That is the only way to get both the music of the words and the music itself.

From this standpoint French is quite different from German, in which one must vibrate certain consonants. The same is true of the double consonants in Italian, which should be sounded very clearly. In French, on the contrary, not only is it forbidden to sing on the consonants, but even the double consonants can only rarely be emphasized in pronunciation.

In vocal music the performance of the literary text must be as perfect as that of the music. The poet must be served as well as the composer. A singer pays great attention to the quality of his voice and his phrasing, and he must give the same care to articulation and pronunciation (which are two different things, for one can articulate well and pronounce badly). In vocal music, the music of the words is an integral part of the music itself. The sonority, the accentuation, the rhythm of the words inspire the music as much as, at times even more than, their meaning. A singer should make the effort to sing each song in its original language, for the music of the poem is as important as the music set to the poem.

It must be emphasized that, in French, as in any other language, the musical line, the *legato*, the phrasing, should never be sacrificed in favour of the words. It is essential that the vocal line should always take first place for the singer's attention. Nothing can be further from the truth than to consider French vocal music, and especially the concert repertoire, as a kind of near speech, of *quasi parlando*. French songs have to be *sung* in the full sense of the word, just as one has to sing a German *Lied*. Of course the style is different . . . but it is obvious that there can be no overall, single style of interpretation for French vocal music. However, a few general characteristics common to all French music can be defined briefly.

Debussy made a revealing remark about French music: 'Music should humbly seek to give pleasure.' What exactly does this mean? First, that the composer must seek the beauty of sonority, subtle harmony, supple modulation and the resulting interplay of colours, while at the same time seeking the beauty and charm of the melodic line. In short, the aim is to give aesthetic pleasure through pure music, stripped of philosophical, literary or humanistic significance such as that which goes so easily hand in hand with German music.

Debussy goes on to write that 'clarity of expression, precision and concentration of form are qualities peculiar to the French genius'. These qualities are most noticeable when compared with the German genius. For the French abhor overstatements, and venerate precision and diversity. The French 'clarity of expression' is also the antithesis of the German ideal; did not Nietzsche say, in speaking of Bizet: 'His refinement is that of a race, not of an individual, it presupposes a listener who is not only musical but intelligent'?

As an example, here are a few indications for the performance and the interpretation of a song by Gabriel Fauré. It is a simple and rather early song, very well written for the voice; and beneath the music, though not for singing, I have put a nearly literal translation by Winifred Radford, because, as I shall show, the meaning of each verse, of each line, is significant in the interpretation.

Along the quay, the great ships,

silently listing to the swell,

are unmindful of the cradles

rocked by the women's hands.

But the day of parting will come,

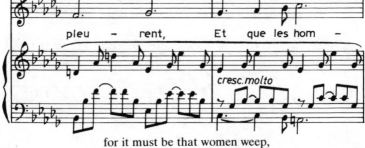

for it must be that women weep,

-mes cu-ri-eux Tent-ent les ho-ri zons qui

and men with enquiring minds

leur — — rent! _____

attempt alluring horizons!

Et ce jour-là _____ les

grands_ vais-seaux, Fuy - ant le port qui di-mi-

And on that day the great ships, leaving the port

growing smaller in the distance

feel their hulls held back

by the soul of the distant cradles.

The original key is B flat minor and certainly the song loses warmth and atmosphere when transposed to a higher key. The metronomic indication ♩ = 58 seems just right. The rhythm suggests both the rocking of the big ships in harbour and that of the small cradles. It must be absolutely steady, with no *rubato* whatsoever. A perfect *legato* is required, and the quavers must be well sustained.

The first stanza, quite descriptive, is *mp* or *mf*, with no change of dynamics. If possible, the lower alternative should be used for the phrase: 'Que la main des femmes balance'. The beginning of the second stanza must be sung *piano*, for after the immobility and the objectivity of the first stanza there now comes a feeling of premonition, of warning. It must also be *piano* because it is the start of a big and long *crescendo* of eight bars, which should not start too soon and must be established gradually. It is possible, but not recommended, to take a catch breath before 'qui leurrent'. The top F on 'leu' sounds better if the singer tends towards the vowel ɔ (No. 6 in the table on page 125) instead of œ (No. 11).

Then the last stanza starts *pianissimo*. It is the expressive climax, the result of the prediction. 'Ce jour-là' (on that day) should be emphasized. The last line of the poem is repeated: *forte* the first time, with very little *diminuendo* when the voice goes down, and *piano*, echo, the second time, with more expression. A little stress on the first syllable of 'lointains' will help give the impression of distance.

The mixture of harmonic sensuousness and clarity of thought explains why French music so well conveys precise and colourful description or the suggestion of a poetic climate. It is possible, indeed, that the art of the greatest French composers is an art of suggestion, more often suggesting moods and impressions than precise emotions. That is not to say that lyricism, or even passion, is absent from French music; but just as severity of spirit controls the sensuousness of sound, so emotions and feelings are refined, purified and controlled by reason. As André Gide said, 'The most beautiful things are those that madness inspires and reason writes.'

There can be no doubt that it is easier for performers to give themselves up to the outpourings of German music and poetry than to re-create the subtle poetic climate and the intellectual refinement of French music and poetry.

French opera

French opera began with Jean-Baptiste Lully (1632–1687), whose opera-ballets with their spectacular scenery were composed for the court of Louis XIV. Opera in France stemmed from Italian opera (Lully himself was Italian by birth), but it is far from Italian *Bel Canto*. Lully's is a much more realistic art. Jean-Philippe Rameau (1683–1764), a great musical theoretician and one of the pioneers of modern music, maintained the specifically French characteristics in his operas and opera ballets, and was indeed the central figure representing French music against the Italian party in the Guerre des Bouffons of the 1750s. Gluck (1714–1787), though born in Bavaria, wrote many of his operas to French texts, and the reforms he introduced, notably the subordination of the music to the drama and the abolition of *recitativo secco*, had a profound influence on French opera. He set out his theories in a preface to his opera *Alceste*, originally written to a German libretto but later, like his masterpiece *Orpheus and Eurydice*, revised to a French text. Giacomo Meyerbeer (1791–1864), also a German despite his Italianized name, composed several of his most successful operas to French libretti.

French *opéra comique*, in which some of the dialogue is spoken, came into being at the end of the eighteenth century; among masters of it were François Philidor (1726–1795) and above all André Grétry (1741–1813), who wrote a remarkable number of such works.

The only great French Romantic composer was Hector Berlioz (1803–1869). His operas proved excessively difficult to mount; *La Damnation de Faust* is now regarded more as a cantata, but the two parts of *Les Troyens* have been seen in recent Covent Garden seasons. If Berlioz found few followers in France, that is because during the main part of the nineteenth century music everywhere was dominated by the influence of Wagner. His influence was felt everywhere, but his expansive, emphatic music was not in accord with the more refined French temperament. It was Charles Gounod (1813–1893) who restored to French opera its characteristics of intimate feeling liberated from grandiloquence, notably with his immensely popular *Faust*. Among his followers were Georges Bizet (1838–1875), whose masterpiece *Carmen* was condemned at first because of its sordid plot, Saint-Saëns (1835–1921), best known perhaps for *Samson et Dalila*, Jules Massenet (1842–1912), whose twenty-seven operas include *Manon* and *Werther*, Lalo, Charpentier and others. The same period also produced some gifted light opera composers. Offenbach (*La belle Hélène*, *Orphée aux Enfers* and many others), Lecoq and Harvé.

The beginning of the twentieth century was marked by the production in Paris of *Pelléas et Mélisande* by Claude

Debussy (1862–1918), which was a complete renovation of the lyric opera. Since that historic production in 1902 almost every leading French composer has produced at least one opera, among the best known being two enchanting works by Maurice Ravel (1875–1937), *L'Heure Espagnole* and *L'Enfant et les Sortilèlges*, and two dramatic and intensely moving works by Francis Poulenc (1899–1963), *Dialogues des Carmélites* and *La Voix Humaine*.

Here is a short list of arias that will help young singers to approach the French repertoire – some of them from operas seldom performed nowadays, but suitable for concert work and very good training material for the young singer. The arias preceded by a number are in the Gevaert Collection published in Paris by H. Lemoine.

Lully. *Alceste*: (385) Air de Caron (bass). *Amadis*: (334) Monologue et déploration d'Oriane (soprano); (310) 'Amour que veux tu de moi' (mezzo-soprano). *Cadmus et Hermione*: (384) 'Belle Hermione' (baritone). *Le Carnaval*: (314) 'Que soupirer d'amour' (soprano). *Thésée*: (312) Chant de Vénus (soprano).

Rameau. *Castor et Pollux*: (308) Air de Télaïre (soprano). *Les Fêtes d'Hébé*: (328) 'Accourez brillante jeunesse' (soprano). *Hippolyte et Aricie*: (313) 'Rossignols amoureux' (soprano leggero). *Les Indes galantes*: (386) Invocation et Hymne au soleil (baritone).

Gluck. *Armide*: (104) 'Plus j'observe ces lieux' (tenor). *Iphigénie en Aulide*: (116) 'Diane impitoyable' (bass). *Les Pélerins de la Mecque*: (259) 'Un ruisselet' (baritone).

Grétry. *L'Amant jaloux*: (97) 'Tandis que tout sommeille' (tenor). *Céphale et Procris*: (45) 'Naissantes fleurs' (soprano). *Le jugement de Midas*: (76) 'Du destin qui m'opprime' (contralto); (99) 'Doux charme de la vie' (tenor). *Richard Coeur de Lion*: (32) 'Je crains de lui parler la nuit' (tenor). *Zémire et Azor*: (33) 'Rose chérie' (soprano); (70) 'La fauvette' (soprano leggero); (98) 'Du moment qu'on aime' (tenor).

Berlioz. *La damnation de Faust*: 'Voici des roses' (bass).

Thomas. *Mignon*: 'Connais-tu le pays' (mezzo-soprano).

Gounod. *Faust*: Cavatine de Valentin (baritone). *Philémon et Baucis*: 'Que les songes heureux' (bass); 'Ah, si je redevenais belle' (soprano).
Lalo. *Le Roi d'Ys*: Air de Rozenn (soprano).
Bizet. *Les pêcheurs de perles*: Cavatine de Leïla (soprano); Romance de Nadir (tenor).
Delibes. *Lakmé*: Strophes; 'Pourquoi dans les grands bois' (soprano).
Massenet. *Le jongleur de Notre-Dame*: Légende de la sauge (baritone).

French songs

It is impossible to use the word 'chanson' to designate the French song (called in the United States the French 'art song'). There is, in French, a very sharp difference between *mélodie* and *chanson*. *Mélodie*, which is the equivalent of *Lied*, denotes a serious song, a concert song; whereas *chanson* refers to a folk song, a popular or night-club song. If some composers of *mélodies* use the word *chanson* in the titles of their songs, it is to suggest a simple or folk song style, as in Poulenc's 'Chansons Villageoises'. It may also be because *chanson* has been used in the title of the poem, as in Duparc's 'Chanson Triste'.

It was almost the middle of the nineteenth century when the first songs were composed in France. They were not derived from the German *Lied* but stemmed directly from the romantic period which had reigned in France since the middle of the eighteenth century. This is obvious in Berlioz's songs, which also show the influence of the lyric theatre.

Charles Gounod was the true creator of the French song. He wrote over two hundred songs; many are of uneven quality, but some are undoubted masterpieces. Their typical French style can be traced in the songs of all French song-writers to the end of the nineteenth century, Bizet, Lalo, Saint-Saëns, Delibes and the others, and even in the early songs of Fauré and Debussy. Other important composers were Duparc, whose songs were closest to German romanticism; Chabrier, who gave back humour and joy to French music, and Chausson, an elegiac post-romantic.

Gabriel Fauré wrote about a hundred songs over a period of sixty years. They show great evolution in his art, which became more subtle in form and harmony and more pure and restrained in expression. Claude Debussy wrote fifty songs in forty years. They too show a progressively greater refinement in the music and subtlety in the setting of the poems.

Albert Roussel was chiefly a symphonist, but he wrote about thirty-five songs in a distinctly personal idiom. Maurice Ravel's output of songs was small; they include harmonizations of folk and traditional songs adapted with such personality and genius that they may be listed as original works. Among later twentieth-century song-writers one must mention Darius Milhaud, Georges Auric, Henri Sauguet, Jacques Leguerney, Olivier Messiaen, André Jolivet and, above all, Francis Poulenc. Poulenc, who wrote about a hundred and fifty songs, is undoubtedly the greatest song-writer of our time.

I have listed below a few rather simple songs, with a very singable vocal line. These songs can be transposed into any suitable key.

Gounod. 'L'absent', 'Au rossignol', 'Chanson de printemps', 'Ma belle amie est morte', 'Mignon', 'Sérénade'.
Franck. 'Nocturne.'
Bizet. 'Chanson d'Avril', 'Les adieux de l'hôtesse arabe'.
Chausson. 'Nanny', 'Le charme', 'Sérénade italienne', 'Le colibri', 'Le temps des lilas'.
Duparc. 'Lamento', 'Sérénade florentine'.
Fauré. 'Chanson du pêcheur', 'Lydia', 'Après un rêve', 'Au bord de l'eau', 'Automne'.
Debussy. 'Beau soir', 'Romance', 'Les cloches'.
Poulenc. 'Priez pour paix', 'Rosemonde'; also a charming song to English words by Shakespeare, 'Fancy'.

Sixteen
The German Lied

Hermann Reutter
  One-time Director of the
Music Academies in Frankfurt,
Stuttgart and Munich where his
master class for singers and
pianists led him to similar classes
in U.S.A., Japan and Korea. He
has toured with Erb, Fischer-
Dieskau, Gedda, Schwarzkopf,
Danco, Fuchs, Wolff, Fischer,
Grummer and McDaniel. His
compositions include 12 operas,
300 songs, 8 piano concertos, a
symphony and an oratorio. His
Credo: Never neglect the most
important elements in all creative
undertakings – Melody, Harmony
and Rhythm.

The German *Lied*: the mind instinctively turns to the incomparable 'classical' Romantic constellation of Franz Schubert, Robert Schumann, Johannes Brahms and Hugo Wolf. These four are the undisputed masters of a form that constitutes the closest possible linking of words and music – a form for which other countries have not even found a word, but still speak of the songs as *Lieder*. The mantle of the four pioneers fell upon the exponents of the late Romantic school, Gustav Mahler, Hans Pfitzner, Richard Strauss and the Swiss composer Othmar Schoeck (Wagner's five *Wesendonck Lieder* are not enough to qualify him as a composer of *Lieder*), and finally Arnold Schoenberg's *Buch der hängenden Gärten* ushered in the twentieth-century *Lied*.

Meanwhile, what of Schubert's precursors, contemporaries and successors? Neither J. S. Bach nor Telemann can really be described as *Lieder*-composers, but both left us one or two important works for solo voice that cannot go unmentioned in a survey of German song, not least Bach's intensely moving 'Bist du bei mir', with which Elisabeth Schwarzkopf used to open so many of her unforgettable recitals, and its counterpart in lighter vein, Telemann's 'Frauenzimmer'. Later the pre-Romantic period produced one or two masters of the *Lied* form, notably Reichardt (b. 1752) and Zelter (b. 1785); Reichardt's 'Beherzigung' and Zelter's heartfelt 'Nachtgesang', both to poems by Goethe, are among their memorable works. Weber too wrote admirable songs, though they did not contain the melodic intensity of his operatic arias.

Joseph Haydn's *Lieder*, a whole volume of them, consist mainly of beautifully written settings of English poems. Three that I find particularly attractive are 'Piercing Eyes', 'Fidelity' and the very slow setting of Shakespeare's lines from *Twelfth Night*, 'She never told her love'. None of Haydn's songs are easy to sing, and the piano accompaniments (like everything else he wrote for the instrument) present daunting technical and interpretative problems. Structurally and stylistically Haydn's *Lieder* display his characteristic mastery of the art of composition. Although his marvellous solo cantatas such as 'Berenice' and 'Ariadne auf Naxos' are really outside the field of *Lieder*, they are admirably suited for opening a recital. Nor of course should Mozart's *Lieder* be overlooked, especially 'Das Veilchen', 'Abendempfindung' (directed to be taken *alla breve!*), 'Als Luise die Briefe ihres ungetreuen Liebhabers verbrannte', 'Der Zauberer', 'Warnung' and one or two settings of French and Italian poems.

Beethoven's contribution to the genre was more varied and comprehensive, including some notable cycles as well as individual *Lieder*. Almost all of them can be built into admirable programmes, beginning perhaps on a serious note with 'In questa tomba oscura', followed by the *Gellert-Gedichte* and culminating in the cycle *An die ferne Geliebte*, which I would prefer to classify as a duo-sonata for voice and piano. Such programmes could also include the delightful 'Andenken' and the glorious 'Adelaide', not to mention Mephisto's grotesque, daemonic 'Song of the Flea' from Goethe's *Faust*, 'Wonne der Wehmut', 'Mailied' and 'Sehnsucht'.

All these *Lieder* by Haydn, Mozart and Beethoven are still as fresh as ever. So too are the lovely *Sechs Lieder* for female voice, piano and clarinet by Louis Spohr and some exquisite songs by Mendelssohn – 'Auf Flügeln des Gesanges', of course, 'Die Nacht', 'Neue Liebe' and the brilliant 'Hexenlied'. Robert Franz, in much the same period, produced some 250 unpretentious songs, some of which, with delightful melodic lines and deeply felt emotional content, are still occasionally heard in recitals. In the lovely 'Herbst', composed in a – a – b form, the last verse contains what I can only describe as a flash of genius; at the words 'Mein Lieb ist falsch' the dreadful word 'falsch' is accompanied not by a dissonance but by an inversion of the Neapolitan sixth chord, a consonance, which is more mordant and penetrating than even the most grinding discord:

The ballad-composer Carl Loewe, a great master in his own field, was himself well known as a singer and was his own accompanist; to judge from the extreme difficulty of some of his accompaniments, he must have been no mean pianist. His ballads and other settings run almost the entire gamut of human emotions, from the relatively simple 'Uhr'

to brilliant ballads like 'Archibald Douglas', 'Edward' and 'Odins Meeresritt'. Some of his settings of verses like 'Tom der Reimer' sound a trifle quaint nowadays, but the *Lied* 'Süsses Begräbnis', an enchanting setting of an enchanting poem, has a melody that can almost stand comparison with Schubert. Loewe also produced a number of light-hearted 'humoresques'. It is a pity that so much of his work, still of real value, is out of print today.

Peter Cornelius, composer of the opera *Der Barbier von Bagdad* and of a number of Christmas carols, including the popular 'The Kings', was also a *Lieder*-writer. Melodically as well as harmonically, such songs as 'Auf ein schlummerndes Kind', 'Auf eine Unbekannte' and 'Ode' – a wonderful siciliano, ardent and fragrant as a bed of red roses – are appreciably influenced by 'Lohengrin'. The cycle *Trauer und Trost* includes the marvellous 'Ein Ton', in which a persistent middle B in the voice part is accompanied by arabesques in which the piano strays into almost every conceivable harmonic field. It is remarkable how many of Hugo Wolf's relations between the vocal line and its accompaniment were anticipated by Cornelius.

And so we come to what I have called the incomparable constellation. Let us look first at Schubert's three great *Lieder*-cycles, *Die schöne Müllerin*, *Winterreise* and *Schwanengesang*, which make up the first of the seven volumes in which Schubert's *Lieder* have been issued. *Die schöne Müllerin* starts artlessly enough as the young swain sets out on his carefree ramble, but in the very next song, 'Wohin,' there is a subtle but unmistakable hint that things will not go smoothly. 'Wohin' should never be sung too fast; it should convey a sense of reflection, of slight hesitation even, a feeling of being urged forward by some mysterious force, the silvery stream that accompanies the victim to his doom. And please, none of those atrocious pauses on the top note at 'Mühlenräder'; the lovely phrase must be sung evenly right through. There follows a sequence of highly poetical descriptions of Nature, interrupted by the impetuous 'Feierabend' and 'Ungeduld', which again should not be taken too fast, nor should the pounding heart-beat triplets in the piano part be so febrile as to suggest an imminent heart attack; excessively fast tempi tend to deaden the emotional impact. And incidentally 'Ungeduld', like many of the other songs in the cycle, is strophic, and the interpreter should allow himself some freedom in adapting his rendering to the exigencies of the verse.

The spirit of elation persists through the lovely three-part accompaniment of 'Tränenregen' and in 'Mein' reaches a climax of absolute certainty; this should be taken in 2/2 and not rushed. In 'Pause' a slight note of misgiving is struck, but in 'Mit einem grünen Lautenbande' the old confidence returns. But only for a moment: in the very next song the hunter appears upon the scene, and against his green attire and vital virility the over-sensitive wayfarer has no chance. 'Eifersucht und Stolz' are of no avail: the Müllerin is captivated by the swaggering newcomer. Interpretations of 'Die liebe Farbe' and 'Die böse Farbe' must bring out the tolling effect of the accompaniment in the former and the passionate dejection of the latter. Once again, not too fast please; the sextuplets should not be allowed to drown the sound of the hunter's horn, and the triplets should be carefully differentiated so as not to obscure the sound of the window opening. 'Ade, ade': the end is near, and after a brief revival in 'Trockene Blumen' the cycle closes with the gentle melancholy of the lover's intimate communion with the stream before he commits himself to it. Yet it is not death that comes with the wonderful final chord, but a gradual metamorphosis into infinity; the pianist should use both pedals with the utmost reticence, holding them down just enough to suggest a sense of being transported into another world.

From this idyllic story let us pass on to *Winterreise* – a 'cycle of dreadfully sombre *Lieder*', as Schubert himself described it to his friends. In all fairness, we should pay tribute to the verses of Wilhelm Müller. He may not be one of the greatest of lyric poets; he does sometimes deserve the epithet 'slushy' that has often been applied to him; but there must be some exceptional quality in his poetry to have inspired Schubert to a song-cycle of such infinite variety and freshness. As the cycle moves to its tragic ending there is a gradual intensification of colour, imagery and feeling, with every now and then a daemonic element, and all this without a trace of monotony despite the unrelieved atmosphere of melancholy. There are a few brief moments of relief, in 'Der Lindenbaum', for instance, or 'Frühlingstraum', perhaps too in 'Die Post', inspired by memories of happier days, but on the whole the tale is one of gloom and despair, with only a fleeting show of defiance in 'Der stürmische Morgen' or 'Mut'. The final scene is one of absolute darkness, of frenzy; in 'Der Leiermann' Schubert's genius comes near to anticipating the world of Mussorgsky. 'Drüben hinterm Dorfe' indicates that this final song is heard at a distance; it must be sung very softly and the piano part, except for one or two outbreaks near the end, must be played as if by fingers numbed by the winter cold. *Crescendi* and *diminuendi* must be scrupulously observed, but otherwise the mood is one of awesome silence (but clear articulation!) above the characteristic 'bagpipe fifth'.

Schubert's settings never degenerate into mere imitations or background music. The rattle of the weathercock, the teardrops in 'Gefrorene Tränen', the rustle of leaves in 'Der Lindenbaum', the flight of the crow, the squawk of the raven, the fall of autumn leaves, the rattle of dogs' chains, barking and growling, the dancing will o' the wisp; all are rendered in purely musical terms. Equally extraordinary is the way in which Schubert succeeds in transposing these motifs into utterly remote harmonic regions within the span of a single *Lied*, in 'Wohin' for example. Similar flashes of inventive genius occur in the much earlier 'Gretchen am Spinnrade', recalling some of the preludes in J. S. Bach's *Wohltemperiertes Klavier*.

The first song of the *Schwanengesang* group, the wonderful 'Liebesbotschaft', is as difficult to sing as it is to play, with its leaps of a tenth (to be sung smoothly and without hesitation), the *legatissimo* demisemiquavers in the right hand and the expressive *declamato* in the left. There follows a series of miniature music-dramas, with one or two lighter songs inserted to contrast with highly dramatic *Lieder* such as 'Kriegers Ahnung', 'Atlas', the impressionistic 'Die Stadt' and the eerie 'Der Doppelgänger'. Among the most effective of these lighter *intermezzi* are the passionate 'Frühlingssehnsucht', the delicate 'Ständchen', the carefree rider trotting out of town in 'Abschied', the 'Fischermädchen' barcarolle on a fragrant summer evening and the winged *sehnsucht* of 'Die Taubenpost'.

If I have already devoted a disproportionate amount of space to Schubert, and still have not mentioned any of the treasures in the remaining six volumes of his *Lieder*, that is because both in quantity and in quality Schubert is far and away the outstanding exponent of *Lieder* in the whole history of music. It is a sad reflection that, apart from a dozen favourites, the contents of these other volumes are far less well known than the three cycles. In selecting some of my own favourites among those that are less often performed, I would venture to include 'Am Grabe Anselmos', 'Erster Verlust', 'Der Zwerg', 'Memnon', 'Prometheus', 'Gretchens Bitte', 'Dass sie hier gewesen', 'Auflösung', 'Verklärung', 'Grenzen der Menschheit', 'Auf der Riesenkoppe', 'Fahrt zum Hades', 'An den Mond in einer Herbstnacht', 'Vor meiner Wiege', 'Heimliches Lieben', 'Freiwilliges Versinken', 'Vom Mitleiden Mariae', 'Totengräbers Heimweh' and 'Die Gebüsche'. All are marvellous; but the three cycles, if equalled in some later individual *Lieder*, are unsurpassed in their entirety.

I shall have to deal with Schumann, Brahms and Hugo Wolf more briefly. As we saw with Schubert, their *Lieder* cycles too are better known than their individual *Lieder*, although some of these are undoubtedly appealing. Schumann's *Liederkreis*, settings of poems by Eichendorff, starts off with a masterpiece, 'In der Fremde'. With his use of melodic imitation Schumann here achieves an intimate relationship between voice and piano that was never subsequently equalled. The second song, 'Intermezzo', confronts its interpreters with daunting difficulties, notably the *accelerando* in the second verse, where the syncopation in the piano part is responsible. 'Waldesgespräch' is an effective, daemonic dialogue; it is really a ballade, and certain liberties in the matter of tempi are permissible. Brightest in this string of precious stones is 'Mondnacht', in which the melodic line is something quite new in *Lieder* composition. Nobody took it so slowly or sang it with such purity as Elisabeth Schumann, and her interpretation brought out the full impact of the clash (which must on no account be mollified) between the D sharp, E sharp and F sharp in the melodic line against F sharp, E, D sharp in the piano part. The ecstatic joy of the final 'Frühlingsnacht' is incomparable.

About *Dichterliebe*, sixteen songs to poems by Heine, there is little new to be said; one can only marvel at its wealth of contrast and of melodic and rhythmic invention, not to mention the lovely Epilogue for the piano – a strikingly original idea. Chamisso's verses for *Frauenliebe und Leben* have not found universal favour, but how beautifully Schumann has set them! I should like to draw attention to some points in the interpretation of these songs. 'Seit ich ihn gesehen' is a song about a girl walking in her sleep; it must be sung softly, without any dynamics, as if with closed eyes, as the composer directs. Not until the final epilogue should the pianist indulge in any marked *crescendi* and *diminuendi*. In the third song, 'Ich kann's nicht fassen, nicht glauben', there is a stroke of genius in the second verse at the words 'Ich bin auf ewig dein', where on the word 'dein' Schumann ties the note F over into the next bar, while the piano has a chord of the seventh with a superimposed F sharp:

Many singers have ignored this subtlety, curtailing their F in order to avoid the clash with F sharp. But Schumann knew perfectly well what he was doing. Nobody can say 'Ich bin *auf ewig* dein' – 'I am yours *forever*'. Death is always lurking in the background, and at the end, after all too fleeting happiness, Death does come, as we hear in the final Adagio.

An even shorter *Lieder* cycle is *Fünf Gedichte der Maria Stuart* in the third volume of Schumann's songs – works of great beauty in an unusual recitative-arioso style, with unpretentious but vividly descriptive piano accompaniments that here and there verge on the imitative. Among Schumann's most beautiful individual *Lieder* are 'Aus den hebräischen Gesängen', which calls for a voice of exceptional compass; 'Dein Angesicht'; 'Aus den östlichen Rosen'; 'Romanze'; 'Belsazar'; 'Der Schatzgräber'; 'Die Kartenlegerin', and 'Das verlassene Mägdlein', which some may find superior even to Wolf's setting, just as I myself find the reticence of Schumann's setting of Mörike's 'Er ist's' more moving than the brilliance of Wolf's. Equally outstanding are the five 'Mignon' settings from Goethe's *Wilhelm Meister*, poems that also inspired Schubert and Wolf; and another favourite of mine is another Goethe setting, 'Nachtlied'. There is also a volume of Schumann's duets for various combinations of voices. My favourite among the more serious of these is 'Zur Nacht', a lovely duet in canon form for soprano and tenor, and among the lighter songs my choice would be 'Unterm Fenster', also for soprano and tenor.

The first volume of *Lieder* by Brahms contains a number of his best known – almost universally known – songs, grave and gay, a cornucopia of melody, rhythm and harmony. All are so characteristic of the composer that one cannot single out individual masterpieces. The most difficult to sing is 'Der Tod, das ist die kühle Nacht', with its very slow, long line and the brilliant climax at 'lauter Liebe' and quiet ending on 'Traum'. I should dearly love to hear again the lovely 'Die Kränze'; it is hard to understand why this song, in Brahms's first volume, is so little known. The individual *Lieder* in the second volume are even less well known. When do we hear 'Nicht mehr zu dir zu gehen' nowadays with the correct rhythm and the proper *portamento* in the second verse? Who sings 'Unbewegte, laue Luft', 'Regenlied' and 'Nachklang' now? And 'Von waldbekränzter Höhe'? But to compensate for this unaccountable neglect, Volume 2 also includes the lovely *Die schöne Magelone* cycle, exuberant music that is as difficult to sing as it is to play, typical of Brahms in melody, rhythm and harmony, the three basic elements of composition. With these songs we are back in the domain of *Lieder* cycles, a domain that includes the superb *Vier ernste Gesänge* – music that transports us from the almost nihilistic darkness and despair of the Old Testament to the rekindling of hope in the New Testament: 'And now abideth faith, hope, charity, these three; but the greatest of these is charity.'

Among the songs in Volumes 3 and 4 I must particularly mention 'O kühler Wald', 'Abenddämmerung', 'Ach, wende diesen Blick', 'Schwermut', 'Spanisches Lied', 'Es träumte mir', 'Wie rafft' ich mich auf', 'Lerchengesang', 'Der Wanderer', 'Verrat' and 'Sommerabend'. Of great interest too are the *Zigeunerlieder*, eight songs for solo voice and seven wonderful four-part songs, and the *Liebesliederwalzer*, with an accompaniment for piano duet. Brahms wrote a number of duets for two female voices, and there is also the beautiful Op. 28 for alto and baritone, including 'Der Ritter und die Nonne' (which sounds almost like a survival from the Crusades), the rhythmic originality of 'Vor der Tür' and the exuberantly melodious 'Es rauscht das Wasser'.

And so we come to Hugo Wolf, one of Brahms's severest critics and an ardent disciple of the music of Richard Wagner, though that did not prevent him from evolving a highly personal idiom of his own. Considering his all too short creative career, Wolf was relatively prolific. The promising *Lieder aus der Jugendzeit* contains several songs of real beauty, and these were followed by settings of poems by Mörike, Eichendorff and Goethe. There is also a volume of settings by miscellaneous poets, but the crowning glory of his oeuvre are the Italian and Spanish song-books and the *Drei Gedichte Michelangelos*. When, occasionally, his inspiration deserted him for periods of anguished inactivity, Wolf wrote nothing: no inspiration, no genius, and that is why in the whole of his output there is hardly one inferior *Lied*, until, still less than forty years old, the creative spark was eclipsed by a totally unbalanced mind.

In my opinion the *Mörike Lieder* constitute the most completely satisfying unity of voice and verse in the history of the *Lied*. They cover the whole range of human moods and emotions from the gaiety of 'Storchenbotschaft', the artlessness of 'Fussreise', the robust humour of 'Rat einer Alten', and 'Abschied', the idyllic contentment of 'Auf einer Wanderung', the eroticism of 'Erstes Liebeslied eines Mädchens' and 'Peregrina-Gedichte', the classical serenity of 'Gesang Weylas', the yearning of 'Verborgenheit', 'Heimweh' and 'Anders wird die Welt mit jedem Schritt',

the religious devotion of 'Schlafendes Jesuskind', 'Kar-
woche' and 'Neue Liebe' to the daemonic, balladesque
'Nixe Binsefuss' and 'Der Feuerreiter'. From a poetical as
well as a musical point of view I find 'Christblume I und II'
the finest of all, truly 'clad in mystic glory'; its colour and
fragrance are not of this world.

From the *Eichendorff Lieder* I would single out 'Der
Freund', 'Verschwiegene Liebe', the 'Ständchen' in triple
counterpoint, 'Soldat I und II' and the wonderful 'Nacht-
zauber', far ahead of its time both harmonically and
melodically. As for the Spanish and Italian song-books, it
seems hardly credible that the former was completed
fifteen years before the three Italian volumes; melodically,
harmonically, rhythmically and contrapuntally, the Spanish book is far bolder and more 'modern' than the Italian.
But that is not to depreciate the latter; as a series of mainly
concise but intensely expressive genre-pictures it combines
profundity with capriciousness, humour with devotion,
and emotion with ardour. The two volumes are as different
as the peoples and countries they depict, and both are
immortal and incomparable masterpieces.

The *Drei Gedichte Michelangelos* (the orchestration by
K. M. Zwissler is as felicitous as his orchestration of
Brahms's *Vier ernste Gesänge*) inhabit profoundly spiritual
domains both in this world and the next; whereas the four
volumes of settings of poems by Goethe transport us to
the uttermost frontiers of human cognition, thus matching
the universality of the poet's concept of life. It would be
invidious to single out any individual songs, but I feel I
must at least mention 'Anakreons Grab', 'Frühling übers
Jahr', 'St. Nepomuka Vorabend', 'Coptisches Lied I and
II', 'Die Spröde' and 'Die Bekehrte' of the Hatem songs,
and 'Locken, haltet mich gefangen' and 'Als ich auf dem
Euphrat schiffte' of the Zuleika songs. As regards
'Ganymed', 'Grenzen der Menschheit' and 'Prometheus',
in my own view Schubert's settings are generally superior
and certainly closer to the sense of the poems; yet in all
three settings Wolf himself was of the opinion that he had

far surpassed Schubert, whom he nevertheless greatly admired.

The late-Romantics Mahler, Pfitzner, Schoeck and Richard Strauss, each one of them a musician of stature, all follow faithfully in Wagner's footsteps yet manage to achieve a highly personal style and idiom of their own. Each of them can point to a number of admirable *Lieder*, notably Mahler's settings of Rückert ('Ich atmet einen linden Duft', 'Um Mitternacht' and the *Kindertotenlieder*) and the *Des Knaben Wunderhorn* settings.

As well as setting poems by his kindred spirit Eichendorff, Pfitzner also found an affinity with a number of other poets: 'Venus Mater' (Dehmel), 'Wie glänzt der helle Mond' (Keller), 'Ich und Du' (Hebbel), 'Mailied' (Goethe), 'Sehnsucht' (Liliencron) and 'Hussens Kerker' (C. F. Meyer).

Othmar Schoeck was a prolific composer of *Lieder*, of which he turned out some hundreds. Somewhat neglected nowadays, the best of them must surely be due for a revival, notably the ten settings of verses by Hermann Hesse and 'Ravenna', 'Auf ein totes Kind' and 'Das bescheidene Wünschlein'. The beautiful 'Mit einem gemalten Bande' shows how Schoeck can at times almost rival Schubert, if not even Mozart, without detriment to his own individuality, and in what is undoubtedly his finest song, his setting of Mörike's 'Peregrina', he convincingly challenges comparison with some of the greatest *Lieder* of Schubert or Hugo Wolf.

Richard Strauss was as highly successful as a *Lieder* composer as he was in every other branch of music he essayed, though he occasionally selected rather unworthy poems for his settings. Among his finest songs are 'Schlechtes Wetter', 'Morgen', 'Ach Lieb', ich muss nun scheiden', 'Ich wollt' ein Sträusslein binden', 'Säusle, liebe Myrthe', 'Freundliche Vision', 'Traum durch die Dämmerung', 'Wiegenlied', 'Sehnsucht', 'Ständchen', 'Ruhe, meine Seele', 'Madrigal', 'Meinem Kinde', 'Drei Gedichte der Ophelia' and 'Befreit' – and, of course, best sellers like

'Heimliche Aufforderung', 'Zueignung' and 'Wie sollten wir geheim sie halten', outwardly at least still effective.

For all his affinity with Bach and Brahms, Max Reger's *Lieder* owe their very existence to the music of Richard Wagner as indisputably as do those of Mahler, Pfitzner, Schoeck and Strauss. Though only 43 when he died in 1916, he bequeathed to posterity an immense amount of music, including a number of *Lieder* of far from secondary importance. As well as individual songs and duets he left four volumes of *Schlichte Weisen* ('Simple Songs', though the word 'simple' is not to be taken in the sense of 'easy'; they are all difficult to sing and difficult to play). The best of them are perhaps 'Waldeinsamkeit', 'Mariae Wiegenlied', 'Aeolsharfe', 'Das Dorf', 'Am Brünnele', 'Wenn die Linde blüht', 'Der Jäger', 'Glück' and 'An die Hoffnung' (which can be rendered with piano accompaniment but, like Mahler's song cycles, sounds better with orchestra). There is no gainsaying Reger's contrapuntal versatility and ingenious harmonic innovations, and in his *Lieder* he gives the lie to the critics who maintain that he lacks melodic invention; yet nowadays he is as neglected as Schoeck.

The *Lieder* of other later-Romantic composers – Joseph Haas, for instance, and Armin Knab, the former mainly influenced by Reger, the latter by Mahler – lacked individuality and are now seldom heard. Let us now look at contemporary *Lieder*, ushered in by Schoenberg's *Fünfzehn Gedichte aus dem Buch der hängenden Gärten* in 1915, settings of poems by Stefan George. Not that the late-Romantic era came to an end. Far from it. Even the new Vienna School of Arnold Schoenberg, Alban Berg and Anton von Webern (Father, Son and Holy Ghost, as the Romanian musicologist Antoine Golea described them) owed its existence to *Tristan und Isolde*. Yet the step from *Tristan's* chromaticism to the twelve-note system, albeit a short one, was one of great ingenuity, and to Schoenberg must go the credit for an immeasurable horizontal and vertical expansion of the melodic and harmonic domains in music.

The very first *Lied* of the *Hängende Gärten* sails peril-
ously close to the twelve-note system, but apart from one
or two atonal passages remains by and large true to
tonality. The cycle is a work of historic importance that is
only surpassed by that of the monodrama 'Erwartung',
which of course requires an orchestral accompaniment. As
for Alban Berg, his *Sieben frohe Lieder*, clearly influenced
by Mahler, are known the world over and feature in the
repertoire of all sopranos, and indeed of many mezzo-
sopranos too, thanks to the beauty of their harmony and
melodic line.

I am not an out-and-out devotee of Webern; what I find
repugnant are his displacement of verbal stresses, the
leaping intervals in the vocal line and a harmonic system
that at times is positively ascetic, if not actually sterile. On
the other hand, I do not gainsay the contemplative delicacy
of his setting of Goethe's 'Gleich und Gleich'; how different
it is from Hugo Wolf's setting of the same poem not very
much earlier! I also acknowledge the melodic beauty of his
setting of Stefan George's 'Einheit'.

But at almost the same time, the early nineteen-twenties
witnessed the exploration of completely new ground in the
treatment of the *Lied* form. The year 1922 saw the
publication of the first version of Paul Hindemith's
Marienleben; the second version, drastically amended, with
only one song, 'Stillung Mariae mit dem Auferstandenen',
left as it was, appeared in the early nineteen-forties. The
work is certainly a milestone in the history of the *Lied*, and
opinions still differ as to which version is to be preferred.
Some find the first version infinitely more inspired, bolder
and more 'modern'; others maintain that the vocal and
piano parts are much better balanced in the second version,
that it shows fewer structural defects and demonstrates
more clearly Hindemith's theories of composition. I know
both versions intimately – I have not only studied them
closely, but have also accompanied them in public; yet I
must admit that I still cannot come down on one side or
the other, though I know well how much of the first version

Hindemith jettisoned. In my view one need only read carefully Hindemith's own foreword to the second version to see eye to eye with the great composer that he certainly was. It is definitely a neo-baroque work, a reversion to the style of J. S. Bach similar to that practised by Stravinsky at the same time.

Ernst Krenek, a neo-Romantic, is known best for his still fascinating *Reisetagebuch aus den Oesterreichischen Alpen*, a cycle that contains some masterly *Lieder* – 'Regenlied', 'Heisser Tag am See' and 'Friedhof in einem Gebirgsdorf'. Joseph Marx wrote many beautiful songs, like 'Japanisches Regenlied', 'Marienlied', 'Hat dich die Liebe berührt', all in late Romantic style. Looking back over the last few decades, we seem to have been regaled with an upsurge of orchestral rather than vocal compositions. Admittedly there have been some striking contributions in the operatic world, neo-Renaissance, neo-Baroque and neo-Romantic. Yet the outlook in the less colourful world of the *Lied* is far from bleak, with composers of the stature of the Swiss Conrad Beck (some lovely autumn songs based on Rilke); Günther Bialas (attractive settings of Lorca); Boris Blacher (*Proverbs of Omar the Tent-Maker* and *Psalms*); Wolfgang Fortner (now composing in twelve-note technique; settings of Hölderlin and Shakespeare, a marvellous setting of Hölderlin's 'Abbitte' and the positively brilliant 'Lied vom Weidenbaum'); Kurt Hessenberg (*Lieder* grave and gay, and some deeply felt settings of Matthias Claudius); Wilhelm Killmayer (expansive and melodious settings of Hölderlin), and Aribert Reimann (highly sensitive settings of verses by Paul Celan, Eichendorff and Sylvia Plath); and finally Winfried Zillig, who despite a tragically premature death left some impressive settings of poems by Goethe.

trans. Richard Rickett

Editor's note

Hermann Reutter's own songs must be mentioned. Besides operas, ballets and orchestral and choral works he has published over two hundred and fifty songs with orchestral or piano accompaniment, as well as an admirable collection of contemporary songs, *Das zeitgenossische Lied*, from Bartók to Webern, one each for soprano, alto, tenor and bass.

His song 'Trommel' is printed on pages 156–7, and the composer comments: 'It is the singer's responsibility to neglect his personal feeling and try to absorb the composer's wishes. Above all his instructions on time, dynamics and rhythm.' Dietrich Fischer-Dieskau has recorded this song with Hermann Reutter on EMI 'A Modern Song Recital'.

Reuter *Trommel*

Zeit sich ver-liert und der Him-mel ver-sinkt und selbst der

Raum im Nichts er-trinkt. Tod, die Trom-mel, ras-selt

trom-trom, ruft al-lem Le-ben: Komm, komm,

komm!

Seventeen
The Italian Singer

Tito Gobbi
  Born in 1913 in the ancient town of Bassano del Grappa in the Veneto. He became the leading operatic baritone of his era and one of the most loved. His interpretation of the rôles of Rigoletto, Scarpia, Wozzeck, Lago, Falstaff, Don Giovanni remain vividly in mind. Now in great demand the world over as producer and teacher.

If one hopes to become a singer of quality it is essential to realize from the beginning that interpretation is every bit as important as the actual voice. The fusion between music and words must be complete – or there is nothing worth discussing. In Italian the language as well as the music is exceptionally rich in melody, allowing of innumerable varieties of expression especially in opera, and this is what makes it irresistible and easily accessible in its tunefulness. No painstaking study of music appreciation is required in order to feel the instant appeal of a great air by Rossini, Bellini, Donizetti, Verdi or Puccini. But, paradoxically enough, it is that very ease of approach for the listener which constitutes the most dangerous pitfall for the singer's attempting to present such music in its full significance and beauty.

For the truth is that one has to be a pretty dreadful performer not to get at least some measure of applause for an energetically sung 'La donna é mobile' or a superficial twittering of Musetta's Waltz Song; even for a lustily bawled Prologue to *Pagliacci* or a carelessly scrambled 'Largo al factotum' delivered with an engaging grin and some leaping around. In other words, it is dangerously tempting to 'milk' a well-loved air to one's own advantage and omit to serve it with the honour, care, love and humility which it deserves to have lavished upon it.

There are certain terms used – quite often inaccurately – to describe various types of Italian vocal music. It might be well therefore to start by defining some of these terms, beginning with '*bel canto*' which tends to be used quite indiscriminately in any discussion on Italian singing. Strictly speaking, this type of singing belongs to a period which was primarily remarkable for the fantastic personal technique required of the singers, a refined craftsmanship which enabled them to perform the most difficult and involved passage work. In the process the real meaning of the text was, it must be admitted, sometimes lost.

'*Recitar cantando*' on the contrary means to express the human emotions with the singing voice in such a way that even with closed eyes one should be able to imagine and follow the action.

The '*arie antiche*', as the term implies, come from a classical period of composition and need to be sung in a style consistent with the period; but this does *not* mean with pitiless rhythm and monotonous tone. Those wonderful composers had heart and feelings and vivid temperament. If their works are made to sound arid and cold their whole beauty and meaning are lost.

For the wide range of Italian folksongs the singing voice must be used in a way to evoke the atmosphere, the regional accent and the place where the song was born and still lives. Not very easy to do, but incredibly rewarding if you will study the background thoroughly, use your imagination and endeavour to convey the scene to the eyes and minds of your listeners.

Then there are the so-called *Romanze da camera* – literally drawingroom songs, or possibly ballads. I am myself particularly fond of some of these songs in which distinguished composers from Tosti, Denza and Brogi to Respighi and Wolf-Ferrari often chose charming verses which they adorned with their delightful melodies. There was an era when these were immensely popular and were sung by gifted amateurs and professionals alike, and also by some of the finest artists of the variety stage. For this wide spectrum of performers the composers created their elegant little works which were ideal to stir the emotions in a 'musical soirée', or evoke a storm of applause when sung from a platform. Let no one suppose that they are easy to sing or that a casual presentation will suffice. On the contrary, they require the right melodic accent not only in the music but in the expression and cadence of the words, with the expected romantic *sospiri* (sighs) essential to their charm. Indeed, in order to sing them properly one should perhaps have reached the stage when singing is as natural to one as breathing.

But let us now go back to a much earlier stage. In fact – to the beginning. You want to be a singer! Well, the first essential is to be well assured that you have a voice, a voice of quality. Sometimes a friend of the family discovers that voice; he may be a musician or a musicologist or even a composer, as in my own case, and so his opinions and suggestions are worth considering. (It is a mistake to listen too eagerly to the admiring but totally *unqualified* friend or relation who raises unjustified hopes. The advice will no doubt be well intentioned and delightful to one's self-esteem, but will almost inevitably lead to disappointment and frustration.) Once the existence of the voice has been reliably established you start looking for a *maestro di canto*. At that point you are going to need a great deal of luck.

Your family will have to face a lot of expense, for teachers naturally tend to live in big cities where living is not cheap, and it may be difficult to find a job to pay for your singing lessons. In actual fact, you put yourself on a waiting list for some years with no guarantee of a successful future. In taking this decision, involving your family, you are supported only by a fragile thread of HOPE. Only later will you realize what a tightrope you have been walking. That fragile hope is like the 'fulcrum' that Archimedes sought to lift the world – a crazy hope which promises nothing because *the voice alone means nothing*.

I myself left my home town with luggage prepared by my dear mother, and dogged my father's footsteps all the way to Rome, relying on the fact that he could then hardly say 'go back' or reject the collective craziness which was infecting the entire family. My sisters and my brothers were happily involved – seven dreamers, including me. I thought that in getting to Rome I had almost achieved my goal. But once I had started serious study I found myself committed to it for life.

I repeat – for this cannot be emphasized too strongly to the young student – that the voice itself is not enough. So, before you involve yourself and your family in a wrong decision which could spoil your life, it is wise to have some alternative in the background; a second string to your bow. In any case, make a realistic and severe assessment of your potential before starting. A singer needs health, strong nerves, presence, musicality, good intonation, sense of rhythm, humility and many other things which you will discover during your career, but which you must already have in embryo and be aware of.

You have all that? Well then, you can go on. How?

Open your eyes and ears and use your brain – and hope for a little luck. You are going to need it. I know that sounds cruel, but that is how it is. Every decision must be yours, even though you may receive suggestions from others which help you. God has already helped you enough. He gave you the voice! The most marvellous gift that a man or woman can receive. Do not spoil or abuse it. Its development and preservation is your responsibility. Engage all your will-power, your determination and your intelligence to make of this supreme gift a joy for humanity.

That is the way to thank God.

Beware of teachers chosen at random and without qualified recommendation. Especially of those teachers who make you vocalize 'KIU'KIU'KIU' or 'MEAW MEAW MEAW' or even 'TRIT TROT TRAT'. I am not inventing that. I could not believe it but I came across that inspired system of lunacy in New York in 1972. Do not change teachers too often. Better to collect the mistakes of only a few.

Breathe properly, as a sportsman breathes, concentrate your whole self at every minute of your life on this world of singing which you are seeking to enter. But avoid becoming a maniac about it, a bore or, even worse, a balloon – a pompous bit of nonsense. Be normal. You are only a very lucky person.

I was myself very fortunate to fall in with my first and only *maestro*, the tenor Giulio Crimi, who kept me for ages on exercises, never tiring my voice or irritating my throat, never insisting on the top notes but just letting my vocal organ develop with practice. After two years of this régime I was allowed to sing 'Malia' by Tosti.*

As I have warned in the beginning of this chapter, a young singer should never underestimate the greatness of a work or an air just because it is easily accessible. Similarly, it is a serious mistake to underestimate a role, however short it may be or unimportant it may seem. The fact is that there are many small performers but few unimportant roles. There are many ways of singing 'Dinner is served'; you may not greatly enhance a scene by doing

* It has been suggested to me that I should provide a list of songs and arias suitable for aspiring young singers, but I am loth to do this. In my experience the equipment, development and basic approach of every artist are individual matters. Consequently, while a so-called simple song may serve to disclose the innate artistry of one singer, it may pander to the deficiencies in another. My advice is: find a teacher in whom you have confidence and then defer to him or her in everything. For my part I should be sorry to have any generalization of mine used as an argument against the particular instruction of a conscientious teacher.

it the right way, but you will very possibly spoil the scene by doing it the wrong way. I have seen it done.

If you are cast for an operatic role – any role, small or large – study the whole work and above all get to know your character intimately as a person. On a simple reading of the libretto the character may seem uninteresting, even what is called 'a cardboard figure'. Do not be deceived. If the composer has touched that character with the hand of genius there will be something in the music to guide and inspire you. Remember he has travelled the road before you, leaving signposts to establish the identity of that character. Look for and pay attention to those signs. Characters are not just funny or touching, noble or devious; they are people and therefore funny, touching, noble or devious in their own individual way. This does not mean that a small-part performer should push forward out of context or balance; it does mean that the artist should always be aware of himself or herself *as that character*.

To take a simple example: much has been written and said about the big roles of Otello, Iago and Desdemona (and rightly so), but suppose you are to play Emilia, what sort of woman do you think she is? Apart from the fact that she attends her mistress here and there, picks up the fatal handkerchief and has it wrenched from her by Iago, most people remember her merely as the person who brushes Desdemona's hair in the last scene. But – she is the wife of Iago and must therefore be more aware of his basic villainy than anyone else on the stage. She also cannot fail to be fond of the eminently lovable Desdemona, who has probably shielded her sometimes from Iago's casual brutality. And yet, because she is a coward, she does not voice her doubts until it is too late. Had she done so she, the unimportant Emilia, might have changed the course of the drama and possibly saved her beloved mistress. It is not possible to show all this on the stage, but it is very important for Emilia to have this constantly in her mind. She will then insensibly become a person, a character. Insensibly, I say; not overacting.

Again in any role, large or small, always remember that a good pronunciation is vitally important. This gives authority to what is said and, incidentally, helps tremendously to project the voice.

Difficulties will always be cropping up in the early years, and you must learn how to correct them. If a certain phrase is particularly difficult to master – because of a note, a breath or a *legato* – you must find the reason. Very often, because of anxiety about that difficult phrase, you did not pay enough attention to what went before and did not place the previous notes properly. In such a case never treat your voice harshly, repeating mercilessly a high note or cadenza. Go back and improve what preceded the difficult passage or note, smoothing the approach as it were. Remember that if you end an aria unduly tired there is something wrong which you must set right.

In order to reach a difficult high note think in terms of reaching the top floor. To get there one has to climb a staircase, step by step, resting the feet firmly but without undue weight. The agility of a voice can be compared to the agility of a body, for much the same technique is required. Again, it is not so important how much you study or practice, but how you do it. Never bully your voice, just bring it firmly under your control, so that gradually you make it ready to follow all the inflections and expressions suggested by artistic talent.

I myself always think in terms of painting with my imagination when I am singing, giving to the sound various colours and degrees of intensity as required. The speaking voice changes when, for instance, you say something happy or something sad. This being so, it is patently wrong to use the same voice when you sing, say, Figaro in *Barbiere di Siviglia* and when you sing Rigoletto. There are, to make the simplest distinction, cold colours and warm colours. But to the singer who will study this side of his or her art there is a splendid palette of shades and colours to choose from. Throughout my career I have found special delight in doing this, sometimes using sharp contrasts, sometimes allowing the shades to merge into each other like water colours, according to the requirements of the occasion.

The term 'to colour the voice' means to dress the notes or phrases with an expression which suggests a colour to tone with the mood. For instance, in *Rigoletto* I feel my voice is yellow in the cruel, mocking phrases of the first scene; but it becomes dark purple with the rage and anguish of Act Three. Similarly Simone Boccanegra has a young voice in the Prologue, but it grows darker with age and worry later in the drama. In the poison scene it becomes sickly grey and tired, but celestial for the final blessing. One could continue indefinitely describing the range of colours applicable to a single character, and I earnestly advise any young singer to try hard to understand and apply this art of 'colouring the voice'. It is the greatest insurance against becoming a vocal bore with an uninteresting 'one tone' voice – a fate which has overtaken more than one singer with an otherwise excellent organ.

It should always be remembered that, just as a fine straight actor conveys his effects by the way he uses his speaking voice, so a singer of any calibre uses his singing voice to convey his every thought and meaning. For instance, when in Act Two of *Otello* Iago is instilling suspicion into the mind of the Moor, the very way he sings, 'Mio Signore—' is of great importance. If he sings it in good, full strong tone it means nothing except that he is calling Otello's attention to the fact that he is there. But if he sings it in an insinuating, faintly hesitant way, the audience becomes aware that he is planning mischief.

Similarly, when Rigoletto and Gilda come on to the stage in the last act the way they walk, the way they look and, above all, the way they sing should express their leaden weariness and despair, the terrible sense of having come to the end of the road. This also is no moment to show what a beautiful full tone you can produce (it is to be hoped you have already done that in the previous act!). At this point I use a foggy grey colour.

There is nothing more intoxicating than living so many different lives and *feeling* them. It is by far the best part of an opera singer's career. The excitement of researching a character, putting him into the right framework, getting to know the places where he lived and the people he had around him; the very way he put on his clothes and boots and therefore how he walked and sat. It is a fascinating work and, along with the proper use of your voice, adds up to making you an artist instead of just a singer. Always listen to the music and you cannot go wrong in your understanding of that character. The music will explain and suggest everything that is required: the tone of voice, the action, the feeling – all is there in the score if you will seek diligently for it.

With time and experience you will naturally learn to find what is good for *your* voice, for every voice must be treated differently. Trying to imitate the voice or the interpretation of another artist, however great, is useless and often dangerous. You have to develop in your own way, for what is good for me may not be good for you, and vice versa.

Learn how to analyse your role and find the pitfalls. And again remember how important it is to lead up to a climax. In *Suor Angelica* for instance, the big air 'Senza Mamma' is a tremendously dramatic one, but it is a fatal mistake to *begin* dramatically. The opening phrases are like a monotonous lament, just the crude facts stated over the chords in the orchestra, with what might be called 'dry tears' in the voice. In contrast the climax of desperation 'Amore, amore, amo-o-or' is almost lacerating in its effect. The temptation there is to waste the impact of the great moment by betraying the mood too soon.

Another, different type of difficulty occurs in the tenor aria in Act I of *La Bohème* – one of those high notes, in fact, which strike terror beforehand. The inexperienced singer tends to imagine that high C is much higher than in fact it is, with a bigger distance between the four ascending notes; consequently he will force and push up too much.

In forcing he probably opens his mouth too far, drops his jaw and therefore closes his throat and cuts off the sound. All that is needed is a calm and intelligent approach. To obtain a well rounded 'La-a spe-e-ran-za' *relax*, then start lifting the sound into the high position from 'ma il furto non m'accora', be lighter in '. . . V'ha preso stanza . . .' then start climbing the staircase, taking care not to put much weight on the previous notes – and you will find that you are already up there.

Yet again there are dangers in connection with the right projection of a *pianissimo*, particularly when this occurs in the opening phrases of an aria, as in 'Una furtiva lagrima . . .' I maintain that a *pianissimo* does not exist without a very strong support of breath, as in a *fortissimo* but without the contrast of a bigger sound; the balance of quantity is then just as important as the quality of the sound. If therefore you start this aria with a poor weak sound, in the mistaken belief that you are going to show what a lovely *pianissimo* you possess, you are in trouble immediately. You cannot reduce the volume of an already weak sound and there is not enough support to increase it, so you start to wobble. What then should be done?

If you are not naturally gifted for the *mezza voce* and not very experienced, better you start with a real note, rich, well-projected and sufficiently strong; then as soon as you are able to do so reduce the quantity of the sound, supporting with more breath and controlling the *quality* and the intensity. It's as simple as that.

Over the years I have come to value singing as such almost entirely insofar as it sheds light and understanding on a character – good or bad. This is a very important part of becoming what is called 'a singing actor', and absolutely essential to the proper performance of Italian opera. To deliver a faultlessly sung aria, making a pleasant and acceptable sound throughout, may be praiseworthy and rate good marks in a students' examination. It will do little for you when you are actually on a stage. And it will do nothing at all for a great musical drama. Witness the slaughter done by people who imagine they can perform *Norma* just because they can sing all the notes.

In this complete identification of the artist with the character it is totally useless to try suddenly to become the character as you enter the scene. This is one reason why I always advocate being in the dressing room some considerable while before going on stage. To play a part, large or small, is not just a matter of coasting along between arias and ensembles, waiting for that precious moment when the attention of the audience will be yours and you can show what a splendid voice you have. Even a silent entry can rivet attention, so that no one in the audience can look at anything but that one figure 'doing nothing' in the most utterly compelling manner.

Among the baritone roles probably the most arresting 'unsung' entry is that of Scarpia in the first act of *Tosca*. It should be absolutely terrifying – and Puccini's music has provided the means to make it so. There are four tremendous weighty chords, and the most effective Scarpia entry demands only that you set down your feet in time to those fearful chords, coming straight towards the audience, who should feel like backing away from your advance. Then you *stand* there. No need to bustle about being a brute. Nothing is more terrifying on the stage than significant stillness. Puccini has done all that is required, relying on a good reaction from the choristers and the sacristan.

In my opinion one of the most important things on any stage is this matter of action and reaction. No action will be remarkable if it does not produce an equally remarkable reaction. Indeed if, during a performance, you want to create trouble for the colleague who is singing to you, all that is necessary is to look straight at him with no expression and no reaction to what he is telling you. He will be utterly put out and probably forget his lines. If, on the other hand – which I trust will be the case! – you want generously to increase the success of the scene (which will be to your advantage too) then follow the action of your 'opponent' and magnify it with the finest reaction you can.

The audience will warm towards you both and you will have behaved as a good colleague should.

And that is important beyond measure. If you really make a good career you will love it and respect it deeply and unconditionally, which means that you will always appreciate all your colleagues and act in a mutually honest collaboration for the sake of the best performance you can achieve.

I hope I have said enough in these few pages to show that in my view an artist does not ask himself or herself, 'What will this role or aria do for me?' but, 'How can I, with earnest work, love, dedication, intelligence and humble respect do justice to what someone else has created?'

Only the mere limited performer works for self-aggrandizement; the artist serves his art. There is no finer goal.

In bocca al lupo!

(arr. Ida Cooke)

Eighteen
Spanish Song

Emilio Nuñez
  Born in Madrid and holds the degree in music from the Conservatorio Superior de Música en Madrid. His publications include a Spanish songbook and several books on musical education. He teaches in Madrid and U.S.A. and has served on many international voice competitions in Germany, France, Holland and Spain.

Spanish song – like Spanish music in general – is not particularly strange, nor particularly difficult to perform, provided the performer has a sound technique, musicality and sensitivity, three qualities I am sure all the young singers reading this book will possess and which indeed they have to employ continually in any aria, song or *Lied* they perform.

Of course, Spanish songs are characterized by distinctive rhythms, cadences, ornaments and so on, but these are always written out perfectly by the composer and can be executed with relative ease. Preparation of this music is the same as that of any other. However, we will discuss later on one of the most difficult aspects of it: the pronunciation of the text.

I have myself heard performances of Spanish songs by non-native singers whose interpretations moved me more than many versions by Spanish singers – exquisite interpretations of songs by Manuel de Falla and Enrico Gran-

ados, for example, by the American Shirley Verrett and
the Soviet soprano Elena Obraztsova. I heard Obraztsova
in Barcelona in 1970; she had just received first prize in
the Francisco Viñas Voice Competition, in which I was a
member of the jury. She was anxious to have a Spaniard's
opinion of her interpretations and came to my hotel one
morning to sing for me. I can assure you that it was one of
the most emotionally inspiring experiences of my life to
realize that this young singer, who spoke only Russian and
a few phrases of French, could offer such a well enunciated,
beautifully phrased and inspiring rendition of Manuel de
Falla's songs. Falla himself named a French singer, Ninon
Vallin, as one of the best interpreters of his *Siete Canciones
Populares Españolas*.

The pronunciation of the text is one of the most difficult
things to master in Spanish song. It is absolutely essential
that the text be properly understood. To gain a basic
understanding of Spanish pronunciation you may refer to
any of the several books on the subject written in English,
many of which go into considerable detail. I would simply
suggest *Collins Spanish-English, English-Spanish Dictionary*, edited by Colin Smith; on pages xxi–xxv in the section
on pronunciation and spelling you will find all the information you need to achieve a more than acceptable
Spanish pronunciation. After all, all singers know Italian,
and Spanish pronunciation is very similar. I need not dwell
on the difficulties that the pronunciation of 'j' or 'c' may
cause; you will soon overcome them. I do wish, however,
to draw attention to something that can prove more
troublesome: those words in Spanish, such as 'querer*te*',
'cant*arte*', 'dive*rt*ida' and so on, which contain a vowel
followed by the consonants 'rt'. To pronounce these words
correctly in Spanish, the vowel must be pronounced purely
and the two consonants articulated strongly. I have often
noticed that the English speaker masks the vowel, does
not roll the 'r' correctly and then pronounces the 't' not as
in Latin but as in English. The proper pronunciation of
words like these may be the most difficult thing you have

to achieve, but once you have mastered it you will have a Spanish diction which sounds genuine and authentic. If possible, listen to songs sung by the Spanish mezzo-soprano Conchita Supervia (EMI Golden Voices Series No. 20, HQM 1220). Even though these recordings were made in 1927–1932 – the artist died in 1936 – you will be able to hear absolutely perfect diction. At the same time you will be listening to one of the few Spanish singers whose interpretation of the songs of their country was truly masterly. But let me offer a piece of advice: do not try to imitate Supervia, or any other singer. You will only manage to imitate the defects, which every singer has, and none of the virtues.

With the problems of Spanish diction solved, we must then understand the meaning of the text to be sung. This is of course nothing new for a singer, but in Spanish song, which is extremely introspective, the text is especially important. I find it difficult to express in words exactly what the character of Spanish song is; perhaps I might call it an 'interior song', a song which is felt deeply in our mind and soul and which is then expressed, though never effusively, with an intensity that reaches down to the very bottom of our hearts. This process is motivated by the text, which also serves as a guide in inspiring us to use the proper quality of voice for the text's interpretation.

Through the centuries, poetry and music have been closely related in Spanish song. Sometimes we have even found the poet and the musician in the same person – in Juan del Encina, for example, without doubt the most distinguished Renaissance poet and musician of the reign of the 'Catholic king and queen' Ferdinand and Isabella. Listening only to the poetry of one of Juan del Encina's songs we might almost feel that a musical setting would be superfluous; the rhythm and sound of the words are so perfect that they create their own music. But it is only after listening to the poetry set to the melody provided by the composer that we can savour the composition in all its beauty, for the melody serves to complement the sad, happy, intimate or picaresque feeling that the poetry invokes. It would be impossible to sing the songs of this poet-musician without knowing the meaning of the text.

We have dealt so far with diction, articulation and the text, but not with any of the vocal difficulties that a song can present to a singer. I am sure that all singers know – they certainly should know – how to make a phrase, to use *legato*, execute ornaments, employ different colours of voice and so forth. These elements of technique are used continually in any aria or song, whatever its national origin. But to perform a Spanish song with sensitivity one must forget one's voice and adjure spectacular high tessituras and other crowd-pleasing vocal effects. One must forget all of this to concentrate on what is being 'said' in the piece and to portray fully the atmosphere, picaresque, joyful or sad, that the text requires.

Let us take as an example one of the *Siete Canciones Populares Españolas* by Manuel de Falla, 'Asturiana'. This song is an *endecha*, which in music means any kind of sad song. It is truly an 'interior song', full of plaintive melancholy, in which the weeping is deeply felt but not heard. The piano accompaniment is like the tolling of distant bells, over which the voice floats – 'floats' because the voice cannot, or should not, look for its support in the accompaniment. This is one of the most beautiful, and at the same time most difficult, songs to perform; phrasing, *legatos* and *ritardandos* must all be perfectly employed to achieve the effect of spontaneity. Here is the text, side by side with an English translation, and then my own notes – not as a correction of Falla's original version but as a guide to interpretation.

Por ver si me consolaba	Seeking consolation
arriméme a un pino *verde*,	I went up close to a green pine-tree,
por ver si me consolaba.	Seeking consolation.
Por verme llorar, *lloraba*	And it cried to see me crying
y el pino, como era *verde*,	Because the pine-tree was green,
por verme llorar, *lloraba*	it cried to see me crying

One mustn't look for a literal translation of the text. Why? The word 'verde' is so beautiful, 'lloraba' is so sad – and both join together in a melody that is so pathetically simple. It is necessary to give special emphasis to these two words: first, to 'verde', by means of a marked articulation which expresses, with utmost intensity, 'life', which in my opinion is what the word symbolizes. Secondly, to 'lloraba'. Each time the word 'verde' appears in the text one must give new life to this song, which is headed irreversibly towards agony ('lloraba' in the fourth line) and ultimately arrives at the definitive rest of death (symbolized by 'lloraba' in the last line).

The colour of voice is very important, a colour veiled by pain but not manifested outwardly. A perfect *legato* and exact *ritardando* are both essential. There are certain breath marks, pauses which are not written in, which give more importance to what follows them. The pause before

the last 'lloraba', symbolizing death, is absolutely indispensable. The phrases can be sung without interruption if
desired, with only half-breaths marking the pauses, but the
song is not intended to show off a splendid *fiato*; it must
move the audience by showing its deep roots in our soul.

This detailed commentary on a single song prompts the
question whether or not classes of interpretation can be
useful to the student. Spain offers very few courses of this
kind. The best I know of at present is that which the
soprano Ana María Iriarte offers twice a year, in the
autumn and in the spring, in Barcelona. (Further information can be obtained from 'Cursos de Interpretación'
Francisco Viñas, Bruch, 125, Barcelona). This professor
guides her students but never obliges them to adopt her
own interpretation; on the contrary, she searches out and
respects the students' own personality, something very
important both for the teacher and for the student, who,
as I said earlier, should never imitate any other singer.

Let us now look briefly at the most important periods in
the history of Spanish song. The Renaissance reached
Spain much later than the rest of Europe, not indeed until
the reign of Ferdinand V and Isabella, proclaimed joint
sovereigns of Spain in 1474. Not until Spain achieved
territorial unity with the expulsion of the Arabs, the period
of the discovery and domination of America, was attention
turned to the great cultural revival. By that time it had lost
the force with which it had originally erupted in other
countries. Consequently in Spain it became a distinctively
Spanish movement, devoid of its earlier Italian overtones.
During this period (the end of the fifteenth and the
beginning of the sixteenth century) the existing song books
are predominantly filled with characteristically Spanish
songs (*villancicos*, *endechas*, *ensaladas*, *estrambotes* and so
on). The term 'madrigal' is applied only to those songs
written in the Italian style. The majority of Spanish
Renaissance songs are composed for several voices, even
though the custom of solo singing had been established by
that time, with one part sung and the others played either

by different instruments or by a simple accompaniment which follows the original harmony as closely as possible. The most popular instrument for accompanying was the vihuela, an instrument shaped like a guitar but strung and played like a lute. We can still find in the repertoire of many singers songs written for solo performance whose original accompaniment is attributed to such important vihuela players as Don Luís Milán, Alfonso de Mudarra, Diego Pisador and others. Other existing accompaniments have been arranged for the guitar, the most suitable modern instrument, by contemporary guitarrists. All these songs require careful articulation. In general they have a small range which presents no problems for a normal, or even a smaller than normal, voice. The singer must concentrate on the construction of the phrase and the expression of the emotion asked for in the text. The interpretation must never be lifeless – something that cannot always be relied on even amongst internationally famous Spanish singers.

Beautiful vocal works can be found throughout the seventeenth century, most of them composed for performance in the theatre. It was at that time that a totally Spanish genre appeared for the first time: the *zarzuela*. Although the *zarzuela* is an exclusively Spanish theatrical form, combining spoken dialogue, song and dance, the *zarzuelas* of the seventeenth century showed heavy Italian influence, understandably perhaps, since Monteverdi's *Orfeo* was premiered in 1607 and Italian opera began to have a great influence on all European countries.

Spain was most strongly influenced by trends in Italian music during the eighteenth century, during which many musicians left Italy to live in Madrid; some of them, such as Domenico Scarlatti and Luigi Boccherini, were internationally famous, while others, far more mediocre musicians, occupied privileged positions in the Spanish musical world thanks to the protection of the *castrato* Farinelli. This Italian influence is obvious in art songs of the period, which are heavily ornamented and elaborate, as well as in the lyric theatre. Italian opera had by now become a spectacle of the masses and reigned in all Europe, and the works presented in the Spanish court and the theatres of Madrid copied the Italian style of the day, with its *secco* and *accompagnato* recitatives and arias. The arias followed the classic a – b – a form and were also ornamented accordingly. Although there are delightful moments in works by Antonio de Literes and Sebastián Durón, two composers representative of this period, they are completely devoid of any uniquely Spanish flavour.

During this period of powerful Italian influence a much more authentic and interesting musical composition sprang up in Spain, primarily in Madrid: the *tonadilla escénica*, a theatrical work of short duration and of popular origin. Unfortunately, although literally thousands of these *tonadillas* are preserved in the archives of the Municipal Government in Madrid, very few of them have ever been published. In the arias or duos of these works we frequently find popular dance rhythms of the day – the *bolero*, the *tirana*, the *fandango* and *seguidillas*. These rhythms presented a special problem to the composer who wished to include them in his works; how to give a special note of popular knavery to the music without descending into vulgarity? The happy solution to this question can be found in works by Blas de Laserna, Palomino, Guillermo Ferrer, Pablo Esteva and a few others.

The best existing anthology that I can suggest, although it was published some time ago, is the song book *Cancionero Musical Popular Español*, compiled by Felipe Pedrell and published by Boileau (Barcelona). The author of this fundamental four-volume work was the founder of the Spanish Nationalist school and the professor to Enrique Granados, Manuel de Falla and others. The anthology contains an ideal selection of Renaissance songs of the seventeenth and eighteenth centuries and of authentic popular pieces of the same period.

The Spanish Nationalist school arose at the end of the nineteenth century. Following the Russian example, its serious works were rooted in popular folk songs. Of the various nationalistic schools formed about that time, it was without question the Spanish school that became the most international of all. The members of it who most successfully cultivated the song were Manuel de Falla and Enrique Granados, creators of a tradition that was to be continued by many other composers up to the present day. The works of these musicians can present obvious difficulties in their popular rhythms, melodies, ornaments and cadences; but, once studied, they can be mastered and performed perfectly. The biggest obstacle that the singer encounters in Falla's songs is the *tessitura*, which is often very low, especially for female voice. Perhaps the most thankless of the composer's works to perform is *El Amor Brujo*; I have yet to hear a satisfactory performance even on record. It is not the singer's fault but the composer's; the range is impossible to sing. The work is very tempting and many top-notch voices have attempted it, but none has achieved the desired result. The opera *La Vida Breve* is a much more reasonable work for the singer, although technically it is not easy. The same is true of the *Siete Canciones Españolas*, the most important collection of Spanish songs, published in two versions, for low voices and for high, with a whole-tone difference in keys.

There are two very interesting collections of songs by Enrique Granados. The *Canciones Amatorias* are composed around poems of the Golden Century. I heartily recommend these songs to you; they are not well known, but the more you work on them the more you will like them. The *tessitura* is very appropriate for soprano, and the pieces present no real technical difficulties. The other collection of Granados's songs, much better known, is *Tonadillas al Estilo Antiguo*. These pieces are inspired by the popular music of Madrid during Goya's lifetime, the end of the eighteenth and beginning of the nineteenth century. All but one are written for female voice, in the typical 3/4 time; the exception is 'El Majo Olvidado', scored for baritone or bass. Three of these *tonadillas* – 'La

Maja Dolorosa', Nos. 1, 2 and 3 – demand an extremely low register for a soprano or even a mezzo-soprano. None the less they are tremendously beautiful songs, which with care can be learned and performed to convey their profoundly dramatic nature.

These compositions by Manuel de Falla and Enrique Granados established the character of the Spanish songs that followed, whether original compositions inspired by the popular rhythms and melodies of the country or adaptations of actual folksong dressed up with a contemporary piano accompaniment. The student of Spanish song should also know the *Trois Mélodies* to French texts by Falla and 'La Maja y el Ruiseñor', for soprano, from Granados's opera *Goyescas*.

Among outstanding contemporary or near-contemporary composers we can name Joaquín Turina, who gives his music a strong Andalusian flavour (*Canto a Sevilla*, *Poema en forma de Canciones*, *Tríptico*); Amadeo Vives, well known for some of his *zarzuelas* and *Canciones Epigramáticas*; Joaquín Rodrigo (*Cuatro Madrigales Amatorios*), who has demonstrated great skill in adapting the songs of earlier composers from their original style to contemporary settings; Federico Mompou (the four songs of *Combal del Somni* and two sets of *Tres Comptines*); and Xavier de Montsalvatge, composer of *Canciones Negras*, songs full of nostalgic Cuban motifs which can be sung either with piano alone or with orchestra. These songs do not require a big voice and are all most enjoyable to sing, notably 'Canción de Cuña para Dormir a un Negrito', which is particularly delightful.

A little earlier in date are Felipe Pedrell, founder of the Spanish Nationalist school (*Cuatro Cantigas de Alfonso El Sabio*) and Román Alis. Others nearer to our own time whose work a singer will find interesting are Jesús Arámbarri (*Ocho Canciones Vascas*), Oscar Esplá (*Canciones Playeras*, for soprano and orchestra), Jesús García Leoz (*Seis Canciones* to texts by Antonio Machado), Jesús Guridi (*Seis Canciones Castellanas*), Cristobal Halffter

179

(*Dos Canciones*), Joaquín Nin (two volumes of *Vingt Chants Populaires Espagnoles*), Fernando Obrados (*Canciones Clásicas Españolas*, three volumes) and Eduardo Toldra (*Seis Canciones, Doce Canciones Populares Españolas*).

Almost all these songs are written for female voice, although often no voice is actually specified. One cannot really distinguish between the songs for soprano, mezzo-soprano and contralto; the singer's common sense should guide her in choosing the songs best suited to her voice. Some of these songs are also frequently performed by male singers.

For a really thorough knowledge of Spanish song, the singer should know the six volumes of *Música Hispana Popular* published by the Instituto Español de Musicología, and the two collections, *Canciones Españolas Antiguas*, songs from the thirteenth, sixteenth, seventeenth and eighteenth centuries compiled and arranged by José María Ramón, and *Canciones Españolas Antiguas*, harmonized by Federico García Lorca.

I have confined myself here to solo songs for the recitalist. Very few Spanish operas have survived; to Falla's *La Vida Breve* and Granados's *Goyescas*, mentioned earlier, we can add Isaac Albéniz's *Pepita Giménez*; but these few examples are not sufficiently significant to allow us to speak about a Spanish opera as we do about the Russian, Italian, French and German opera.

Finally, I have to say that it has always been very difficult for a Spanish composer to publish his works in his own country. This lack of support by the Spanish people of their country's musicians has been evident throughout all our history. Fortunately there has always been another country which, drawn to Spain's music, has taken up the role of patron and protector of our composers and their works. For this reason many editions of Spanish music have been published in other countries: Italy in the seventeenth century, England in the eighteenth, France in the twentieth century, and so on.

Nineteen
A Singer's Survey of American Song

Helen Boatwright
  Has been known throughout her career for her penetrating interpretations of American song, particularly those of Charles Ives of which she has recorded fifty-two. She has taught at the Eastman School of Music and Syracuse University and holds master classes at the Ecole Hindemith in Switzerland.

At the time of our Bicentennial (1976), American singers turned their attention toward American song. Programmes were given on college campuses and at various festivals displaying the richness and diversity of our heritage in this art form. An annotated bibliography on 'Art Song in America' was compiled by the National Association of Singing Teachers, containing some 2,500 titles by nearly 500 composers. These entries are all available in published form. Many other songs exist in manuscript on the shelves of composers themselves and the singers to whom they have been sent. I, for one, have more than one hundred such manuscripts, and I have sung most of them. The title of my article is one I have used for recitals of American song from 1750 to the present and I shall direct my attention in this article mainly to the art song with piano accompaniment. I am writing not as an historian, but as a singer who has performed most of the music discussed and with the reader's indulgence, I will turn to an autobiographical approach when my contact with the more recent literature becomes direct. In some cases the songs mentioned were performed with or for the composers themselves or their close associates.

Francis Hopkinson (1737–1791), a singer of the Declaration of Independence, claimed that he could not be denied the credit of being the first native of the United States to produce a musical composition when he wrote the preface to his '*Seven Songs*' (actually eight) issued in Philadelphia in 1788. An even earlier song, 'My days have been so wondrous free', is perhaps his best known. Its lovely lyrical melody may be elaborated with ornamentation in the second verse. An attractive song from the 'Seven Songs' is 'My generous heart disdains the slave of love to be'. In rondo form it is more extended than 'My days have been so wondrous free' and bears a resemblance to the songs of the English composer, Thomas Arne. I have used it successfully to open a group of early American songs.

Benjamin Carr (1769–1831) came from England to America in 1793, settling in Philadelphia. Particularly beautiful is his setting of Sir Walter Scott's 'Hymn to the Virgin', published in 1810, fifteen years before Schubert made his famous setting of the same text, 'Ave Maria'. The arpeggiated accompaniment calls for the use of the 'harp stop', suggesting that he had in mind either the harpsichord, or a pianoforte with a special stop. Of this song, Upton says, 'Here begins (American) art in song, conscious, beautiful art'.

Another effective and historically interesting song by Carr is his 'Dead March And Monody', composed to mourn the death of George Washington. The 'Dead March' has a sixteen-bar introduction in sombre harmonies and solemn dotted rhythms followed by simple strophic treatment of the text. While the 'Hymn to the Virgin' attains lyrical beauty, the 'Dead March' achieves a certain measure of grandeur.

Contemporaries of Benjamin Carr were Alexander Reinagle (1756–1809), Raynor Taylor (1747–1825) and James Hewitt (1770–1827). All three of these men came to America from Great Britain (Reinagle, of Austrian descent, had studied with Taylor in Scotland before both came to America). I should like to mention Reinagle's lovely 'I have a silent sorrow' to a text by R. B. Sheridan, and Taylor's charming 'Jockey and Jenny'. James Hewitt's 'In a far distant clime' and 'In vain the tears of anguish flow' are rather Mozartian in their melodic contours. Hewitt also wrote a patriotic text and arranged 'A new Yankee Doodle' with piano introduction and postlude in 1798. This stirring song makes an excellent final song for an early American group.

Another source of vocal music from the eighteenth century is the music of the Moravians who came to America in the 1730s and founded Bethlehem, Pennsylvania, in 1741. Composing mostly for the church, they modelled their style after the pre-Classical Central Europeans, using instrumental accompaniment. One song that stands out and can be performed with piano is John Antes's 'Go, congregation, go!' Both its text, by Christian Gregor (1723–1801), and its melodic line are strikingly stark, depicting a sombre procession to the Garden of Gethsemane.

Outstanding among the next generation of American composers were William Henry Fry (1813–1864) and George Frederick Bristow (1825–1898). Fry and Bristow were both born in America, and both considered themselves champions of American music. Both men progressed technically beyond the solo song to the larger dimensions of opera; Fry's *Leonora* was performed in Philadelphia in 1845, and Bristow's *Rip Van Winkle* in New York in 1855. An aria from *Leonora*, 'Every doubt and danger over', is a charming, though somewhat primitive, echo of Donizetti. Bristow's 'List, the merry bells' for soprano with chorus is Handelian, recalling 'O, had I Jubal's lyre', and the bass aria 'Alas! they know me not' is a genuinely impressive piece. In a–b–a form with an extended ending, it has a beautiful melodic line above a rich harmonic texture, giving the true bass an opportunity to display a full two-octave range, from low E to e^1.

By far the best known songwriter in America during the nineteenth century was Stephen Foster (1826–1864). William Austin of Cornell University has written a penetrating book about Foster, his songs, and the deep effect they have had on 'all the world'. Besides the almost too well-known 'The old folks at home', 'Susanna', and 'Jeanie', there are many other Foster songs which retain their freshness. I am particularly fond of a ditty called 'There are plenty of fish in the sea', about a girl who flaunts her beauty but never chooses a lover until it is too late. 'Summer longings' is a dignified and sad little song to a text by the Irish scholar, Denis Florence McCarthy. These are but two of many Foster songs worth reviving for inclusion in song recitals.

Stephen Foster never set foot off American soil, but after the middle of the nineteenth century most of our gifted young musicians went to Germany for their training, or in some cases to France or Italy. European training set the course for American music for about the next seventy-five years.

The first American composer to achieve high status in Europe as well as America was the German-trained Edward MacDowell (1861–1908). His songs are patterned on German models, but they are by no means merely derivative. My favourite among the songs of MacDowell is 'Midsummer lullaby'. Though it encompasses only a narrow range of a sixth, the ever changing seventh chords of the accompaniment (not too far removed from the accompaniments of Hugo Wolf) sustain interest. For a time, MacDowell's music, like the furniture of the Victorian period, was out of fashion. At the present distance, however, we can appreciate its warmth and fine craftsmanship.

Other gifted Americans trained in Germany at about the same time as MacDowell were George Chadwick

(1854–1931) and Arthur Foote (1853–1937). Both had distinguished careers in the Boston area and their songs reflect the professionalism and craftsmanship which American composers of that time had acquired, compared with their somewhat amateurish predecessors of the early nineteenth century. Horatio Parker (1863–1919) a friend and contemporary of Chadwick, and also German trained, achieved more recognition outside America than any composer other than MacDowell through his oratorio *Hora Novissima*. First performed at the Worcester Festival (USA) in 1893, it met with great success at the Three Choirs Festival in Worcester, England, thereafter gaining many performances in both England and America. In 1911 Parker's opera *Mona* (libretto by Brian Hooker) won the $10,000 prize given by the Metropolitan Opera Company for the best grand opera in English by an American. I have sung the aria 'Mona's Dream', with piano reduction by John Kirkpatrick, in many recital programmes, and find that its dramatic quality commands attention, and that its tonal language does not seem dated; it is more complex than any other work by Parker.

In the early twentieth century some composers in America turned away stylistically from classical German models. One direction was towards impressionism and the other (following the lead of nationalist composers in Europe) towards native American sources. The songs of Charles Martin Loeffler (1861–1937) and of Henry Hadley (1871–1837) show the impressionist influence and yet could hardly be called imitative. Loeffler, Belgian born, came to the United States as assistant concert master of the Boston Symphony. His song 'To Helen' (Edgar Allan Poe), written in 1906, modulates freely and has a melodic line of tender beauty. Of Hadley's more than 150 songs, his 'Il pleut des pétales de fleurs' (Alfred Samain) stands up to the songs of his French contemporaries in its subtlety and use of chromatic harmonies.

Charles Griffes (1884–1920) best known for his early impressionist piano piece 'The White Peacock' (from *Four*

Roman Sketches), experimented with oriental scales and Scriabinesque harmonies. His death at the age of thirty-six was a tragedy for American music. He had composed over thirty songs between 1911 and 1918 which showed the promise of a rich contribution to this medium. Many of his songs have luxuriant piano accompaniments – for example, the brilliantly conceived 'Lament of Ian the Proud' from his *Three Poems of Fiona MacLeod* – and one of his best known songs, 'Auf geheimem Waldespfade' (the same text by Nicolas Lenau set by Alban Berg as the second song of his *Sieben Fruehe Lieder*), reflects Griffes's German education. Often sung in the excellent translation by Henry G. Chapman ('By a lonely forest pathway') it depicts the mood of the text with a soaring melodic line supported by undulating figures in the piano accompaniment.

Arthur Farwell (1872–1952) followed the trend started by Dvořák during his American years in turning towards native American material. In 1901 he founded the Wawan Press in Newton Center, Massachusetts for the artistic publication of compositions by Americans, particularly music based on Indian themes. He was also one of the first composers to set a substantial number of poems of Emily Dickinson (*39 Songs*).

The traditions of German song with some mixtures of French colour here and there were continued in the work of several facile and successful song writers of the post World War I period. Winter Watts (1884–1962) was described by William H. Austin as 'thoroughly American in his work' because of abounding enthusiasm in the construction of his songs and a certain flamboyance in their piano accompaniments. John Alden Carpenter's (1876–1951) *Gitanjali* poems by Rabindranath Tagore, are expressive songs with opulent vocal line and romantic accompaniments. Richard Hageman (1884–1966) also made two beautiful settings of Tagore poems 'Do not go my love' and 'When the two sisters go to fetch water' which should be a part of every soprano's repertoire. They are difficult to sing, but fine programme material.

Of the next generation of composers, Samuel Barber (b. 1910) has given us a rich supply of songs, beautiful in their variety of texts and textures. Barber grew up in a family deeply rooted in the tradition of song. His aunt was the famous operatic contralto, Louise Homer (1871–1947), and his uncle the prolific song composer, Sidney Homer (1864–1953). Having begun his career as a singer himself, it is not surprising then that all of his songs are melodically interesting and grateful for the voice. Three early songs (1939) that bear the mark of genius and stand the test of time and many performances are his Opus 10, to texts by James Joyce: 'Rain has fallen', 'Sleep now' and 'I hear an army'. Each evokes the mood of the text and as a group they give the singer a chance to sing lyrically, dynamically and dramatically.

'Knoxville', composed in 1947, for soprano and orchestra is considerably longer than an ordinary song and can be sung with its effective piano reduction. Barber's agile, melodic idiom fits well the poetic prose of James Agee, depicting the scene of a family sitting out under the stars on a hot summer evening in a small town in Tennessee in 1915. This is a bit of Americana at its best.

While the above song composers were having their works published and performed, the most important contribution to American song had been made by a composer who at the time was almost completely unknown – Charles Ives (1874–1954). The curious chronology of Ives' career has had no parallel in music history. After his graduation from Yale in 1898, where he studied with Horatio Parker, he entered the insurance business in New York with outstanding success. For a period of about twenty years he led a double life, conducting his business, but devoting all the rest of his time to composition. A health crisis in 1918 led him to bring together the bulk of his songs and his *Concord Sonata* for piano to be engraved at his own expense. In 1922 he circulated privately a collection of *114 Songs*. They were largely ignored until 1932, when Aaron Copland and the baritone Hubert Linscott performed seven of them at the Yaddo Festival, near Saratoga, New York. These songs were subsequently published by simply reprinting them from the original plates Ives had had made for the *114 Songs*.

It is at this point that I wish to make my discussion somewhat autobiographical, for the volume of *Seven Songs* by Ives played an important role in establishing my own commitment as a young singer to American song in general, and to Ives in particular. I was a student at Oberlin conservatory in the late thirties, and at that time the professor of theory and composition was Normand Lockwood (b. 1906). Lockwood was a member of the post World War I group who went, not to Germany, but to Paris, to study with Nadia Boulanger. In his classes at Oberlin, Lockwood introduced his students to new American music – the *avant-garde* of that time – Roger Sessions, Aaron Copland, Theodore Charler, David Diamond, Ives and others. Lockwood himself wrote a great many songs during his tenure at Oberlin, and one of the most important aspects of my training in learning to cope with the problems of contemporary music came from singing his songs before the ink was dry on them. I have since sung many Lockwood songs on my programmes and still treasure them.

After I finished my work at Oberlin, I married Howard Boatwright, violinist-composer, whose interests and career led me further into by-paths of contemporary music not usual for every young singer. In 1945, my husband decided to go to Yale to study composition with Paul Hindemith, and after a few years joined the faculty there. Yale, partly because of Hindemith, was a magnet which attracted gifted young composers. In the atmosphere of Yale at that time, what was considered 'advanced' elsewhere was the normal thing, and I was constantly singing new works.

In 1946, my husband and I were invited to participate in a two-week festival of contemporary music at Yaddo, the same festival at which Ives's songs had been introduced fourteen years earlier. American art song was well represented at the 1946 festival; I performed songs with piano by Ludwig Lenel, Jack Beeson, Godfrey Turner, Howard Boatwright and Kent Kennan. With chamber orchestra I sang Elliot Carter's 'Warble me now for joy of lilac time' (Whitman), still tonally oriented, but already displaying the long line and complexity of texture which were to characterize the later Carter, and Normand Lockwood's 'Mary who stood in sorrow', a kind of 'Pietà' in which music and text (Sarah Moore) are blended in stark and angular gestures. With John Kirkpatrick at the piano, I sang a somewhat derivative French but sensitive song cycle, *Terre de France*, by the Boulanger pupil, Louise Talma, whose subsequent career has included an opera to a libretto by Thornton Wilder. The most important outcome of the Yaddo Festival was the beginning of my association with John Kirkpatrick, who had already performed much of the music of Charles Ives and had recorded the *Concord Sonata*, an event which resulted in the first general recognition of Ives as a major figure in American music. A concert of Ives's music at Yale in 1953 with Kirkpatrick led to our making the first long playing record of Ives's songs in 1954 (Overtone Records). In 1974, the year of Ives's centennial, Kirkpatrick and I recorded an additional twenty-five songs for Columbia Records, including eleven songs edited by Kirkpatrick from manuscript sources.

It is possible to learn much of the depth and complexity of Ives, the man, from his songs – because they are so varied and reflect the many aspects of his personality, background and pattern for life itself. 'Autumn' (reproduced with technical notes on pages 190–03), 'Walking', and 'Maple Leaves' express his fervent love for a New England autumn, and the changing of the seasons, so similar to the procession of life to death.

Ives *Autumn*

to hush her song and close her 'tired eyes,

She turns her face for the sun to smile up-on and

ra – diant-ly, ra – diant-ly,

thro' Fall's bright

Throughout this song the melodic line in the right hand of the accompaniment is as important as the vocal line itself and the descending interval on the first and second beat of bars 2–14 and again 19–22 makes for an expressive unity which heightens the expression of the quiet simplicity of the first two words of the text in bar 2 and throughout. 'Earth rests' must be stretched by singing a long vowel on *earth* and omitting the *r* entirely. To obtain the right sound say the English word 'fur' but stop the sound before pronouncing the *r*. Then say quietly the *th* and flip the initial *r* of *rests* with one quick movement of the tip of the tongue. Elongate the *sts* with as little hiss as possible but making sure each consonant is pronounced. Having sung these two words effectively continue to think through to the next entrance using the melody of the piano line to guide the mood. The beautiful low entrance in bar 6 should be sung with a solid, resonant but quiet sound, with a slight crescendo to 'her fields like bare' (bar 7), remembering again not to pronounce the *r* in the words *her*, *work* and *bare*. The lovely turn of phrase in bars 8 and 9 indicates a little crescendo to 'of win' diminished again on '-ter comes' (bar 9). Ives indicated exactly how 'to hush her song and close her tired eyes' in bars 10 and 11 should be sung; the dots and phrase marks meaning that these words should be pronounced as delicately and clearly as possible, being careful to pronounce the *h* and *sh* of the word *hush* and to spread the dipthong of the o-oo in *close*. On beginning the crescendo in bar 16 take care to pronounce *thro'* with a good *th* and a flipped *r* and enunciating clearly the *ll*s and *z* sound of 'fall's' and the *br – t* and *gl* of 'bright glow'. The *Più animato* which begins in bar 12 continues to the *firmata* between bars 17 and 18. This *firmata* gives the singer the opportunity to finish the word 'smiles with a good 'z' sound. The support of the accompanist holding the pedal through to the *firmata* is very important. Then the pedal can be lifted before the beautiful *adagio* begins. The effectiveness of the song lies in the way bars 18–23 are sung – a fitting reminder of Ives's love for the beauty of a New England autumn and his Emersonian belief that God is found in such moments of beauty.

Three patriotic songs, each in different mood, show Ives's ardour and sympathy for those who fought in World War I. 'In Flanders Field' is a setting of the touching poem written by John McCrae about our soldiers who were buried overseas, made strong by Ives's use of dissonant chords in martial rhythm and the melodic surge that flings up on the words 'We throw the torch. Be yours to hold it high'. 'Tom sails away' is impressionistic in its contours yet thoroughly American with its quotation of the familiar war song 'Over There'. 'He is there' suggests a folk song in strophic form with march-like introduction and an extended second ending giving a moment of reminiscence to other tunes, 'Tenting on the old camp ground' and 'Star Spangled Banner'.

Ives wrote his own texts for many of his songs, describing his passionate feelings for the rights of man in 'Majority', his loud protests against machines, their noise and their smells contaminating his beloved Nature in 'The New

River', and his admiration of 'that old time religion' as shown in 'Down East' and 'The things our fathers loved', in which Aunt Sarah hums gospels, or plays the old melodeon in the parlour after the Sunday morning chores are done.

Ives's sensitivity to great literature is shown in his settings of Milton's 'Evening' from 'Paradise Lost'; a short excerpt from *Leaves Of Grass* titled 'Walt Whitman'; and the first gentle lines of Longfellow's 'The Children's Hour' capturing the essence of the poet's idyllic home in New England at the turn of the century.

In 'General Booth Enters Into Heaven' (Vachel Lindsay), generally regarded as his greatest song, Ives depicts the powerful panorama of a revivalist scene, making real for all listeners those words, 'Are you washed in the blood of the Lamb' by repeating them in a variety of contexts throughout the song. In this, as in many of his other songs, he quotes the tunes of his favourite gospel hymns, thus bringing his child's soul into everything that he wrote.

It is clear that Ives has been a central figure in my own repertoire and it gives me pleasure to observe that the same is now true for any serious American recitalist, and for students preparing for such a career. Ives has become for us a cornerstone, giving support to the whole modern American repertoire as Schubert supports the repertoire of the German *Lied*. This is not to disparage other gifted American song writers; the success of Ives has been encouraging to his successors. I think especially of John Duke (b. 1899) and Ernst Bacon (b. 1898) of the older generation of living composers, and Ned Rorem (b. 1923) and Dominick Argento (b. 1927) among the younger. Duke, a pianist and pupil of Schnabel, has devoted almost all of his extensive output to the art song. Throughout, his songs are distinguished by great sensitivity to the voice and textual values, and they are supported by piano accompaniments that are effective and highly idiomatic. 'in just spring' (e.e. cummings) is a lighthearted description of this poignant text, and 'Chill of eve' (James

Stephens), in extreme contrast, with sombre harmonies and a slow steady swing, describes penetratingly the passing of the chill day to an even chillier eve.

Bacon, also a pianist, is a prolific composer in all media, but possibly has made his greatest contribution in his more than one hundred settings of the poems of Emily Dickinson. The extraordinary union of poet and composer in these songs reminds one of that same blend of text and music in Schumann's setting of Heine's *Dichterliebe*. My confidence in the value of Bacon's songs springs from the experience of singing many of them in recitals and recording twenty-eight of them with him for Cambridge Records in 1964. Two of my favourites are: 'It's all I have to bring today', which achieves great depth of expression with a broad melodic line, spanning an octave and a fifth, and 'The grass so little has to do', so contrasting with its infectious, delightful melody and bouncing rhythm.

Rorem's importance in the American repertoire springs first from the fact that there are so many of his songs available in print (over fifty), secondly from their great variety, and thirdly from the fact that unlike many composers he writes specifically for all voice ranges.

Argento, the youngest of the four composers mentioned above, shows in his solo songs the same sure sense for effective treatment of texts which has led to his considerable success as an opera composer. His *Six Elizabethan Songs* are a cycle of great variety and lyricism, especially fine for young, high voices. His imaginative *From the Diary of Virginia Woolf* won him a justly deserved Pulitzer Prize in 1975.

Of the composers I have mentioned, only the oldest, Ives, is regarded seriously by the present *avant-garde*. They are attracted to him because of his extraordinary anticipation of nearly every compositional advance of the twentieth century, and perhaps because of a certain nonconformity in his musical personality, a trait always appealing to the young. Although Aaron Copland (*Twelve Songs of Emily Dickinson*), Vincent Persechetti (*Harmonium* –

20 Poems of Wallace Stevens), George Rochberg (*Songs in Praise of Krishna*) and David del Tredici (*Four Songs on Poems of James Joyce*) have carried on the tradition of writing art songs with piano accompaniment, most composers of 'new music' have more or less abandoned the solo song with piano in favour of vocal works with instrumental ensemble, works which in that sense descend from Schoenberg's *Pierrot Lunaire* (1912) through *Le Marteau sans Maître* of Boulez (1955). While some of these composers, especially George Crumb with his *Madrigals* and *Ancient Voices of Children*, have contributed works of great beauty and effectiveness to the vocal literature, most of them lie outside the provenance of this article in that they are a new category rather than an extension of the solo song with piano.

A good omen for the future of the art song in America is the announcement of the 1979 Vocal Competition, John F. Kennedy Center – Rockefeller Foundation International Competition for Excellence in the Performance of American Music. The list of works that is provided for singers to choose from is a catalogue of contemporary American song in itself, and the fact that contestants are given additional time to perform other works of their own choice is heartening.

Technical Aspects

The problems of diction encountered when singing in English are numerous. Americans, who have many regional accents, must work for a neutral, standard English that is used on the stage, in the pulpit, or on television and radio. When I was a student some forty years ago, *An English Pronouncing Dictionary* by Daniel Jones was my Bible for correct pronunciation. Using the International Phonetic Alphabet, it offered an elegance of speech like that of the British stage. Such elegance was perfect for most poetry but it sounded stilted in songs that have regional or character implications, such as Copland's

'Ching-a-rung chaw' from *Old American Songs* or Charles Ives's 'The greatest man'. We are fortunate today to have *The Singer's Manual of English Diction*, prepared by Madeleine Marshall, who teaches at the Juilliard School of Music in New York and coaches singers from the Metropolitan Opera Company. This book aims to give rules that make it possible to sing 'one English'. It also gives enough exceptions to permit us to choose, with what I like to call 'an artist's taste', when or when not to apply these rules.

Particularly troublesome is our American 'r'. The use of it identifies Americans immediately wherever we travel. The Marshall book gives three basic rules for omitting it or sounding it:

(1) *Never sing 'r' before a consonant* e.g. 'chahming' instead of cha*r*ming, fo-get instead of fo*r*get.

(2) *Do not sing 'r' before a pause.* I think this rule should be applied without exception (the Marshall book gives one – as in the words fi*r*e or dea*r* on a high tone). For the sake of a better tone, the clarity of diction can be sacrificed here.

(3) *Always sing 'r' before a vowel sound.* (This rule remains in effect whether the 'r' and following vowel sound are within the same word or in adjoining words of the same phrase) e.g. *spirit, for us, great, drab*. There are no exceptions to this rule; however, our 'artist's taste' will tell us when to flip the 'r' or when to use the American 'r'.

Of vowel sounds perhaps the most abused is the sound in *cat* or *hand*. Although this vowel is prevalent in our speech (e.g. magic, glad, thank, gather, shall), singers rarely learn to make a pleasant sound of this vowel because in the great tradition of *Bel Canto* we are taught to vocalize on the five Latin vowels – a, e, i, o, u. It is possible, however, to correct this often twangy sound, making it sound smooth and natural, if the resonance is kept high in the nasopharynx, the tip of the tongue forward, and the jaw loose. An interesting comparison in the use of this vowel can be made in listening to three recordings of Charles Ives's 'Shall we gather at the river'. Fischer-Dieskau (Deutsche Grammophon) sings it with the studied tone and cultivated diction of traditional European training; Jan DeGaetani (Nonesuch) adopts a precious sound, somewhat too unnatural for this text; Marni Nixon (Nonesuch) sings with a certain nasality that fits the camp meeting atmosphere from which it is derived. No doubt Ives himself was referring to an affected type of singing, for he wrote in his 'Postface to 114 Songs', when does a song have to be 'sunk by an operatic greyhound'?

The complexities of diction can be overcome in part if a singer's technique is free of conditioning, allowing for flexibility of colour and purity of intonation. Many teachers and students today place too much emphasis on the importance of developing only an operatic sound, one that is heavily dramatic and will carry over our full orchestras. The great singer is, above all, a musician whose perceptions are keen enough to discriminate how his technique can best serve a piece of music, be it an art song or an aria.

Twenty
Russian Song

Martin Cooper, C.B.E.
Born 1910. Educated
Winchester, Oxford and Vienna.
Music critic successively –
London Mercury (1934), *Daily
Herald, Spectator, Daily
Telegraph* (1950–78).
Publications – *Gluck*, 1935; *Bizet*,
1938; *French Music, 1869–1924*;
Opéra Comique, 1949; *Russian
Opera*, 1951; *Ideas and Music*,
1966; *Beethoven – the last decade*,
1970.

The repertory of Russian song begins for practical purposes
in the second quarter of the nineteenth century, at least as
far as Western European singers are concerned. Until that
time the liturgical chant of the Orthodox Church, and the
folksong which in many cases formed its foundation,
represented singing in Russia as a whole. Italian opera,
introduced to the court of the Empress Anna Ioannovna
in 1736, only gradually assumed Russian characteristics,
and even the production of Glinka's *A life for the Tsar*
(now performed as *Ivan Susanin*) some hundred years
later, while of the utmost importance to the minute circles
of the court and cultivated upper bourgeoisie, left the huge
proportion of the vast population untouched. Interest in
Russian folksong and collections by enterprising amateurs
gave no more than a new veneer to the music enjoyed in
the theatre or performed in the drawing-rooms of the
educated minority, which was Italian, German or – particularly in the case of the solo song – French. For French

199

remained the language of polite society until late in the nineteenth century; and although society was divided into the so-called Slavophils (or conservative nationalists) and the 'progressive' Westernizers, the musical nationalists who gathered round Balakirev in St. Petersburg remained a minority, regarded as uncouth, or at least eccentric, at any rate until 1880. They were, in fact, like Glinka himself, fundamentally amateurs as opposed to the thoroughly Westernized professional composers centred in Moscow and led by the Rubinstein brothers, Anton and Nikolai.

The Nationalist composers, who based their music on the folksong of the Russian past, had little interest in symphonic and less still in chamber music. They were concerned with operas based on Russian historical themes or folk-tales; and their comparatively few solo songs were for the most part either dramatic vignettes of Russian contemporary life (Mussorgsky) or lyrical evocations of a half-imaginary Orient modelled on scenes from Glinka's opera *Ruslan and Lyudmila* (Balakirev, Rimsky-Korsakov). Both Glinka and his rather younger contemporary Dargomyzhsky wrote drawing-room songs (*romansy*), fundamentally French in character but often marked by melodic turns with an unmistakably Russian (i.e. folksong) flavour, though Dargomyzhsky eventually began the exploration of a vocal style based entirely on the rhythms of Russian speech and virtually inseparable (like French song) from the language in which the songs were conceived. The Moscow 'Westernizing' composers, led first by Anton Rubinstein and then by Tchaikovsky, were characteristically grouped round the Moscow Conservatory founded by Nikolai Rubinstein in 1864 and included men who were primarily scholars (Taneiev) or pianists (Rachmaninov, Skryabin, Medtner). Opera was of wholly secondary importance to them; but with their knowledge of Western models they were aware of the German *Lied* (Schubert and, more importantly, Schumann) and wrote consciously 'contemporary' settings of Russian (and in some cases German) lyrical poems.

There was of course no firm or clear dividing line between the two 'schools', such as this schematic account might suggest. After the death of the great amateurs (Glinka, Dargomyzhsky and Mussorgsky) and Rimsky-Korsakov's belated conversion from an extremely gifted amateur to a highly professional, and eventually academic, composer the dividing line became even harder to draw. Tchaikovsky, for instance, wrote a large number of works, including songs, which were only distinguished from those of the Nationalists by their greater professional skill (the second symphony and the opera *Christmas Eve*), while Rimsky-Korsakov himself composed in *Mozart and Salieri* what is in effect a pastiche of an eighteenth-century Western European opera. Only the trio of great pianists remained all but totally aloof from the ideals of the Nationalists. Skryabin wrote no songs; and those of Rachmaninov and Medtner, though often intensely Russian in feeling, mood and occasional melodic turns of speech, follow the pre-Nationalist formula established by Glinka. With the death of Rimsky-Korsakov in 1908 the last trace of the old division in Russian musical life had virtually disappeared, though it is interesting to note that of the two major representatives of the younger generation Prokofiev continued the Moscow tradition of the composer-pianist, while Stravinsky followed the operatic (or in his case balletic) tradition of the St. Petersburg school. Neither was a prolific song-writer, nor were Glazunov and Lyadov, who belonged to the intermediate generation.

The composers who grew up in Russia after the revolution of 1917 found themselves faced with an entirely new situation. The distinction between Nationalist and Westernizer, conservative and progressive in the old sense, had gone; but in fact extra musical (now called ideological) loyalties continued to play a large part, eventually a much larger part than before, in determining the character of their music and the language in which that character expressed itself. The traditional revolutionary mentality in Russia had been opposed to any 'art for art's sake'; and now music, like the other arts, was expected to make a social contribution, exactly as in Plato's ideal republic – to 'improve' the listener's potential as a citizen, to fortify his courage and patriotism and to lead his mind to 'higher' things. A very similar demand had been made of the arts by Leo Tolstoy, and it is a common mistake to suppose that the Communist Party's claim to direct the arts towards approved goals is either unfamiliar in Russia or resented to anything like the extent that it would be in Western Europe. All composers have been compelled, at least superficially, to conform. As far as song-writing is concerned the texts chosen by the composer are plainly targets for criticism, but so too are the manner and idiom in which he sets them. The composers who concern us here are Shostakovich and to a lesser degree Prokofiev. The former brought to a fine art the form of expression which the Russians themselves call 'Aesopian' – that is to say, oblique reference to 'forbidden' subjects and opinions through parable or fable. There are excellent examples of this in the solo songs which make up his thirteenth and fourteenth symphonies. But he sometimes went much further in his resentment of official guidance, as in his *Five Romances to words from 'Krokodil' magazine* and *Preface to the complete collection of my works*, which are more openly satirical. Prokofiev, though no doubt sharing Shostakovich's sense of frustration and resentment, had lived nearly twenty years in Western Europe and sown his musical wild oats liberally. In his early Op. 9 and again in his Op. 36 (1928) he had chosen to set poems by one of the leading 'decadent' poets of the pre-revolutionary years, Konstantin Balmont, also a favourite with Stravinsky and regarded with sour disapproval by the Soviet authorities. In fact, the solo song itself had a slightly suspect character as the expression of subjective, individual and often unedifyingly melancholy sentiments unworthy of a good Soviet citizen. The alternative to an 'Aesopian' was often an impregnably 'classical' text, and in fact Kabalevsky's settings of a

number of Shakespeare's sonnets (in Marshak's translation) are among the best Russian songs of comparatively
recent years.

Language and texts

The Russian language is itself rich in a very wide variety
of beautiful and intensely musical sonorities. In many ways
it combines the consonantal strength of German with the
smooth, vocalic liquidity of Italian, and it is very much
easier than French for an English-speaking singer. In all
good songs the relationship between text and music is
close, but it is much closer in some instances than in others.
Thus the songs of Schubert and Brahms suffer much less
(though they still suffer a great deal) from translation than
those of Schumann and Wolf; and whereas Fauré's or
Duparc's songs might conceivably be translated, the
relationship between text and music is so close in Debussy's
that it is foolish to attempt a translation. It is equally
foolish to translate Mussorgsky's songs, in which the
musical rhythm is often determined by that of the naturally
spoken Russian text, and it is impossible to reproduce in
another language anything approaching the raciness of
purely Russian characters ('Savishna', say, 'the Seminarist'
or indeed Tsar Boris or Dositheus in the operas) or the
atmosphere of *The Nursery* and *Songs and Dances of
Death*.

The first difficulty facing a singer who wishes to sing
Russian is of course the alphabet; he cannot even read
what he has to sing. But the Russian alphabet, largely
borrowed from the Greek, is not a main problem for
anyone with moderate linguistic interests and abilities.
There are, however, a fair number of traps in Russian
spelling as well as in pronunciation and it is absolutely
essential to find a thoroughly competent coach, preferably
of course a native Russian. Apart from learning the exact
meaning of each word and the sense, and at least something
of the atmosphere, of the poem, a singer who wants to give

a convincing performance in a language that he does not in fact know should learn by imitation, to recite the poem intelligibly and with expression before he even attempts to sing the song. There is always the cautionary tale of the singer who actually recorded a French song pronouncing the word *ailes (de l'amour)* – the wings of love – as though it were *ail* (garlic). Many of what look on paper impossible groups of consonants in Russian (kvsd, vp, mgn, shch) prove to be much less formidable in a Russian mouth, and though the hard *i* or *yery* (ы , generally transliterated as y) and the 'soft sign' or *myagky znak* (ь, generally transliterated as an apostrophe) may present initial difficulties, these are child's play compared with the nasalized vowels of French.

Russian poetry is dominated as that of no other European language by a single figure. Alexander Pushkin, who was killed in a duel at the age of thirty-eight in 1837, was the first to give the Russian language a purity and simplicity of diction and expression, which he combined with an unique variety of mood and style, ranging from an almost Greek economy to the most extravagant romanticism and a relaxed conversational style rivalled only by Byron. Russian song-writers have been attracted to his poems more than to those of any other poet, just as Russian composers for more than a century found inspiration in the music of Glinka. Like all poems, Pushkin's lose all that is unique in their character when translated into any other language, and similarly it is difficult for non-Russian musicians to understand what his fellow-countrymen find the inexhaustible inspiration of Glinka's music. The singer who wishes to specialize in Russian songs should ideally immerse himself in a study, however handicapped by linguistic ignorance, of these two men's works, which are the foundations of the vast majority of any songs they are likely to sing. A number of Pushkin's poems, long and short, are obtainable in paper-backs with the text and its translation facing each other; and even a few hours spent on familiarizing himself with some of these – especially the lyrical poems repeatedly set by Russian song-writers – would be extremely valuable to any singer who means to take up the Russian repertory seriously. And with the linguistic standards of today it would be most unwise to embark on it unless he is prepared to do some serious preliminary preparation.

Second to Pushkin in the affection of Russian song-writers has been Mikhail Lermontov, his contemporary, who also died young in a duel. Lermontov has not Pushkin's variety or range, either of style or of subject matter; he is more exclusively romantic and has neither the wit nor the humour of Pushkin, though he has a comparable verbal magic in his own sphere. Most of the poems by these two men chosen for setting by Russian composers are lyrical, concerned with human relationships or the relationship of man to nature. Ballads and narrative poems form a smaller class. Born rather later, Fyodor Tyuchev and Afanasy Fet, both deeply indebted to Pushkin like all nineteenth-century Russian poets, explore the same fields of human reaction to the fundamental experiences of life and to nature with rather more sophistication and, in the case of Fet, with a pantheistic tinge. Among lesser poets favoured by composers perhaps the most important is Alexey Tolstoy, a distant cousin of the great novelist, frequently set by Tchaikovsky and also by Rachmaninov. The names of Polonsky, Apukhtin, Pleshcheyev, Mey and the fashionable Nadson recur with variable regularity among the song-lists of most nineteenth-century composers and the name of Merezhkovsky begins to appear at the end of the century and even later (Tchaikovsky, Rachmaninov). Dmitri Merezhkovsky was an early and important member of the Symbolist or 'decadent' school of poetry, which began to appear during the 1890s, much concerned with a variety of religious mysticisms and deeply influenced by French and Belgian poets of the day. The most popular members of this school with composers were Konstantin Balmont (Stravinsky, Prokofiev, Rachmaninov) and Valery Bryusov (Prokofiev's opera *The Fiery*

Angel), while the greatest of them, Alexander Blok, has provided texts for a number of more recent songs by Miaskovsky, Shaporin and, most notably, Shostakovich.

Repertory

There are plainly two sources on which a concert-singer can draw: the solo song conceived as such with piano accompaniment and the opera, conceived with orchestral accompaniment and as a succession of 'held' moments in which a solo singer expresses his reactions to a given dramatic situation. The more isolated such moments are from the main body of the work, and the more self-contained, the easier they are to extract from their context and the more successful they are in the concert-hall. Operas composed according to Wagner's ideal and contemporary works in which there is no clear dividing line between formal aria and lyrical recitative will provide little for the concert singer; and many of the opera arias or scenes recommended below require not only an exceptional power of dramatic projection in the singer but in many cases an exceptional pianist to suggest orchestral colours and dynamic shadings. Since the composers concerned are the same in both groups – song proper and operatic – it will perhaps be simplest to list recommendations under the names of individual composers.

Glinka. Many of Glinka's early settings are elegant, rather sentimental drawing-room romances, but a number of these are well worth singing. Among these are 'Do not tempt me needlessly' (Baratynsky), 'Disenchantment' (Golitsyn) and the touching 'A voice from the other world' (Zhukovsky, after Schiller). Two Pushkin settings show Glinka at his best as a song-writer – 'Where is our rose?' and 'I remember a wonderful moment'. From the song-cycle entitled *Farewell to St. Petersburg*, with texts by Kukol, 'The Lark' has an exceptionally beautiful melody and 'Travel Song' is a lively patter song in a popular style.

No bass or baritone should neglect 'The midnight review' (Zhukovsky), a brilliantly evocative dramatic ballad in which Napoleon's ghost rises from the tomb and reviews his troops.

From the operas there are perhaps four pieces which will bear transplanting to the concert-room. The cavatina sung by Antonida (soprano) in Act 2 of *A life for the Tsar (Ivan Susanin)* and the superb recitative and aria sung in Act 4 by Susanin (bass), 'They guess the truth'; and in *Ruslan and Lyudmila* the romance sung by Ratmir (contralto) in Act 4, 'She is my life', and the comic rondo sung in Act 2 by Farlaf (bass). Only a very confident singer, with much previous dramatic experience, should attempt to project any of these in concert-hall conditions.

Dargomyzhsky. There is an exquisitely simple and touching song beginning 'I am sad' (Lermontov's 'Mne grustno') at which every woman singer should at least glance (and if possible hear Netania Davrath's recording), and operatic basses might well consider the Miller's song from Act 1 of *Rusalka*, one of the very few 'mad songs' for a male voice.

Tchaikovsky. Everyone knows 'Mid the din of the ball', 'I bless you forests' and 'None but the weary heart', but Tchaikovsky wrote over eighty songs, many more of which are admirable. Besides the kind of tragic or elegiac lyricism that we generally connect with his name there are a number of dramatic romances and ballads that have great possibilities for an experienced singer. Those with popular Russian or gypsy characteristics include the gripping ballad 'The Corals' (Syrokomla), 'Reconciliation' (Shcherbina), 'Why did I dream of you?' (Mey) and 'He loved me so much' (anon.). Love songs include the brilliant 'Don Juan's Serenade', the passionate 'Does the day reign?' (Apukhtin), and the many of a more melancholy nature are well represented by 'If I'd only known', 'On the golden cornfields' and 'Do not believe, my friend' (all Alexey Tolstoy), 'To forget so soon' (Apukhtin) and the six settings, Op. 73, of poems by D. Rathaus dating from the last year of the composer's life.

Although Tchaikovsky wrote eleven operas, the concert-singer outside Russia is not likely to want to look beyond the two familiar favourites. From *Eugene Onegin* there is of course Tatyana's 'Letter' scene, which needs a very skilled and experienced soprano if it is to be effective in the concert-hall. Olga (contralto) has an admirable recitative and aria in Act 1 ('Ah! Tanya, Tanya, you dream in broad daylight') which is in effect a self-portrait; and in the Duel Scene in Act 2 Lensky (tenor) sings his passionate *arioso* farewell to life ('How far, how far'). In Act 3 Prince Gremin (bass-baritone) sings an aria ('All men should once with love grow tender') which loses absolutely nothing in the concert-hall and only needs a beautiful tone and perfect control. From *Pique Dame* sopranos have the choice of Liza's two impassioned monologues, 'Whence come those tears' from the final scene of Act 1 and 'Midnight is already approaching' from Act 3. Polina's sentimental romance 'Dear friends', from Act 1, is very rewardingly written for the contralto voice, and in the same act Tomsky's narrative 'ballad' could be made very effective in the concert-hall by a theatrically experienced baritone. Prince Susin's declaration in Act 2, 'I love you', has a noble dignity very much like that of Gremin's aria in *Onegin* and only needs a good bass with an absolutely steady line. Finally I see no reason why tenors should not sing Herman's defiant, devil-may-care 'What is our life? A game', from the gambling scene in Act 3, in the concert-hall.

Mussorgsky. The songs fall into three sections: one, the three cycles, two, the vignettes of Russian life and character, many with texts by the composer, and three, miscellaneous songs, some with texts by Heine or Goethe, such as 'The song of the flea', one of the composer's best known songs, immortalized by Shalyapin. Of the cycles, *The Nursery* belongs preeminently, though with some exceptions, to women singers, and *Songs and Dances of Death* to men. The texts of *The Nursery* are by an assortment of authors, including Dargomyzhsky and the critic Stasov, and each of the four songs in *Songs and Dances of Death* is by a different poet, the last by Golenishchev-Kutuzov, who also provided Mussorgsky with the texts of all six songs in the third cycle, *Sunless*. Whereas the other two cycles are closely identified with the Russian scene and Russian humanity, *Sunless* is more universal in its appeal, less confined to time and space. The suggestion of intimate introspection and narrowness of space in No. 1 ('Between four walls') and of open space and wide-ranging thought in No. 5 ('Elegy') and still more in No. 6 ('On the river') is almost physical; and the gusty, dusty moods of No. 3 ('The idle, noisy day is over') and No. 4 ('Ennui') have a character which we may feel as modern rather than belonging to the nineteenth century. It is perhaps in fact universal and timeless. These superb songs are equally suited to men and women singers, but they are full of difficulties and subtleties and should not be attempted by the inexperienced. The Russian vignettes are different and need primarily an ability to dramatize with the voice alone – and, it must be added, an excellent command of the Russian text. The music of 'Between four walls,' is printed on page 210–11, with a translation of the Russian words.

Boris Godunov is the best known of Russian operas and it is not necessary to list the possible excerpts from the title role. On the other hand I have never heard in the concert-room either Xenia's lament (soprano), the Nurse's story of the gnat (mezzo), both in Act 2, or the marvellously serene *arioso* of the old monk Pimen (bass) in Act 1 ('But one more page'). Varlaam's roistering ballad about the siege of Kazan in Act 2, also for a bass or bass-baritone, is a virtuoso piece which either raises the roof or falls flat on its face.

From *Khovanshchina* the final prayer of the monk Dositheus (bass) and the Act 2 scene of 'divination' for

Mussorgsky *Within Four Walls*

Little room, quiet, friendly,
shadow impenetrable, shadow mild,

pondering deep, song despondent,
cherished hope in a beating heart,

swift flight of moment after moment,
motionless gaze on distant happiness,

much perplexity, much endurance –
that is my night, my lonely night!

Martha (mezzo-soprano) might perhaps be transferred to the concert-hall by clever singers with the right operatic experience.

Borodin wrote only a handful of songs, but they include some masterpieces. Three of the best have a vividly epic quality, 'The sleeping princess', 'The song of the dark forest' and 'The sea', all with texts by the composer. There are also three romances, 'My songs are filled with poison' (Heine), 'From my tears' (Heine) and 'The false note'; Borodin again provided the text for this last song, in which a woman's insincerity is suggested by an intrusive wrong note in the piano part. Perhaps best known of all is the exotic 'Septain' – generally known by its opening words 'Wonderful garden' – written for Borodin's Belgian patroness the Countess Mercy-Argenteau. All these songs need a very strong sense of atmosphere.

In *Prince Igor* the Act 1 *arioso* of Jaroslavna (soprano) is rewarding, but it is also long. From Act 2 the cavatinas of Konchakovna (contralto) and Vladimir (tenor) are vocally very effective, though technically demanding. For a baritone, Igor's complaint at his imprisonment ('No sleep, no rest') has great dramatic as well as musical appeal and the attempt of his captor Konchak (bass) to restore his spirits is a superb piece of character-drawing. (Great bass-baritones often sing both roles.) For the high bass (Borodin's specification) Galitzky's recitative and air at the opening of Act 1, 'There's no denying it – I hate boredom', is another brilliantly effective portrait, alternately swash-buckling and lecherous, only possible in the concert-hall for a singer of great experience and confidence.

Rimsky-Korsakov. It is a strange thing that of Rimsky-Korsakov's eighty songs two of the best known belong to his Op. 2, written very early in his career. The cradle song from Act 1 of Mey's *Maid of Pskov* has a haunting melody and the oriental fantasy of 'Enslaved by the rose, the nightingale' (Koltsov) is a mood which the composer frequently exploited both in his songs and in his operas. Songs in the same, or similar, vein are 'In the dark grove the nightingale is silent' (Nikitin), 'My voice for thee is sweet' (Pushkin), 'Thy glance is radiant' (Lermontov) and 'Hebrew Song' (Mey). Other early songs that are well worth investigating are 'The golden cloud has slept' (Lermontov), 'Night' (Pleshcheyev), 'Quietly evening falls' (Fet), 'What is my name to thee?' (Pushkin), in which Rimsky elaborated a particularly Russian kind of *arioso*. Among his later songs are 'In moments to delight devoted' (Byron), 'Softly the spirit flew up to heaven' (A. Tolstoy), 'Thou and you' (Pushkin). At the end of his life he wrote two very ambitious songs for the bass Stravinsky (father of the composer), 'The prophet' and 'The upas tree', both poems by Pushkin.

From the operas, the tenor aria 'Sleep, my beloved' from *May Night* Act 3 and for contraltos Lel's two folk-like songs from *Snow Maiden* Act 1 are obvious choices. From *Sadko* there are the magnificent Viking Song (bass) and the so-called 'Chanson hindoue' (tenor), while *The Golden Cockerel* contains the Queen of Shemakhan's andantino ('Answer me, gleaming mirror') for a light soprano with impeccable command of florid passages.

Balakirev. As with Rimsky-Korsakov, two of Balakirev's early songs are among his best known, 'Cradle song' and 'Selim's song' (Lermontov). His 'Hebrew melody' (Lermontov, after Byron) is perhaps only surpassed by the 'Song of the golden fish' (Lermontov), a superbly glittering and seductive mermaid piece, and 'The song of Georgia' (Pushkin), one of the best of the many 'oriental' evocations by Russian composers. Only singers with virtuoso accompanists should attempt the two Khomiakov settings 'Starless midnight coldly breathed' – an eagle's vision of Prague from the night sky – and 'November 7', which describes the opening of Napoleon's tomb on St. Helena; and the piano part is almost as important, though not as demanding, in 'Sleep' (also Khomiakov). Two settings of

Fet, 'I came to thee with greeting' and 'A whisper, a timid breath' are delightful, and much less ambitious.

Rachmaninov, like Rimsky-Korsakov, composed some eighty songs, including some well known favourites – 'Spring waters' (Tyuchev), 'Lilacs' (Beketova), 'Before my window' (Galina), 'To the children' (Khomiakov) and 'Sing not to me' (Pushkin), from the early opera *Aleko*. He also explored the oriental mood, as in 'She is as lovely as the noon' and 'In my soul', both texts by Minsky. Some, though by no means all, of Rachmaninov's accompaniments, like those of Balakirev's just mentioned, reveal the piano virtuoso, but in the best of them, especially those of his Op. 21 (1902) the balance and interweaving of voice and instrument are perfectly contrived, as in 'How fair this spot', a perfect miniature in Rachmaninov's exquisite elegiac manner. A number of Rachmaninov's songs are dedicated to the great bass singer Shalyapin – 'You knew him', 'The raising of Lazarus', 'The peasant' – and others to the sopranos Nezhdanova ('Vocalise' – a fascinating piece for wordless voice and piano) and Litvin ('Discord'). All of these are well worth looking at. Rachmaninov's last (1916) songs are settings of contemporary Russian poets and include 'Daisies' (Severyanin) and 'The dream' (Sologub), which are excellent examples of a slightly new style, which, however, he never went on to develop.

Medtner, like Rachmaninov, was a great piano virtuoso, and the piano part in some of his songs is overloaded, in the sense that only a really superb performer can play it properly and still remain a partner rather than a soloist. Medtner's family was of German origin and he himself had a lifelong admiration and affection for German poetry and wrote over forty songs to German texts, primarily Goethe but also later Romantic poets. His Russian songs are mostly settings of Pushkin, Tyuchev or Fet. From the six Goethe songs of Op. 18 'Die Spröde' is particularly good, and later Goethe sets contain memorable settings of

'Wanderers Nachtlied', 'Meeresstille' and 'Nähe des Geliebten'. Two of Medtner's finest songs are to be found in his Op. 24, 'Willow, why for ever bending?' (Tyuchev) and 'Whispering nature' (Fet); and 'Day and night' (Tyuchev), 'Sea-swell and memories' (Tyuchev) and 'Greeting' (Fet) are almost as fine. Among the many settings of Pushkin that any singer interested in the Russian repertory should consider are 'To a dreamer', 'I loved thee well', 'The flower', 'Waltz' and 'The waggon of life'. Like Rachmaninov, Medtner also wrote a piece for wordless voice and piano, entitled 'Sonate Vocalise', with a Goethe motto.

It is of course not possible to give an exhaustive list of Russian songs suitable for inclusion in an English-speaking singer's repertory. What seem to me unsuitable are folksongs themselves, and I am therefore listing none of the many collections in which these can be found. But a few further hints may not be out of place. I have already referred to Kabalevsky's settings of Shakespeare sonnets; Taneiev, the great Russian contrapuntal expert, also wrote some fine songs, among them 'And the enemy trembled' (Hérédia) and 'Surrounded by enemies' (after Nietzsche). Both of these are bass or baritone songs. It may be worth looking through the vast production of Alexander Grechaninov, two of whose songs have won popularity, 'Over the steppe' and 'The captive', both superbly recorded by Alexander Kipnis. Shostakovich's late songs – besides those mentioned earlier there are the *Four verses of Captain Lebyadkin* – are too exclusively Soviet in their references, open and veiled, to tempt English-speaking singers.

Western Slav Song

The Western Slavs possess almost as rich a repertory of folk music as those settled within the boundaries of the old Russian Empire; but when national musical consciousness began to dispute the claims of the Western classical tradition (as represented primarily by Vienna) it became clear that the supreme musical endowments of the Czechs, Moravians and Slovaks – the 'Bohemians', as they had been called – were in the field of instrumental music rather than vocal. In the works of the 'founding fathers' of Czech musical nationalism, Smetana and Dvořák, the rhythms and melodies of folk-dance are quite as important as folksong, and the so-called 'art song', for solo voice and piano, tempted neither of them. Both Dvořák and Smetana however were attracted by the poems of Vítězslav Hálek and both wrote a set of his *Evening Songs* in the late 1870s. Smetana's five songs are simple, predominantly slow and somewhat autumnal pieces which reflect the ideals which inspired him through a life which was now declining. These songs are a challenge to any singer who can afford to stake all on the expressive quality of his singing. Neither voice part nor accompaniment offers any scope for virtuosity or display of any kind. Linguistic problems with both Czech and Polish are similar to, though by no means identical with those of Russian. Neither language should be attempted without expert tuition.

Dvořák, who had already written earlier sets of songs without marked success (*Cypresses, Queen's Court Songs*) set twelve of Hálek's *Evening Songs*. The best are the lighter ones – 'Spring came flying through the air', 'I am that knight of fairy tale' and 'Like a linden tree'. More interesting than these are the *Gypsy Melodies* written a few years later and very characteristic of the composer, if not so much of gypsy music in general. By far the finest of Dvořák's solo songs, however, were written at the end of his life, during his second year in the United States. These are the ten *Biblical Songs*, Op. 99, with texts chosen from the Psalms. Nos. 2, 4 and 10 recall the composer's interest in negro spiritual and the quality of the set as a whole is a transparent simplicity and trusting faith, such as only Bruckner among the great composers can parallel. Here again the chief demand on the singer is unaffected expressiveness and a tone and style that can only be achieved by complete imaginative identification with the songs.

The supreme achievement in the field of Czech solo song is Janáček's *Diary of a young man who vanished*, written between 1917 and 1919. It is written for tenor, alto and three female voices, with piano, and is in effect a mono-drama based on a newspaper story – a peasant boy, after many searchings of heart, leaves home to follow a gypsy girl. In these twenty-two songs, as in the songs of Smetana and Dvořák, everything is reduced to bare expressive formulae, without ornamentation of any kind. The natural setting is hinted at – the forest at night, the twittering swallows, the heavy tread of oxen; and the melodic forms themselves are closely related to those of folk music – two-bar phrases, with frequent changes of barring and accentuation and harmony very closely modelled to the text, as in Mussorgsky.

Poland. It is unlikely that foreigners will be tempted to explore the 270 songs in Moniuszko's *Spiewnik domowy* ('Song-book for home use'), and Chopin's handful of songs lose a great deal of their fragile charm in translation. Experienced singers who are interested in the modern repertory, have sung Debussy and are not daunted by a Slavonic language, would be very well advised to consider Szymanowski's songs. The outstanding sets are *Lovesongs of Hafiz*, *Songs of the Fairy Princess*, *Four Songs*, to texts by Rabindranath Tagore, *Songs of the foolish Muezzin* and *Wordsongs*. All these are the very opposite extreme to the Czech songs that we have been considering. Szymanowski's music is highly sophisticated in harmony and texture, with piano parts of great delicacy and elaboration. Translation of these texts would largely destroy the subtle, verbal-musical web of sound; and in *Wordsongs* (*Slopiewnie*) Julian Tuwim's texts are in themselves fantastic word-structures in which sonority plays quite as important a part as grammatical meaning. Szymanowski's songs can in fact only succeed if the performance is superlatively fine, and only those with special qualifications should attempt public performance.

Twenty-one
The Songs of Scandinavia

Kim Borg
  Finnish bass, internationally famous in such roles as Don Giovanni, Boris, Sachs, Hagen, Mephisto, Scarpia and especially 'Jesus' in Bach's *St Matthew Passion*. Author of *Suomalainen laulajanaapinen* (A.B.C. for the Finnish singer). Many compositions including orchestral music and song cycles. Professor at the Royal Conservatory of Music in Copenhagen. Member of juries in international competitions and gives T.V. master courses for singers.

For a group of nations – Iceland, Norway, Denmark, Sweden and Finland, together with Greenland and the Faroe and Åland Islands – with a total population of no more than 22 million, Scandinavian singers have won a remarkably prominent place in world music, displaying a great deal more versatility than might have been expected. If they have done little to propagate Scandinavian song, it is perhaps because Scandinavian song writers have tended to restrict their song writing within narrow limits, the result perhaps of the strong folklore tradition together with a strange feeling of being at once outside Europe and part of it. The moment one delves into Scandinavian song one is overwhelmed by thousands of unknown songs – unknown and unsung, some because they are too old-fashioned, others because they are too modern, many because they simply do not fit into the standard repertoire of concert singers; but unsung most of all because of the unfamiliar languages.

The roots of Scandinavian music come from Germany, both because the Central European tradition was easily accessible in Berlin, Leipzig, Prague and Vienna and because German musicians often travelled north in search of fame and fortune. We find this reflected especially in Danish music. The famous Danish composer N. W. Gade (b. 1817) became a professor in Leipzig and later influenced his pupils in Denmark by his 'Mendelssohnian' writing, unconsciously bringing his master's voice to his native country and perhaps thereby inhibiting the growth of a national style. Later Grieg studied in Leipzig, Sibelius in Berlin and Vienna, and so on; but by then Scandinavian musicians, even abroad, were consciously nationalistic.

The history of music in the Nordic countries is not outstandingly one of vocal works. There are splendid accounts of choral singing in places where no orchestras were available, but I shall concentrate here on the solo song, the Scandinavian *Lied* or 'Nordic *romans*' – not least because it is in this field that the traditional influences are strongest and the echoes of Central European music least heard. Opera in Scandinavia is worth a book of its own, but that is another story.

For the student of Scandinavian song a general understanding of Scandinavian culture would do no harm; we are no longer barbarians and have a flourishing musical life. A foreigner – unless he is a musicologist – can with a clear conscience skip the history and jump straight to the end of the nineteenth century, when the Nordic *romans* began to blossom. As most of our music is written in local idioms it is chiefly performed by local artists, though it is sometimes used to give an exotic touch to international recitals by Scandinavian singers. The songs lose freshness and originality in translation, and since the touring singer now always sings in the original language – a *Lied*, song, *mélodie* or POMAHC – the Scandinavian song remains neglected.

Most Scandinavian songs are naturally in the local language, but there are many in other European languages, and a foreigner should perhaps begin with these, for there he has the lowest fence to scale. Then he should get someone to coach him in Swedish. Sibelius wrote nearly ninety songs to Swedish texts, and Kilpinen also wrote many fine songs in Swedish as well as in Finnish and German. Next, Norwegian, which is phonetically near to Swedish, and there of course Grieg comes first. After mastering Swedish and Norwegian the student should study the Finnish language, followed by Icelandic and, finally, Danish. Danish poses a real problem, for although contemporary Danish music includes many works in English or German, the great majority of the best songs are in Danish, by no means an easy language to sing in.

Language, then, is the main factor that discourages the propagation of Scandinavian songs. Idiomatic pronunciation of all five languages is difficult. It would be impossible to give detailed instruction here; a student must have recourse to the *International Dictionary of Phonetics*, or, better still, seek instruction from a national teacher.

My knowledge of Icelandic, that ancient Norse tongue, is limited. The rules for its pronunciation are complicated; a knowledge of Norwegian *landsmål* (see below) will help. The alphabet contains two unfamiliar consonants, denoting sounds similar to the 'th' sounds in English 'the' and 'smith', as well as a whole range of unfamiliar vowel sounds.

The grammar of Swedish, Norwegian and Danish is relatively simple, but their pronunciation is difficult and complex. Without attempting to go into it here, I should perhaps mention the three vowels that don't occur in other European languages, and come at the end of the alphabet: Å å (be careful; this is written as 'aa' in older Norwegian and quite recent Danish texts), which sounds like a very open 'o', as in Italian or Welsh; Æ æ, equivalent to the Swedish ä and near enough to the same letter in German or to the vowel sound in English 'there' or French 'cher', and Ø ø in Danish and Norwegian, ö in Swedish and older Danish texts, like 'ö' in German or 'eu' in French.

In Icelandic and Finnish the accent is on the first syllable. The same is often true in Danish, Norwegian and Swedish, but not invariably. In every phrase there must be *one* extra emphasis pointing to the most important word. The colouring of a sentence is determined by the dominant vowel and the general feeling. The pitch of the speaking voice seems to mirror the contours of the country, covering a remarkable range among people who live in mountainous regions, but flat and monotonous in flat country, and this is something that must be taken into account in the colouring of singing. Short syllables tend to disappear in speech, as they do in English, but in singing they must still have an independent existence – something that easily gets muddled in Scandinavian song.

The pronunciation of Danish is unlike that of Norwegian or Swedish and in Denmark, a country of many islands, the dialects differ enormously. High Danish, generally used in songs, must in singing be made more 'inter-Scandinavian' or it won't be understood. The spoken language is built on half-vowels and makes use of *stød*, the glottal stop bringing a vowel sound to a sudden halt – almost impossible for a singer in serious music. Danish pronunciation is so complicated that even other Scandinavians seldom learn it. Sung with melodic feeling, the language has a certain poetry, but it would be impossible to translate, say, an Italian opera into Danish, let alone to sing it.

Norwegian is found in two forms, *riksmål* (or *bokmål*), the old official language, and *nynorsk* ('new Norwegian'), a revised form of *landsmål*, the 'country language'. Both now have official status. It is an advantage for foreign students that both forms are, in writing, highly phonetic. A feature of spoken Norwegian is the great range covered by the voice, sometimes more than two octaves when speaking emotionally or emphatically. If this speaking line reflects the mountains, the clear vowels reflect the fresh arctic air.

Swedish is the best of the Scandinavian languages to sing in. In speech the 'position' is almost the same as for singing. You just open your mouth and sing! Swedes complain that their language has too few open vowels. It may be so, but the consonants are clear cut, the vowels placed high 'in the mask', and there are few breath control problems.

Finnish has nothing in common with the languages of either its eastern or its western neighbours. It is neither Slav nor Nordic, but a Finno-Ugrian language, the northern counterpart of Hungarian in the south; an extremely complicated and highly developed language with a grammar, it has been said, 'for scientists'. But it is written phonetically and is easy to pronounce, sounding more like Spanish than any other language. One important rule: double vowels such as 'oo' and 'aa' and double consonants such as 'kk' or 'tt' are very long, while the single letters are very short. To sing 'katu' (street) may take half a second, but 'kaatuu' (falls) takes three times as long.

Few operas were composed in the Scandinavian countries until quite recently, when the art saw a sudden flowering. Unfortunately, like virtually all modern opera, these newer works contain few arias that can be performed separately in concert programmes or recitals. There is however a wealth of solo songs and vocal chamber music, some of it not yet available through commercial channels, and I have confined my accounts below to this field. All the major Scandinavian countries now have music information centres in their capital cities:

Iceland: Iceland Music Information Centre, Laufàsvegur 40, Reykjavik

Denmark: DAMIC, Music Information Centre, Skoubogade 2, Copenhagen

Norway: Norwegian Music Information Centre, Tordenskjoldsgt. 6 B, Oslo

Sweden: Swedish Music Information Centre, Tegnérlunden 3, Stockholm

Finland: Finnish Music Information Centre, Runeberginkatu 15 A, Helsinki.

The Modern History of Scandinavian Solo Song

Iceland. It is astonishing that a tiny nation of less than a quarter of a million people can have produced its own musical culture. In the circumstances choral singing has been of greater importance than the luxury of *Lieder* recitals, and composers have concentrated less on solo song than on orchestral, choral and chamber music. The song writers Arni Thorsteinsson (b. 1870) and Sigvaldi Kaldalóns (b. 1881) were notable for their sincere quality. A versatile figure in Icelandic music was Páll Isólfson (b. 1893), while Emil Thoroddsen (b. 1898) combined national elements with profound German schooling. Arni Björnson (b. 1905), Hallgrimur Helgason (b. 1914) and Jón Porarison (b. 1917) lead the way to the dominating figure of Jón Nordal (b. 1926). Central European technique linked to Icelandic tradition is growing fast; the country is no longer an isolated saga-island and is growing increasingly close to America. My knowledge of Icelandic is slight and I write with deference, basing my opinions on personal experience of this very special country.

Denmark is closer to German cultural life than the other Scandinavian countries, and not only for geographical reasons. Danish music (including a rich collection of solo songs) began with two German immigrants, Kuhlau (b. 1786) and Weyse (b. 1774). Gade, as we have seen, had strong connexions with the German school and his contemporary J. P. E. Hartmann (b. 1805), though now regarded as a classic, never found a Danish romantic style. Today the songs of that period – though not the instrumental music – have become more or less *passé*. It is a paradox that the German-born C. E. F. Weyse was more Danish in his strophic songs than his successors. The tradition of strophic composition, with no variation from verse to verse, inspired by Goethean ideas, has been disastrous to Danish vocal music – an obsession that has continued down to our times and limits the songs to Danish audiences

223

(and even they can easily get bored by them). The nineteenth century saw a boom in vocal chamber music in Denmark; Henrik Rung (b. 1807), Peter Heise (b. 1830) and P. E. Lange-Müller (b. 1850) attained artistic merit comparable at times with Schumann and Brahms. Although Heise died relatively young in 1897, his output was the largest and historically the most valuable. His last work, and probably his best, was the song-cycle *Dyvekes sange* for soprano or mezzo, mainly *durchkomponiert*, a love story between Prince Christian and his mistress. It was a great pity he wasted so much of his talent on strophic songs. The melodic richness in Lange-Müller's work is appealing and some of his songs, like the serenade for tenor from the play *Det var engang*, have real class.

But the greatest name in Danish music is Carl Nielsen (b. 1865), a master whose reputation is still growing. He wrote little vocal music, but some of his songs, miniature sketches strongly influenced by Danish nature and poetry, are quite lovely. In his compositional style he was a strenuous opponent of German romanticism. His little lullaby 'Sænk kun dit hoved, du blomst' (excerpts are on pages 225–6) is a very typical Danish song, and very characteristic of Nielsen. It is in strict strophic form; the accompanist has only nondescript broken chords and the necessary variation must come from the singer. The tempo must be fairly fast, to avoid sentimentality; Nielsen's directions *poco rall* and *a tempo* in each stanza need only be hinted at, but a tiny *ritenuto* at the end, on 'halvt og sukker', improves the intimacy. The effect of peacefulness depends on singing the quavers in dactylic rhythms *long*, keeping the pulse in crotchets. The singing must be mellow, very *legato*, avoiding big dynamic jumps. The singer must take care not to sing a series of two-bar phrases; the phrases must be given different lengths, at least four bars, by following the words. The German translation should *not* be used.

Bars 1-10

Quasi allegretto 1) *legatissimo*

Sænk kun dit Ho-ved, du Blomst,___

bøj det i Bla – de – ne ned,

(*poco f*)

vent kun med luk – ket Kro – ne

Nat – tens liv-sa – li – ge Fred.___

Bars 12-19

2)

Nat – ten, den mil – de, den ty – ste,

poco cresc.

kom – mer – o bøj dig til Blund.

poco rit.

Sov un-der gyld – ne Stjær – ner,

a tempo

sov dig sa – lig og sund.___

Bars 21-28

3)

Sov som et Barn, der vug – ges

225

blidt i sin Mo - ders Favn,

vaag - ner kun halvt og suk - ker

smi - len - de Mo - ders Navn.

A generation of Danish composers grew up in Nielsen's shadow, learning from his sophisticated simplicity to create natural melodies in different styles; practically all of them have written something for the voice. Poul Schierbeck (b. 1888), Ebbe Hamerik (b. 1898), Flemming Weiss (b. 1898) and Finn Høffding (b. 1898) have written beautiful songs, notably Schierbeck's cycle for soprano with piano or orchestra *Den kinesiske fløjte* (The Chinese Flute).

In the next group, names like Otto Mortensen (b. 1907), Herman D. Koppel (b. 1908), Vagn Holmboe (b. 1909, with an international reputation as a symphonist) and Svend S. Schulz (b. 1913) have shown individuality in works for the voice; Mortensen especially. The younger generation, now extremely active, displays a healthy traditionalism in its vocal music, though they make too much use of that damned strophic form; some of them have established their names internationally. The youngest generation is still feeling its way. If solo song is to survive, a reaction against *avant-garde* techniques is absolutely necessary. Professional singers have something better to do than gurgle *solfeggi* and destroy their voices.

Norway. If you don't know Norway, they say, you don't understand Grieg. But Grieg wasn't the first in the field. He learned his profession in Germany, but he went on writing music in a very Norwegian style. But the real creator of the Norwegian national song was Halfdan

Kjerulf (b. 1815). He was a friend of Bjørnson's, who wrote many poems specially for him to set, and besides over a hundred solo songs he wrote choruses and quartets for male voices. The early death of Rikard Nordraak (1842–66), composer of Norway's national anthem, was a tragedy for Norway. His ideas and influence came alive through Edvard Grieg (b. 1843); the two men were friends and together determined to create a truly Norwegian music. Grieg's songs are a 'must' not only in Norway, where they appear in every recital, but throughout Scandinavia. The best perhaps are those written to texts in *landsmål*, notably the cycle *Haugtussa* to poems by Arne Garborg and the Vinje songs. Most of Grieg's songs are for soprano or mezzo, many of them written for his wife. Grieg's German songs, like the popular 'Ein Traum' ('En Drøm') are almost always sung in Norwegian even abroad, and the songs to Danish lyrics, like Hans Andersen's 'Jeg elsker dig', also sound more genuine in Norwegian. Written Danish and Norwegian were of course identical in Grieg's time; the difference between the two languages only appeared when they were spoken – or sung.

The shadow of the master was long. The generation of composers that followed him – Agathe Backer Grøndahl (b. 1847), Christian Sinding (b. 1856), Eyvind Alnaes (b. 1872) and Arne Eggen (b. 1881) – all showed warm interest in the Nordic art song. In the inter-war period David Monrad Johansen (b. 1887) was a central figure; both he and Ludvig Irgens Jensen (b. 1894) introduced neo-classical elements in their composition. Fartein Valen (b. 1887), Harald Saeverud (b. 1897) and Klaus Egge (b. 1906), though mainly composers of instrumental works, all contributed to the treasury of Norwegian song. Valen's music is notable for his individual use of dodecaphonic construction. Geirr Tveit (b. 1908), in contrast, builds his folkloristic works on modality; there are a few songs in his vast output. Gunnar Sønstevold (b. 1912), a film composer, has written beautiful melodies. A Norwegian national style with traditional elements is still to be found in the work of a number of twentieth-century Norwegian composers, but the 'modernists' seem to have little feeling for songs. Perhaps we must wait for the next generation. Meanwhile a foreigner to Norway must never forget that Nature in that country is so monumental, so overwhelming, that no artist can possibly ignore it. Even the most academic works have in them something of this enormous power, reflected by a people living on a narrow strip of land between the sea and the mountains.

Sweden is not so rugged. Once a great power and still an important one, the country has become very international, very Central European, American perhaps. That has put Swedish music in a somewhat weaker position than one might have expected, for this internationalism has destroyed something of Sweden's own national image.

The earliest composers had little interest in song-writing. There was of course a famous opera house, founded by King Gustaf III (1746–1792), but his contemporaries preferred to write works on a big scale and regarded solo songs as no more than a hobby. It is still puzzling that Swedish composers should have ignored the inspiration to be found in folklore and in nature. The nineteenth-century masters Franz Berwald (b. 1786) and August Söderman (b. 1832) concentrated on music in other fields, but in time, as a national-romantic feeling developed, the 'Svensk romans', the Swedish song, began to blossom. Emil Sjögren (b. 1853) wrote hundreds of such songs; he had studied in Germany and still leaned heavily on German traditions, but with Wilhelm Stenhammar (b. 1871), Edvin Kallstenius (b. 1881) and Ture Rangström (b. 1884) one can speak with confidence of a true Swedish style. Rangström is unsurpassed among Swedish song writers; he has written a most effective song-cycle for baritone and piano (or with orchestra), *Ur King Eriks Visor*, to lyrics by Gustaf Fröding. Older men, too, Wilhelm Peterson-Berger (b. 1867) and Hugo Alfvén (b. 1872) wrote in the same romantic idiom, their strength being in older styles and their songs maybe over-sweet. But all credit to the Swedes; in their song writing they never abandoned the *Svensk romans* but only modernized it. Hilding Rosenberg (b. 1892), and Lars-Erik Larsson (b. 1908) are among Swedish composers who have retained a Nordic impressionistic style with no intrusion of modernism. The younger generation, Rosenberg's pupils, have worked mainly in instrumental music, but there are some little known but very fine songs by Karl-Birger Blomdahl (b. 1916), Sven-Erik Bäck (b. 1919) and Ingvar Lidholm (b. 1921), and Laci Boldemann has turned out a number of simple, artistic songs. The youngest generation is very European, very up to the minute, which means that they have written little for the solo singer. The true Swedish song was, and is still, national-romantic or neo-romantic.

Finland. Culturally as well as politically, Finland occupies a peculiar position among Nordic countries. Strictly speaking it does not belong to Scandinavia, but its culture is so firmly anchored to it, consciously and unconsciously, that we are justified in speaking of Finland as Scandinavian. The claim that Finnish music is influenced by music from further east (Sibelius by Tchaikowsky, for instance) is nonsense. The Karelian (East Finnish) thread was, maybe still is, strong, but Karelia is part of Finland's cultural history, which is quite different from North Russian. Foreigners sometimes forget, too, that Finland is bilingual; Swedish is the second official language and many famous songs by Finnish composers were written to Swedish words.

The history of music in Finland is short. We look on Fredrik Pacius (b. 1809) as the 'father of Finnish music'; an immigrant from Germany, he quickly settled down in Helsingfors (Helsinki) and organized a regular concert life. There had been fine musicians before him, but they had been forced to move into Sweden to earn a living. The period after Pacius is mainly of historical interest; I should like to mention Karl Collan (b. 1828), a talented songwriter, but otherwise his generation concentrated on choral

229

and chamber music. We have to come straight down to
Jean Sibelius (b. 1865), that amazingly gifted man who not
only created a true Finnish music but gave his people a
cultural identity. Cultural life at the end of the nineteenth
and the start of the twentieth centuries was dominated by
the Swedish language. It is not surprising, therefore, that
most of Sibelius's songs were written to Swedish poems,
which in fact makes them more accessible to singers from
other countries. Sibelius's songs are now sung world-wide;
they form as it were a partnership with Grieg's.

Another composer of Sibelius's generation, Oskar Meri-
kanto (b. 1868) wrote in a popular style and is now
enjoying a well deserved revival. Erkki Melartin (b. 1875)
and Selim Palmgren (b. 1878) both produced some gems
for the voice. Toivo Kuula (b. 1883) wrote little during his
short life, but some of his songs have lasting quality. Leevi
Madetoja (b. 1887) combined national with pan-European
characteristics. But the most powerful figure in Finnish
song – indeed, the strongest in the whole of Scandinavia –
is Yrjö Kilpinen (b. 1892), composer of more than seven
hundred songs to Finnish, Swedish and German texts.
Kilpinen is one of the few real masters of the *Lied* and a
towering figure not only in Scandinavia. His music can be
arctic, archaic, ascetic, not always easy to get acquainted
with, but it well repays special study. I would rate as the
best his Finnish songs to the folk poems from *Kanteletar*
(a huge collection), his Swedish songs to Pär Lagerkvist's
lyrics and the settings of German poems by Morgenstern,
which include a very effective and dramatic cycle for
baritone and piano (also arranged for orchestra), *Lieder
um den Tod*.

Of later composers, a master who often found inspiration
in the written word is Erik Bergman (b. 1911), who wrote
a great number of songs in different styles. Ahti Sonninen
(b. 1914), Tauno Pylkkänen (b. 1918) and Bengt Johansson
(b. 1914) lead into the younger generation, among whom
Ilkka Kuusisto (b. 1933) and Leif Segerstam (b. 1944) are
very capable and versatile musicians.

Twenty-two
Hungarian Song

Rosemary Hardy
  Studied at the Royal College of
Music and the Franz Liszt Music
Academy in Budapest. She
has wide experience of
contemporary music – Boulez,
Berio, Brian Fernyhough and
Harrison Birtwistle – in England
and France. She made her 'Prom'
debut in 1979 in Ravel's
'L'Enfant et les Sortilèges' and
her recordings include *King
Arthur* and *Tempest*, Purcell;
Psalm 112 and 'Salve Regina',
Handel; Cavalli's Opera *Ercole
Amante*, and works by
Monteverdi.

Hungary in the 1880s, the Hungary into which Béla Bartók
and Zoltan Kodály were born, was a very different country
from the Hungary we know today. It had been occupied
by foreign powers for a major part of its history; as a part
of the Austro-Hungarian Empire under the yoke of the
Austrian Hapsburgs, virtually all its culture was Germanic,
and German rather than Hungarian was the language
spoken by educated people in Hungary. Bartók was born
in Transylvania, now a part of Romania; Kodály, born at
Kecskemet in Hungary, was educated in Slovakia, now
belonging to Czechoslovakia. But it was the great German
musical tradition that was to be the staple musical diet of
both men during the formative years of their youth. Early
influences on Bartók were Brahms and Strauss, the latter
a composer widely disapproved of by the musical establishments of Budapest and Vienna; later Liszt and Debussy
were to have a much more profound effect on Bartók's
music.

231

The Singer's World

In the first decade of this century Bartók and Kodály, along with their contemporaries, were caught up in the feverish reawakening of Hungarian nationalism that was taking place. Bartók in his letters appealed to his family and friends to use Hungarian, and it was at this time that both composers formed their ideal of creating a musical language that would be truly Hungarian in character. This aim led them to embark upon their famous folksong-collecting tours, on which they discovered that genuine folk music was still thriving amongst the peasants in the Hungarian countryside. The systematic and scientific study of their discoveries proved no easy task, as original folk music had come to be submerged under a plethora of pseudo-folksongs, 'csŕdás', and what Bartók described as 'the usual gypsy slop'. It proved however to be the decisive influence on both composers' work, and consequently on the whole of Hungarian musical life up to the present day. The successful fusion by Bartók and Kodály of deep-rooted folk traditions with their own highly individual language has meant the realization of their dream of bringing true Hungarian music to international recognition. The folksongs themselves, however, are still not widely known outside Hungary.

The Hungarian language

The main stumbling block for many British singers who wish to acquaint themselves with these songs is the Hungarian language, which seems positively terrifying at first glance. Of course, a deeper understanding of the songs can only really be achieved with a knowledge of Hungarian, a language of great beauty, with a richness of vocabulary that makes its literature one of the finest in Europe. Translations, however lovingly prepared, will always seem inadequate to the sensitive singer.

Formidable as Hungarian is grammatically, there are only a few sounds in it that create difficulty. It is pronounced as it is written and the stress is always on the first syllable.

232

Rules for the pronunciation of consonants are similar to those of Italian consonants. They should always be distinct and clear even at the end of a word; they should always be unaspirated as in Italian, and double consonants should be at least twice the length of single. There are some special individual sounds that the student will have to learn. 'C' and 'cc' sound like the German 'z' in 'Zeit', or 'ts' in 'hats'; 'cs' and 'ccs' are like English 'ch' in 'church'. 'J' and 'jj' are like the English 'y', and so are the combinations 'ly' and 'lly'. A single or double 's' sounds like English 'sh'; the unvoiced 's' sound is written 'sz' or 'ssz', and the voiced 'z' or 'zz'. The sound of the 's' in English 'treasure', the French 'j' in 'je', is written 'zs'. Finally there are three more difficult sounds, using the letter 'y' – 'ty' and 'tty', 'gy' and 'ggy', 'ny' and 'nny'. They should be formed by the flat of the tongue raised up against the back teeth, so that the two letters become a complete unit, as opposed to two separate sounds obtained by pronouncing the letters with the tip of the tongue as in English (as in 'onion'). Note that 'gy' is nearer to the English 'dj' heard in 'during' or 'dupe'.

Hungarian vowels should be very open and clear. Basically they are similar to the vowels in German, including the modified vowels 'ö' and 'ü'; but the short 'a' sounds very much like the 'o' in English 'hot'. An accent on the vowels ('á', 'é' etc.) – doubled on the modified vowels, 'ő' and 'ű' – indicates that they are long. Beware of any kind of a diphthong; the vowels must remain pure. The best method for an English singer to get the right sound for the long vowels is to speak them as if with a Yorkshire accent!

Once the singer is confident of the pronunciation, he should go on to try to master, preferably with the aid of a Hungarian speaker, the subtle variations that should take place on written rhythms because of the stress of the words. This may seem a little strange at first, but it is something that happens unconsciously to a native Hungarian speaker and is vital if the words are to sound convincing. In the first song of Bartók's 'Twenty Hungarian

Folksongs', the first phrase gives an example. Written thus:

Minden ember szórencsésen._____

it should be sung thus:

Minden ember szórencsésen._____

Though one's musical instincts may lead one to put a stress on the ' . . . csé . . .' because of its place in the musical phrase, that would give a wrong emphasis.

Hungarian Folksongs

English folk music, while undoubtedly loved by many musicians, tends to be regarded as less worthy of the close attention which is given to other, more 'serious' music. It is perhaps hard to imagine the deep reverence in which folk music is held by Hungarians, who see in it the root of their whole musical culture.

The number and variety of Hungarian folksongs is seemingly inexhaustible, and Bartók and Kodály chose some of the best of their collections in preparing arrangements for voice and piano. In addition to the four volumes of *Twenty Hungarian Folksongs* from which I quoted above, Bartók also published a volume of *Eight Hungarian Folksongs*. Kodály's great collection of *Magyar Népzene* (Hungarian Folk Music) fills ten volumes, while there is a volume of *Magyar Népdalok* (Hungarian Folk Songs) edited by both composers. All these, suitable for medium or high voice, are published by Editio Musica Budapest and are available in Britain through Boosey and Hawkes. The whole range of human emotion is to be found in them, as well as the more basic pleasures of eating, drinking and dancing. They extol the virtues of local heroes or the grander exploits of historical or legendary figures.

The melody of 'Árva vagyok' (I am an orphan), from Volume X of Kodály's *Hungarian Folk Music*, expresses through its haunting melismas the touching melancholy of the lonely orphan. The song, reproduced below, should be sung quite freely, with *rubato*, whilst the decorations should emerge quite naturally as emotional impulses out of the melody.

tár - sat vá - - laszt.

Jaj Is-te-ném kit vá - lasz - szak,

sostenuto Tempo I accel.

Hogy ë-gye-dül ne ma-rad-jak.

♩=100

Szép a ta vasz, de szebb a nyár,____

Hej! de szép, ki

Più lento ♩=76

pár - já - - val jár!

Hej, de szép a pá - - ro -

- su - lás, ____

sostenuto

A ki el - ta - lál-ta ëgy - -

- mást.

A contrasting song is Bartók's setting of the Székely Friss, a Transylvanian dance. This exuberant song with its almost oriental melody should be sung in absolutely strict rhythm. It illustrates another element of Magyar folk culture, the dance. Hungarian peasants have a legendary capacity for celebrating, and their wedding feasts can last for two or three days, or until the food and drink, not to mention the participants, are exhausted! Kodály's 'Dudan-óta' (Bagpipe Song) from Volume V is another good example, with its marvellous drunken middle section, and is a real *tour de force* for the pianist.

The Art Song

Bartók and Kodály did not neglect the art song. Kodály wrote many more than Bartók, who, apart from some early compositions, wrote only two song-cycles, his Op. 15 and Op. 16. The latter, some of Bartók's finest music, is a setting of five poems by Endre Ady. Ady was a major literary and political figure in Hungary at the turn of the century, and these poems reflect the great sadness of a dying man abandoned by the woman he loves. One senses Bartók's deep sympathy for the poems, and they seem to presage the loneliness of his own last years, fatally ill with leukaemia and cut off from his beloved country.

Kodály also set poems by well-known contemporary writers such as Endre Ady and Béla Balázs, the distinguished poet who wrote the libretto for Bartók's only opera, *Duke Bluebeard's Castle*. But often he chose the work of much earlier Hungarian poets, suggesting a desire to bridge the time-span during which Hungarian urban culture had been suppressed by constant foreign occupation and interference. The passionate love songs of Op. 14, to words by Balassa (1551–94) and two unknown seventeenth-century poets, as well as the *Megkésett Melodiák* (Late Melodies) with words by early nineteenth-century poets, seem to fulfil that wish to create songs that might have been written if history had taken a different course.

The influence of folksong is never far away in Kodály's music, and in *Énekszó*, Op. 1, he set 16 folk poems.

Contemporary composers

The flourishing musical life in Hungary today bears witness to the great pioneering work and example of Bartók and Kodály. The younger generation of composers, many of them pupils of Kodály, are making fine contributions to twentieth-century vocal repertoire in a language that is at once distinctively Hungarian and international. Kurtág, Kocsár, Kadosa and many others are writing demanding music for today's singers that can be judged at the highest level. Some of the following suggestions would make a valuable addition to the singer's contemporary repertoire.

Kurtág, Gy. *The Sayings of Peter Bornemisza*, concerto for soprano and piano Op. 7.

SK-*Remembrance Noise*, seven songs for voice and violin Op. 12, suitable for medium or low voice.

Farkas, F. *Fruit Basket*, twelve songs to poems by S. Weores

Naptár (Calendar), Twelve Miniatures for soprano, tenor and piano or chamber ensemble.

Kadosa, P. *Seven Songs* to poems by A. József (high voice).

Four Songs to poems by Nelly Sachs (high voice).

Three Radnóti Songs (high voice).

Mihály, *Attila József Songs*, soprano and piano.

Fly, Poem! for baritone, choir and orchestra.

Kocsár, M. *Lamenti* for high voice and piano.

Three Petőfi Songs for soprano and piano.

Soproni, J. *Three Radnóti Songs* for soprano and piano.

Szőllősy, A. *A Restless Autumn*, cantata for baritone and piano.

Maros, R. *Two Laments* for soprano and chamber ensemble.

Vass, L. *Floating Landscape* for soprano or tenor and piano.

Bozay, A. *Paper Slips*, Op. 5, for soprano, clarinet and cello.

Two Landscapes, for baritone, flute and zither.

Lendvay, K. *Ride at Night*, song-cycle for contralto and seven performers to poems by Endre Ady.

All the above are published by Editio Musica Budapest except Farkas's 'Naptar', which is published by Universal Editions.

The rewards to singers exploring this rich and unfamiliar realm of Hungarian song will be more than just an interesting expansion to their repertoire. If, in immersing themselves in the songs, they are led to learn the Hungarian language, make a visit to Hungary and experience the generosity and warmth of the Hungarian people, they will have discovered a whole new world.

Twenty-three
Choral and Vocal Ensemble

Sir David Willcocks, C.B.E., M.C.
Beginning musical life as a chorister at Westminster Abbey, he went on to study at Clifton and Cambridge. After war service his appointments were: Fellow of King's College, Cambridge; Organist of Salisbury and Worcester Cathedrals; conductor at the Three Choirs Festival; Director of Music at King's College 1957–73; conductor of the Bach Choir since 1960; and Director of the Royal College of Music since 1974. He holds many Honorary Degrees at home and abroad.

There is delight in singing, though none hear
Beside the singer.

Walter Savage Landor

There can be few things more rewarding in life than making music with others, and of all types of concerted music-making choral singing is surely the most satisfying. The human voice is certainly the most natural medium for the creation of musical sound and it is probably the most delicate and expressive of all instruments, capable of subtle gradation of pitch, volume and colour.

The possibilities of dramatic utterance inherent in solo singing are intensified when singers are in consort and a choir can corporately be the expression of ecstatic joy on the one hand or poignant grief on the other.

A choir is not unlike a football team in that its success depends partly upon the ability of each individual and partly upon the degree to which each individual's effort is co-ordinated. The similarity does not end there, for membership of a choir demands, like membership of a football team, physical fitness, mental alertness and enthusiasm; it demands too a degree of dedication and a long-term commitment to the regular training necessary for the acquisition of knowledge and experience of the art; it demands loyalty and unselfishness, and to some extent the subjugation of individuality for the collective good.

Consideration of the ways in which individual singers can develop fully the natural vocal talent with which they are endowed belongs to other chapters of this book. It is only necessary here to stress the importance for all choral singers of acquiring a sound basic vocal technique, and of building upon that secure foundation by regular individual practice, if the contribution that they make to their choirs is to be of maximum value.

It is recommended therefore that all choir members should, if possible, receive some individual instruction concerning posture, breathing and tone production from an experienced teacher; and that time should be found each day for vocal exercises designed for the development of tone, the extension of range and the cultivation of flexibility and control. It is taken for granted that those who aspire to play in orchestras require individual tuition followed by regular practice, but the need is just as great for choralists.

Ensemble singing can take many forms ranging from the duet, trio, quartet, quintet, sextet in which each singer has a separate voice-part – through the chamber choir where two, three or four singers are allotted to each part – to the large choir where there are many singers for each part.

Blend

It is perhaps not surprising that the fewer the singers engaged in a performance, the more difficult it is for them to achieve a good blend, satisfactory balance and security of intonation.

Good blend is largely dependent upon the cultivation of types of tone that are compatible with each other and upon securing uniformity of vowel treatment. As an exercise, this may be sung by the choir,

the conductor (i) listening for any deviation from the pure vowel sounds and (ii) checking on the position of the lips (forward and rounded for *oo* etc.) of each singer. The composition of diphthongs (e.g. NIGHT=NAH-ĭt; MU-SIC=Mĭ-ōō-ZICK) needs to be explained to each singer. Poor blend in ensemble singing frequently occurs when singers are incapable of controlling their vibrato, or when they fail to realize that the degree of vibrato needed to give vital warmth and intensity to the singing of a solo line may be disturbing in a choral group. Choirs need to practise attacking chords clearly at all dynamic levels and holding them *senza vibrato*:

Balance

Satisfactory balance requires mutual understanding between singers and a realization that certain parts of the voice are apt to be weak in relation to others. Particular problems occur in the performance of polyphonic music where, ideally, the listener should be aware of the detailed movement of all the parts. In practice clarity is obtained by bringing to the fore those voices which are engaged in imitative counterpoint, and lightening those which are temporarily engaged in supplying harmonic support. Low-lying phrases need to be sung relatively loudly with a warm sound, and high-lying phrases lightly with more delicacy. Take, for example, the 'came running down amain' phrases in the madrigal 'As Vesta was' by Thomas Weelkes. This example presents no problem since tenor and bass are both well placed:

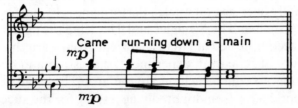

This example is more difficult since the tenor must be careful not to drown the alto:

This example is more difficult still and the alto will have to sing relatively *much* louder than the tenor to achieve satisfactory balance:

Assuming that the lower part sings *mp*, the upper part should be *mp, mf* and *f* respectively in these three passages.

Ensemble

Small vocal ensembles, like string quartets and small wind groups, often function best without a conductor, provided that they can have regular and intensive rehearsal. Sometimes a natural leader emerges within a group and the rehearsals and performances bear the stamp of that leader's authority. At other times tempi and style are discussed by all the singers and an agreed interpretation built up gradually over several weeks. Performances by professional groups such as The Swingles and The King's Singers or the most accomplished amateur madrigal groups are the result of hours of rehearsal, experiment, discussion and detailed planning, to which each one in the group has contributed.

A conductor is undoubtedly necessary for the successful operation of any large group of singers, as for any sizeable orchestral body. It is to the conductor that the singers look for guidance over interpretation, for attention to detail at rehearsal and for inspiration at performance.

Choir direction

What then are the qualities that the director of a choir should possess?

(1) A wide experience of music, so that the repertoire of the choir can be interesting and varied.

(2) An awareness of style and authentic performance practice, even though there may often be convincing arguments for a departure from strict authenticity.

(3) Complete understanding of the technique of conducting, so that not only the choir but also any soloists and orchestra who may work with the choir receive the necessary direction and recognize the significance of every gesture.

(4) A knowledge of singing technique, including good posture (sitting and standing); tone-production; treatment of pure vowels and diphthongs; treatment of consonants.

(5) A keen ear, so that the choir can be made to cultivate habits of good intonation, and so that inaccuracies and faulty balance can be detected and corrected wherever and whenever they appear.

(6) Imagination, so that rehearsals are well planned and stimulating and the necessary repetitive work is made interesting.

(7) Personality – a word that not only embraces courage, leadership, integrity, tact and sympathy, but also unbounded energy and infectious enthusiasm for life in general and music in particular.

How can those qualities be obtained?

(1) By means of radio and recordings, if not through live performances, for it is now possible for people in almost any part of the world to gain a wide knowledge of music. It is particularly important that choral directors should undertake an extensive study of orchestral and chamber music, since choral and orchestral textures and phrasing are closely inter-related.

(2) By careful comparison of different styles of performance on record, and by detailed study of the composer's autograph scores when available in facsimile editions.

(3) By watching other conductors, and preferably singing or playing under them, noting the gestures that are meaningful and those that are superfluous.

(4) By having a course of singing lessons, or observing the work of a qualified and experienced singing teacher.

(5) By developing systematically aural perception. This can best be done through regular singing in a small choir and by following musical performances with a

245

score whenever possible. An effort should be made to imagine the sound from a perusal of the score and then to compare the imagined sound with the real sound.

(6) By devising ways and means of adding interest to rehearsals, e.g. by having competitions between one section of the choir and another; by changing the normal seating arrangements of the choir; by transposing up or down a semitone.

(7) By taking a personal interest in the individual choir members and sharing with them their joys and sorrows, their excitements and their anxieties.

Rehearsal planning

How should a rehearsal be planned?

(1) The singers should be seated in a formation approximating to a semicircle, so that those seated on the wings can hear each other clearly. It is desirable for the basses to be central, since singers should be trained to listen to the bass part. If the tenors are few in number it is best for them to be concentrated and placed centrally in the front of the choir. All singers must be able to see the conductor, so it may be necessary either for the conductor or for some singers to be raised.

(2) Frequent changes of position throughout the rehearsal (sitting and standing) are desirable; in general it may be best to study new music seated but to stand for an initial run-through, any revision and any 'performances'.

(3) Warm-up exercises, which may be scales, arpeggios or other technical exercises hummed or sung to different pure vowels, are beneficial at the start of a rehearsal, both for the cultivation of good tone and blend and for the development of good intonation. In addition to singing major and minor scales

(melodic and harmonic) singly and in octaves, it is good to practise chromatic scales in contrary motion pausing at the half-way mark to check tuning:

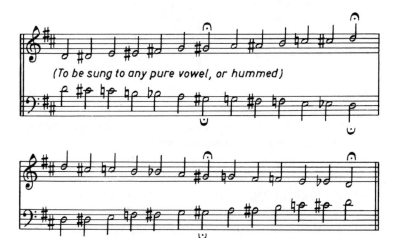

(To be sung to any pure vowel, or hummed)

Other useful exercises are the singing of all the modes:

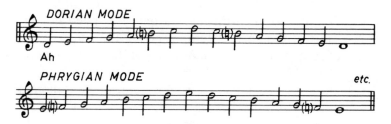

DORIAN MODE

Ah

PHRYGIAN MODE

etc.

and of whole-tone scales in either direction or in contrary motion:

WHOLE-TONE SCALE

Advanced choirs can profitably practise moving all parts of a chord down or up by steps of a semitone:

(4) It may be best to begin the main rehearsal with something that has been studied at a previous rehearsal, so that confidence is gained before embarking on the unfamiliar.

(5) With a new work, give the choir the opportunity to read through the words before attempting a run-through at sight and be prepared to give a brief outline of the history of the work . . . when it was written and for whom, and when and where it was first performed. If the text is in Latin, give a free translation, or at least the gist of the story, in English. Give the choir a general idea of the structure of the piece and any climactic points.

(6) For the first run-through, attempt a speed not far short of the correct tempo, giving the singers a lot of support from the piano, so that they get a general idea of the work.

(7) Do not stop at every mistake – but make a mental note of all mistakes during the run-through. Some mistakes will correct themselves; others will need to be pointed out and the reason for the mistake explained. It may be a good thing to tell the choir members that there was a mistake in a certain bar and let them discover for themselves what the mistake was and why it was made.

(8) Keep everybody occupied all the time, if possible. If the tenors are rehearsed on their own for any length of time the other singers may begin to whisper and cease to pay attention. Consider therefore whether the sopranos could sing the tenor part an octave

higher with the tenors and thereby gain experience. Consider too whether the sopranos, altos and basses could be asked to hum their own parts during a rehearsal of the tenors, or alternatively to comment on the progress of the tenors.

(9) Choirs love competitions. If there is a difficult run to be mastered (e.g. 'sit singing' in Tomkins's 'Adieu, ye city-prisoning towers'), hear each voice part separately and judge which is best. Then test the men against the women; those who are married against those who are not; those who have birthdays from January to June against those who were born between July and December.

(10) Some choral conductors slave away to get the notes right first and then 'put in the expression'. It is best to make even the note-learning stage expressive and musical.

(11) A good deal of rehearsal can profitably be unaccompanied, but be very careful to ensure that the pitch is maintained. If the conductor does not possess perfect pitch frequent piano checks will be necessary.

Intonation

Secure intonation is a matter of habit. Some choirs always sing flat because they have never been checked. Others sing in tune because they are aware of the danger spots and react to them. There is a tendency for choir members to make upward tones too small:

Thy wealth thine hon - ours man - i - fold,

and downward semitones too large as here and on p. 250:

Keep   me   from sin   in   heart   and   thought,

Con - strue my mean - ing,

so the careful singing or humming of upward whole-tone scales and downward chromatic scales can be helpful in counteracting this fault. More common still is the tendency to lose pitch when singing repeated notes:

With mourn-ful tunes I fill the air,

particularly when there is a change from a 'bright' vowel (e.g. *ee*) to a 'dark' (*ah* or *aw*). Even the monotone singing unaccompanied of the Lord's Prayer poses intonation problems for many a parish church choir. It is sometimes necessary for singers to imagine that they are starting each phrase on a very slightly higher note than the last in order to maintain pitch.

Phrasing

Just as in speech, where some words or syllables receive more stress than others, so in vocal music every phrase has its individual shape and its greater or lesser accents. Furthermore, just as there may well be more than one satisfactory way of reading a sentence:

'*God* is our hope and strength: a very present help in trouble'
or 'God is our *hope* and strength: a very present *help* in trouble'
or 'a very *present* help in trouble'
or 'a *very* present help in trouble',

so in choral singing a conductor is responsible for deciding (i) where breaths shall be taken (ii) the degree of *legato* and/or *staccato* to be used, (iii) the degree of stress to be used for each note in relation to the others within the phrase, thus obtaining a performance which has unity of style. In choir work it is sometimes desirable to 'stagger' the breathing-places, so that the impression is conveyed of *legato* throughout a phrase that is longer than any individual singer could manage. Other choral techniques, not suitable for solo singers, are the separate aspirations of notes in florid passages, e.g. in Handel's *Messiah:* 'For unto us a child is bor-haw-haw-haw-haw-haw-haw-haw-haw(n)', which can lead to greater clarity of detail and not sound offensive. However, this form of singing should only be used to assist clear articulation by normal means.

Repertoire

The ideal repertoire for any choir, be it a large choral society, a village choir, a school choir or a small madrigal group, is one that balances 'old' and 'new' music (i.e. includes classical, romantic and twentieth-century works), familiar and unfamiliar, difficult and easy, polyphonic and homophonic (i.e. chordal), so that the horizons of the individual singers are constantly being enlarged and their experience broadened.

Those responsible for school choirs have to be especially vigilant to ensure that the music selected imposes no unreasonable strain on the voices, and especially on immature tenors. The problem of the changing voice is one that demands careful consideration. Whereas some recommend that boys should not sing at all during the one to two years of change from treble/alto to tenor/bass, others, of whom I am one, feel that the risk of any damage to the voice is less than the risk of losing the enthusiasm and commitment to choral singing of the boy concerned. I would advocate therefore the continuation of singing *within the limited range which is comfortable*, provided there is no feeling of strain.

Advice on repertoire for church choirs can be obtained readily from the Royal School of Church Music, Addington Palace, Croydon, Surrey, which has done so much to improve the standards of church choirs since its formation in 1927. For choral societies the National Federation of Music Societies, Francis Street, London S.W.7, produces regularly an invaluable catalogue of choral works, both accompanied and unaccompanied, giving full details of publisher, price, orchestration, timing etc.

Fortunately there are few if any parts of Britain where anybody who wishes to participate in the joys of choral singing cannot find either an established choir or like-minded people eager to meet regularly.

> 'Sing we at pleasure
> Content is our treasure.
> Fa la la.'

Twenty-four
Studying a Role

Thomas Allen
Studied with Hervey Alan at the Royal College of Music. His career has been closely associated with the Welsh National Opera, the Royal Opera Covent Garden and Glyndebourne. Main roles to date – Count Almaviva, Papageno, Don Giovanni, Pelleas, and notably Billy Budd, a part in which he has justly earned the widest acclaim. He also continues to give concerts and recitals.

There is a great deal more to studying an operatic role than learning the words and the music. You have to immerse yourself deeply, not only in the character, but in the whole work and the background against which it is set. By way of illustration I have set down here some thoughts on *Billy Budd*.

I first sang the role of Britten's 'Billy Budd' in September 1972 in a new production for the Welsh National Opera, by Michael Geliot. I was not to know then how much more channelled and finely focused my interest in maritime matters was to become as a result of the experience of those first performances.

Visits to Portsmouth, Greenwich or, as happened on two occasions, to the Maritime Museums of Paris and Barcelona, now meant rather more to me than they had done before *Billy Budd*. This feeling partly describes some of the more physical aspects that attract me to the opera. Now I would like to go on to deal with some of the points

253

of detail arising from the libretto of Eric Crozier and
E. M. Forster.

Perhaps the incident most often quoted from the opera
as being rather hard to swallow, is Billy's exultant farewell
to the *Rights of Man*, and its misinterpretation by the
officers as the protestation of a disciple of Thomas Payne
(Act 1, figs 32–34). Indeed, with the merchantman *Rights
of Man* still in sight, it is hard to see how such a
misunderstanding could have arisen.

For my own peace of mind I find it essential to remember that these are the days following the Floating Republic, of the mutinies at Spithead and the Nore. The fact that the officers witnessed these events explains to some degree their over-watchfulness. In the novel, Melville described the incident as 'a breach of naval decorum' and no more.

During the revival of the opera at Covent Garden in March 1979, it seemed to me during rehearsals that Billy's violent reaction towards Squeak stemmed from a very disturbing mental state. This may be an inapt medical description but it is one which helps me uncover some of the problems of portraying this naïve character. On its own, the incident may not seem important, but it illustrates the possibility of finding something new in a role, no matter how familiar it may be.

Success in portraying Billy lies partly in the success of treading a narrow dividing line, one side of which lies a simpleton, and on the other side a nauseating do-gooder.

Ample evidence of his strength of character is provided by his vehement refutation of the charges brought against him at his court martial (Act 2, figs. 84–85).

This and the subsequent refusal of Vere to say anything on his behalf is, perhaps, the greatest emotional moment in the opera. How thoroughly dejected Budd must feel, when the man in whom he has placed so much trust remains unmoved in the face of his most urgent appeals.

King. It is true I'm a

BILLY   *simply* / *semplice*

no - bod - y, ___ who don't know where he was

born, and I've had to live

cresc.

rough, but ne - ver, ne - ver could I
Hn.

It is essential for me to remain uninvolved *internally* at this moment, otherwise the scene could easily become too overwhelming. I have talked here of the emotions experienced by Budd. Those of Vere, of course, would require a book to themselves.

The Soliloquy

For the scene of 'Billy in the Darbies' (Act 2, Sc. III) Britten has written an accompaniment suggesting gently lapping water. It is very early morning (Melville says four o'clock) and, as though out of respect, the sea slumbers with Billy on the eve of his last day. Each call of the piccolo announces a gradual stirring in the ship, as the new day approaches. Melville's words are a joy to sing and offer the baritone the materials with which to paint an epic picture of the scene:

259

Billy continues: 'It tips the GUARD'S CUTLASS and SILVERS (bright) this nook (dark).' Then, the words 'Ay, ay all is up', with their naval connotation, but in this context, and as set by Britten, heralding the passing away of all former cares and the beginning of Budd's resignation to his fate.

Billy soon faces the horror of the realization that perhaps one of his friends will have the task of hauling him up. But who? Red Whiskers? Dansker? – not Donald, for he has promised to shake his hand before he sinks – but again no;

how could he for 'it will dead then I'll be'. Billy quietly humourizes the situation. Again, so many colours in the words. In 'drop me deep' a hollow cavernous quality, then 'fathoms down, fathoms' with all that that implies – the first light, shallow waters, the darkening blue, blue green, ever colder, until darkness is everywhere. Next the sensuousness of 'I feel it stealing now'. He sees himself awash in the greatest depths – 'rocked in the cradle of the deep'. The gentle lolling flow, back and forth of the currents, his body wrapped round with heavy, thick-bladed fronds of weeds, lashed by the finer branches of 'oozy weeds' – the lashing he was so anxious to avoid following the novice's punishment.

Billy has a simple, layman's instinct of sensing the dangers, physical and mental, that he and Vere face, though he lacks the vocabulary or intellect to explain their situation. Knowing his own torment to be soon at an end, he has it in him to use Dansker as his agent, in order to avert a tragedy brought on by the crew's reaction to his hanging.

In the section beginning 'And farewell to ye' (fig. 115) my task is to present as clearly as possible the image Billy has of his previous happy shipboard life in the exalted position he enjoyed as Foretopman, which now affords him the vision of a far-shining sail that is eternity. In this vision he can rest contented, for it provides the strength he requires to deal with the predicament in which he finds himself.

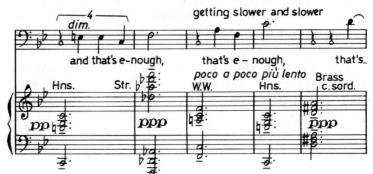

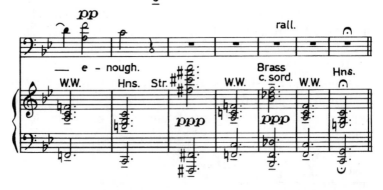

It is my firm belief that, in order to convey the depth and strength of these emotions and visions, it should be necessary for me to do no more than remain still. Not an easy thing, but essential if one is to concentrate the attention at this time. I allow myself an energetic movement to reinforce the words 'I'll stay strong' and for the rest, as Billy himself says 'that's enough'.

Twenty-five
Light Opera

Frederic Lloyd, O.B.E., Hon.
F.R.A.M., Hon. R.C.M.
For many years General
Manager of the D'Oyly Carte
Opera Company. He is Chairman
of the Board of Governors of the
Royal Academy of Music, a
Governor of the Royal
Philharmonic Orchestra, member
of the Associated Board of Royal
Schools of Music, and erstwhile
President of the Theatre
Manager's Association. He is a
Regional Director for the Arts
Council of Great Britain.

What is the most important ingredient for light opera? Well of course you will say singers, orchestra, scenery, costumes, production, are all vital too; but what kind of singers?

It is quite wrong to assume, as some people do, that almost anyone can sing in light opera. This field of music is as specialized (and should be) in its own way as that of grand opera, and so those who feel that their métier lies in this direction should clearly understand that certain qualifications are essential to achieve success.

There has always been a place for light opera in the theatre, and in France and in Germany in particular a high level of achievement was reached both by composers and performers in the eighteenth and nineteenth centuries. So much so that the Vienna Volksoper was established as a suitable opera house in which works of a lighter nature could be undertaken by singers who often sang in grand opera and were just as accomplished in either field.

263

Offenbach and Messager wrote many popular works during the nineteenth century, which became very well known in London; but in England composers were few, and when Richard D'Oyly Carte engaged Gilbert and Sullivan in 1875 to write 'Trial by Jury' he did not realize that in doing so he was creating an English *Opéra Bouffe* – something which in over one hundred years has established an important chapter of English musical history. The dozen comic operattas that these two men wrote set an example that so far has not been surpassed, and if performed by good singers and Gilbert and Sullivan's instructions followed, then they are still one of the most popular sections of the English music theatre.

After the Gilbert and Sullivan era came many other worthy attempts to follow them but without much success. Edward German, for an example was a splendid composer, but was let down by his librettist.

Musical Comedy has in the last fifty years or so developed from the amusing frothy type of production to the mammoth American musicals, especially those of Rodgers and Hammerstein, which in their own way are as interesting as Gilbert and Sullivan.

From my own knowledge as General Manager of the D'Oyly Carte Opera Company, for many years, I am going to take this organization as an example of how Artists were recruited and trained so successfully over a long period, until owing to inflation and lack of essential financial support the company had to close.

Auditions were held regularly either in London or in the provinces, and many people who came to sing were from amateur operatic companies who aspired to become professional, so that many had played in the Savoy operas in their own locality. Many others came of course from other professional companies. All auditions are ordeals, but very necessary ones. If the singer was being auditioned for a principal part then of course consideration had to be given, not only to the singing abilities, but the speaking voice, movement (very important!) and general appearance, all these points to be assessed in connection with the parts to be played. When listening to Choristers, then of course a well balanced voice, again movement and spoken dialogue were required, together with the ability to sight read.

Light opera requires all these ingredients for its singers, and more so today when the modern stage demands such a very exacting standard, and the eyes and ears of the audience both in the theatre and often in front of the television screen are expecting perfection. In view of these demands I think it is vital for the singer or would-be singer to consider most seriously several facts before going to any audition: have they got the necessary experience, vocal training, breath control, sight reading, knowledge of dancing? If so then they should go and try at any audition and, if they are lucky then be prepared for an interesting but hard training ahead.

Beginning a career in a light opera company entails a long period of rehearsal, and good stamina and general fitness are most essential because the singer will not only be working in a new environment, absorbing music, learning movement, and perhaps dialogue, but also living away from home, in theatrical lodgings out in the provinces, while the production is on tour.

All that I have said may sound somewhat depressing to the would-be singer, who aspires to go into the field of light opera: I may well seem to be discouraging. But if after careful thought about the points I have mentioned, the singer feels he or she has the qualifications then a most exhilarating, interesting and rewarding life can lie ahead.

Twenty-six
The Conductor and the Singer

Sir Charles Groves
While still a student at the Royal College of Music he accompanied Toscanini's choral rehearsals for the B.B.C. He became conductor of the B.B.C. Northern Symphony Orchestra and later Director of the Welsh National Opera. From 1963 he spent fourteen years with the Royal Liverpool Philharmonic Orchestra. After four years as Music Director of the English National Opera he decided in 1980 to give up the post and devote more time to freelance work in opera and concert at home and abroad.

Sooner or later most singers will have to work with conductors, so perhaps a conductor's view, subjective as well as objective, of singers may be helpful.

First, the subjective view: what does a conductor expect from a singer whom he is meeting for the first time either on the concert platform or in the opera rehearsal room? I think he prays first that the singer, given a good voice, should have a musical instinct as well. To be an instinctive musician is nothing to do with training but, like a good ear, can be developed with practice. I know that it is sometimes very difficult for someone coming late to a musical career compared with an instrumentalist to learn music, languages and movement at the same time as studying his technique, but we have in this country today many, yes, many splendid young musicians who can coach singers, can teach them how to listen to themselves and how to turn a lovely phrase. Nobody need be without help in this direction, and a fine coach can develop a singer's personality side by side with his musical and vocal skills to produce an artist with a strong personality, making collaboration between him and a conductor creative and not sterile.

A strong personality can be a delight or a menace; most conductors have come across singers whose egos can be quite destructive of musical atmosphere either in an oratorio quartet or in an opera cast. However this sort is only slightly worse than those who have nothing to contribute, so I think I prefer a singer with a strong personality and clear ideas as a musical collaborator.

Collaboration, a particularly happy word to use when speaking of music-making, means partnership and this is difficult to achieve if one or other of a group wants to dominate the rest. I know that I am being controversial when I say that for me the ideal collaboration of the string quartet can be extended into larger forms of music. Objectors will immediately say: 'What is a conductor for if not to impose his own personal stamp on the music and its performers?' If we go into this more carefully we shall see that a conductor who pays no heed to the musical instincts of his players and singers will soon lose their interest and so it is necessary for ideas to be flowing back and forth between singer and conductor. For example, what tenor would enjoy singing the role of 'Gerontius' with a conductor who would not allow him some latitude in 'Sanctus fortis'? Or what conductor could bear to suffer a Rodolfo in *La Bohème* pulling 'Che gelida manina' all out of shape merely for the sake of his top notes? No, we must collaborate even if collaboration is born out of initial struggle.

I suppose singers vary more than most musicians in the speed with which they learn their work; some read quickly while others have to proceed slowly by painstaking repetition. Conductors can quickly sum up a singer's capability and will work accordingly but they do dislike to find that a work has not been well learnt. This emphasizes again the need for good coaching.

Punctuality is a splendid virtue in everyday life but it is becoming a vital necessity for performers now that rehearsals are becoming more and more expensive and so more exactly planned than they used to be. It is extremely annoying for everyone concerned if a singer essential to the rehearsal of a song-cycle, a certain section of an oratorio or a specific operatic scene is late. I always leave enough time for my car to break down or have a puncture and for a taxi to rescue me and get me to the rehearsal or performance. Get the earlier train!

Looking now at things objectively it is equally annoying for singers if rehearsals are not carried out roughly as planned and I should always expect to be criticized for lack of respect to my colleagues if this happened except for reasons beyond my control.

I always try to remember that singers are themselves their instrument; playing the violin or the cello carries enough pain with it caused by unnatural muscular strains but a singer's daily physical condition is a barometer of his performance and very often of his mood too. My advice is: 'Try not to become obsessed with your throat'. We all know singers who doctor themselves incessantly and who often frighten themselves into trouble. *Mens sana in corpore sano* is a good motto for singers and when you are preparing to sing with orchestra fitness is important. Do not rush to the rehearsal and arrive flustered and without time to meet your colleagues and perhaps, discuss what you are singing with the conductor. Know your music if necessary by heart and try to understand the basic elements of the score because it will help you enormously to know what to expect when you hear the orchestra instead of the piano with which you have practised. Remember that however skilful conductor and players are they cannot follow all your idiosyncrasies like a pianist.

Be firm about tempi and balance; as I have suggested, conductors who are musical will always discuss these things and enjoy collaboration to achieve a good result.

Nowadays a singer's repertoire must include music of

many different styles from Monteverdi to Tippett, not to mention the *avant-garde* which calls for special gifts again. It must be sensible to take advantage of the great amount of coaching expertise available not only in London but in the regional centres too. It may cost you money you can ill afford to start with but you will reap big dividends from it as your career develops.

Above all be yourself. Our profession is so easily and so often a prey to cant and artificiality both in the way in which we relate to one another and, more dangerously, in our response to music. It is sometimes hard in the face of fashionable opinion to take an independent and honest view of performances and performers and more difficult still to see one's own achievements and limitations clearly. There are always the select and happy few, the great stars in the firmanment who can be, and often are, a law unto themselves, but most of us can do our best work and fulfil ourselves most completely in working with others, in collaboration.

Now – 'Sing – sing. Music was given to brighten the gay, and kindle the loving'.

Twenty-seven
The Accompanist and the Singer

Gerald Moore, C.B.E., Hon. D. Mus. (Cantab), F.R.A.M.

His professional life has been spent as an ensemble pianist, associated with the world's greatest singers and instrumentalists. Schubert has been his idol and he recently recorded nearly 500 of his songs with Dietrich Fischer-Dieskau. His publications include *The Unashamed Accompanist*; *Singer and Accompanist*; *Am I too loud?* (Memoirs); *The Schubert Song Cycles*; *Farewell Recital* (Further Memoirs). He holds many Honorary Degrees at home and abroad.

What inspires a pianist to become an accompanist? What is the magnet? Speaking for myself I can say it was the glory I found in the immense field of song and chamber music and, most important, the stimulation of taking part in a joint enterprise.

It is a magical moment in the partnership between singer and pianist when, in the course of their rehearsals, they realize they are one in musical understanding, their rapport so perfect that they are inflamed.

A good ensemble cannot be realized without a sensitized understanding between partners. The first element to be studied by singer *and accompanist* is the lyric and when discussion is necessary, it is focused on the poem's mood and meaning, its influence on line, dynamics, general colour and basic tempo. The song is seen as a whole (before the first note is sounded) as a map spread out before them, where emotional or expressive high points are agreed, where tension should gather and relax, pulse beat quicken or retard.

Of all virtues with which a good accompanist is compounded, I declare the most essential is sensitivity; all the others – fine musicianship, technique, imagination, temperament, taste, industry – are sterile without it. Sensitivity exercises its delicate and dictatorial sway by one inescapable medium, the ear. Listening, acute and self-critical, must for ever be the watchword.

First, because it is obvious, let us look at the part sensitivity plays in judging balance of tone between voice and pianoforte. At all times, even when he is playing *fortissimo*, the player's ears are keenly aware of his partner, for only thus can balance of tone, for which the accompanist alone is responsible, be gauged. He gives as much tone as he dare without covering the voice; he plays as softly as he dare without leaving the voice unsupported.

Again, and to be taken for granted, it is sensitive anticipation that enables the partners to float along arm in arm, ensuring unanimity of attack in minutest fluctuations of tempo.

Much more subtle than these considerations is the prescience which tells the accompanist *exactly* when the singer starts to make a *crescendo* or *diminuendo* so that their curves coincide, their nuances are similarly shaped. Pace too, is matched in an *accelerando* and *rallentando*. They are as one in shaping their *rubato*. Elasticity, or freedom from strict tempo, occurs frequently, and this only becomes undesirably obvious to the listener if the partners are not as one, or if, tastelessly, they exaggerate their *rubato* and distort the music. Anticipation would not be strained if obedience to the metronome were mandatory.

Phrases are shaped identically though this precept is not a *sine qua non*. It is a fallacy that the accompanist should always 'breathe' with the singer. Sometimes he should, but often the punctuation mark in the lyric, which gives the singer a chance to take in air, should be disguised by the accompanist, for if he too makes a musical comma it draws attention to the gap in the vocal line; this gap is bridged by sustained pianoforte tone.

In 'Feldeinsamkeit', by Brahms, the singer has to be a virtuoso to contain in one breath the long slow phrases at the close of each verse; only a few artists, in my experience, can do it; generally a breath is necessary and the pianist covers it by his *sostenuto* which enables the singer to breathe calmly – rather than agitatedly.

Again in Schubert's 'Du bist die Ruh' there are two slow seven-bar ascents, each wanting ever increasing tone from a *piano* to a *forte*, severely testing for a singer. The pianoforte supports the voice and maintains a steady flow of sound, more especially if the singer is forced to take a breath in mid-stream.

In fact the examples above suggest that the accompanist should use his imagination. There is no law in heaven or earth that prohibits the singer's partner exercising this faculty and playing as poetically and colourfully as he knows how. He, like the singer, will find imagination stirred by the lyric which inspired the composer in the first place: the more he understands the poem's essence, the more he will be at one with the composer and with his partner, the more will the spirit of the words be reflected in his playing.

In emphasizing that the accompanist listens to his partner, it goes without saying that he previously learned to listen to himself. It is for him to infuse colour into his playing and shades of colour, and this is a subtle affair, not a mere matter of *forte* and *piano*. Within the restrictive range of *pp* and *p* there are different shades.

Take Schubert's 'Litanei'; the postlude has a pale attenuated quality of tone, the slight undulations in the melodic line are scarcely noticeable. At the other extreme 'Von ewiger Liebe' by Brahms has an introduction, portentous in mood, the colour sombre and heavy. Yet in these widely diverse songs each composer asks for a *piano*. Does the pianist think for a moment that there can be any similarity whatsoever in the quality of tone between them?

If the touch desired for 'Von ewiger Liebe' were employed in 'Litanei' the result would be deplorable.

Schumann's introduction to 'Mondnacht' with its unhurried phrasing, its punctuation marks and its jewelled starlight is a world apart from Fauré's 'Clair de lune', whose masked dancers seem not to believe in their *bonheur*. Fauré could not be commonplace if he tried and this song needs elegant handling, but it is intentionally more sophisticated than the Schumann song; less secret and less profound. The contrast in colour between them is not so wide as that between the Schubert and Brahms examples, but in mood they are a world apart. The high treble notes in 'Mondnacht' are affectionately touched by the fingers – not bound together – and the sustaining pedal's overtones make them shimmer. 'Clair de lune' needs a finger *legato*, cool in colour; its movement has an even tenor, with no suggestion of the *rubato* implied by the phrasing in 'Mondnacht'. Yet both songs are *softly* performed.

This principle applies when the basic dynamic is *forte*. From Schumann's *Dichterliebe*, the harsh quality used in the course of 'Ich grolle nicht' would be out of place in the majestic unpercussive 'Im Rhein im heiligen Strome', where the accompaniment suggests the diapason sound of an organ.

All these examples give an idea of the discrimination required by the complete accompanist.

Imagination spurs him again when coping with a strophic song, where his response to the lyric (every word being understood) stimulates his partner.

If I seem to have spoken too glibly of 'variety of colour' or differing qualities of tone, it must be emphasized that the search for these can only be realized by conscientious practising, keen listening and patience – before rehearsing with your singer. Eventually, the result of your response to word and music will be transmitted to your fingers; here technique takes over. Imagination proposes; technique disposes.

What is technique? Agile fingers are indeed an asset and

no musician will neglect to study an accompaniment where speed is the essence. But this is an obvious hazard. There are deeper considerations.

Three difficulties confront any and every pianist:—

(1) To achieve perfect smoothness (*legato*) between one note (or one chord) and another.
(2) To effect this *legato* in slow tempo.
(3) To make the listener unaware that the pianoforte is a percussive instrument.

It is scarcely possible on our instrument to play a slow *legato* without the sustaining pedal. Schubert's 'Nacht und Träume' Wolf's 'Wenn du zu den Blumen gehst' and Duparc's 'Extase' are types of accompaniment needing particular study. Each one of them presents a different problem. The first named is handled with care since it lies in the most resonant part of the piano, and for this reason is played *una corda*; one must not be aware of separate semi-quavers but of a soothing undertone and the fingers creep from one harmony to another with no daylight intervening: the Wolf song is contrapuntal in style, where each note is clearly articulated but it is none the less *legato* (a finger *legato*, technically not unlike 'Clair de lune' but much warmer and intimate). Duparc's song is more rarefied than either of the others, it floats on a white cloud, is again played *una corda* and has a counter melody as obbligato to the voice, and is as soft as gossamer.

A young accompanist will read these songs with ease at first sight, and will assume that further penetration is unnecessary. He must undeceive himself: your true artist finds after a lifetime that his grasp on them in the act of performance is not always to be relied on and frequently leaves much to be desired.

Where does rhythm come in the order of things? I have hardly touched on it save in connection with that life-enhancing quality known as *rubato*. Paderewski, who was considered the king of pianists in his era, declared that rhythm was the soul of music. Rhythmic control is the hallmark of authority. Lack of control manifests itself by a wretched tendency to get quicker and quicker, *in fast movements*. Schubert's 'Erlkönig' loses impact if the horse bolts, and occasionally a singer gripped by excitement will hurry, taking each phrase faster than the last so that words become unintelligible, characterization non-existent, the accompaniment unplayable. Schubert marks it 'fast', not 'very fast' and certainly not *presto*, and it should be performed, paradoxically, under a strong rein if its desperation and drama are to be projected. The introduction may be taken at a reasonable gallop but if the singer gets the bit between his teeth, it is almost impossible to restrain him. The same, to some extent, applies to 'Der Musensohn'; it is marked *Ziemlich lebhaft* (somewhat lively) and on more than one occasion my partner has raced away as if the devil were after him: my right hand, in order to keep pace, was dashing to right and to left, dabbing away at the notes like a feather duster.

On the other hand, in a slow moving song, it is the singer who can be embarrassed. What can she do in Schubert's 'Ave Maria' if the introduction is taken too slowly? She listens to the accompanist's pedestrian tempo and realizes, with increasing anxiety, that she will be unable to contain her long phrases in one breath. She is helpless; her sustained notes make it impossible for her to urge her dreaming partner forward. The song is ruined for her. Instead of spiritual ecstasy, her soul is filled with longing for the opportunity to strangle the pianist. At all events the latter was certainly not alert at rehearsal.

No, the accompanist with personality, eagerness and life will warm the heart of the singer.

Never, in the course of much advice offered over the years have I suggested the accompanist should be self-effacing. Modesty is a cloak he has been schooled to assume for generations and he almost regards it as a prerequisite. No, if we recognize our contribution is a vital one, and are worthy of our responsibility by giving it the thought, hard work and time it requires, we may possibly do justice to the composer. Several accompanists came before us and we would do well to remember them – Schubert, Schumann, Wolf, Strauss, Debussy, Fauré, Poulenc, Britten – they did not want their pianoforte parts to be unobtrusive, of that we can be certain. Let us play their songs as they played them, with pride and authority. Pride, yes, and love; a deep and abiding love – this comes before everything.

Part Four

Some Remarkable Voices Preserved on Gramophone Recordings

Some Remarkable Voices Preserved on Gramophone Recordings

Adelina Patti (1843–1919)

'The undisputed Queen of
Song from 1860 to 1890.'

The undisputed Queen of Song from 1860 – 1890. Her
legacy of recordings made in 1905 and 1906 preserve only
a shadow of the vocal brilliance and art that captivated
Rossini and Verdi, but are an important legacy stylistically,
incorporating as they do, Pasta's embellishments in the
second verse of 'Casta Diva'. Her trill and ascending run
at the beginning of the 'Jewel Song' are magically perfect
and know no rivals! She studied some of her interpretations
with Maurice Strakosch who had been Giuditta Pasta's
accompanist.

Lilli Lehmann (1848–1929)

One of the greatest phenomena in operatic history for
glory of voice, variety of repertoire and length of career.
She appeared with equal success as Violetta, Costanze,
Philine in Thomas's *Mignon*, Norma, Donna Anna, Isolde,
Brünnhilde! Her recordings made in 1905 and 1907 still

279

demonstrate a formidable technique. She achieved further fame as a teacher, amongst her most famous pupils being Geraldine Farrar the American soprano – for many years a leading light at the Metropolitan Opera House.

Francesco Tamagno (1850–1905)

Verdi's own *Otello*, and the foremost dramatic tenor in Italy. In his prime his *tenore robusto* reached up to a pealing high C sharp. His recording of the 'Esultate' from *Otello* is probably the most wonderful example of sustained declamatory singing on records and of course invaluable historically. Blessed with iron lungs, and clarity of diction, in his prime he was also noted for a truly marvellous *mezza voce* (a quality not generally associated with him today).

Pol Plançon (1854–1914)

'The great bass.'

This great French bass, was probably the most perfect singer (other than Mattia Battistini) ever to have made records. A pupil of Duprez of the famous High C from the chest, and later of Sbriglia, his name is a by-word for *bel canto*. A trill that would be the envy of most coloratura sopranos and a velvet-like legato allied to superb musical taste make his recordings a must for all students of singing. The trill is admirably demonstrated in his 1906 recording of the 'Air du Tambour-Major' from Thomas's *Le Caid*, and in his 1907 recording of the 'Porter Song' from Flotow's *Martha*.

Mattia Battistini (1856–1928)

'Probably the greatest baritone produced by Italy.'

Known as *La Gloria d' Italia*, he was probably the greatest baritone produced by Italy. He enjoyed a career which carried into the 1920s, singing with a voice miraculously untouched by time. Fortunately the voice recorded well, and he has left us a wonderful legacy of recordings. Even a trifle such as Tosti's 'Amour, Amour' is elevated by the genius of his singing, ending on a magical hushed *pianissimo* high F. His recordings of the baritone music from *Ernani* (particularly the 'Vieni meco') *La Favorita* and *I Puritani* should be prescribed listening for all would-be baritones.

Allessandro Moreschi (1858–1922)

The last of the breed of castrati, and soprano soloist at the Sistine Chapel; he made a series of nine recordings in Rome in 1902–1903. Though by no means a Farinelli or Velluti his recordings give a fascinating glimpse of the castrato voice.

Marcella Sembrich (1858–1935)

This Polish soprano was a pupil of the younger Lamperti. A brilliant singer, she was also an accomplished pianist and violinist. On the occasion of the benefit evening for the Met's manager Henry Abbey, Sembrich as violinist played Beriot's Violin Concert in F; as pianist, a Chopin

281

Mazurka; and ended with a brilliantly sung 'Ah, non giunge'. Her recordings give a fair impression of her singing. The duet 'Vado, coro' with Antonio Scotti from *Don Pasquale*, and the 'Sull aria' duet with Emma Eames from *Le Nozze di Figaro* are particularly beautiful specimens. Her recording of 'Une voce poco fa' incorporates Patti's decorations, presumably those that occasioned Rossini's remark to the latter Diva 'A very pretty song my dear; who wrote it?'

Emma Calve (1858–1942)

Studied with Puget, briefly with Marchesi, and later with Rosine Laborde. She was an extraordinary person and the most famous Carmen and Santuzza of her day. She took lessons from the famous castrato Domenico Mustafa from whom she learnt the secret of what she called her 'fourth voice'. These are those 'strange, sexless, disembodied' altissimo notes which are heard in her 1907 recordings of 'Charmant Oiseau' from David's *Perle du Brésil* and 'Magali' (the Provençal song that Massenet incorporated into the opera *Sapho* which he wrote for Calve).

Leon Escalais (1859–1941)

His voice was likened to Duprez's in range and brilliance: a dramatic tenor with a clarion quality to his high notes. His recording of the 'Sicilienne' from Meyerbeer's *Robert le Diable* demonstrates a brilliant voice of remarkable range and a well turned trill.

Fernando de Lucia (1860–1925)

The *bel canto* tenor par excellence – as he is remembered today – was particularly famous for his intensely dramatic portrayal of Canio in *I Pagliacci*, deemed to be as memorable as Jean de Reske's *Romeo*, Terninas's *Isolde* and Calvé's *Carmen*. Very few tenors had the technical facility that de Lucia shows in coloratura work. His early 1904 recording of 'Ecco ridente' for *Il Barbiere di Siviglia* is a wonderful exhibition.

Nellie Melba (1860–1931)

The most famous of Salvatore and Mathilde Marchesi's pupils. Her voice in its prime, wrote W. J. Henderson 'extended from B flat below the clef to the high F. The scale was beautifully equalized throughout and there was not the smallest change in quality from bottom to the top'. Her voice was described as having a clarion quality on the stage – one that her recordings could not capture owing to the rather primitive conditions obtaining in the early recording studios and apparatus. Her 1904 recordings of 'Nymphes et Sylvains' by Bemberg, 'Il pensieroso' by Handel, the 'Mad Scene' from Thomas's *Hamlet*, the 1907 recording of 'Ah forse lui' and 'Sempre libera' from *La Traviata* and the memorable 'O soave fanciulla' with Caruso, all give a vivid impression of a marvellous voice and impeccable technique.

Ernestine Schumann-Heink (1861–1936)

A magnificent contralto voice, with a range extending from D below middle C to a firm high A and B flat. She sang Donizetti, Verdi, Mozart, Wagner, Meyerbeer and eventually in a musical comedy (*Love's Lotter* by Julian Edwards) with great success. A great Waltraute in *Gotterdämerung*, her recording of the Narrative is justly famous. Her recordings of the Brindisi from *Lucrezia Borgia* and Arditi's Bolero 'Leggiero invisibile' have been standards by which other recordings have been judged for years.

Emma Eames (1865–1952)

Another famous Marchesi pupil, this American soprano studied the role of Juliette with Gounod himself and has left a lovely memento of the 'Waltz Song' from his opera. She was a great Aida and Tosca. Her recordings of duets with her second husband the baritone Emilio de Gogorza are beautiful examples of the art of duet singing, as is the 'Letter Duet' with Sembrich. her autobiography *Some reflections and memories* makes fascinating reading.

Ellen Beach Yaw (1869–1947)

Another Marchesi pupil, she exhibits a remarkable color-atura facility and an extraordinary trill. Her Berliner recordings made in London in March 1899 of 'L'Éclat de rire' from Auber's *Manon Lescaut* and Paer's 'O Dolce contento' variations have recently been re-issued.

Alessandro Bonci (1870–1940)

Once considered to be Caruso's only rival in the lyric tenor field, he had a lovely voice with a wonderful sweetness of quality, and an apparently continuous flow giving the impression that he did not need to take a breath! (a characteristic matched only by John McCormack). His recording of 'A te O care' from *I Puritani* is justly famous.

Luisa Tetrazzini (1871–1940)

Gifted with an enormous voice of superb quality and a technique bordering on the phenomenal, she was undis-puted Queen of Song wherever she appeared. Significantly Melba never appeared as *Lucia* anywhere that Tetrazzini had sung that role previously! Her recording of 'Sempre Libera' from *La Traviata* fully justifies her great reputation as does the 'Saper Vorreste' from *Un Ballo in Maschera*.

Enrico Caruso (1873–1921)

Probably the most famous tenor ever. His voice is marvel-lously captured even by the early recording techniques.

His essentially lyric tenor voice darkened perceptibly after 1908 when a vocal nodule had to be excised from his vocal cords. His 1904 recording (with piano) of 'Una furtiva lagrima' and particularly that of the second verse beginning 'Un solo istante' is a wonderful memento of one of his famous roles, while his 1906 recording of 'Spirto gentil' from *La Favorita* remains unrivalled. The voice on his later recordings sounds baritonal, but still unmistakably Caruso's.

Dame Clara Butt (1873–1936)

'A voice of immense power and beauty', with her husband Kennerley Rumford, baritone.

This great contralto had a voice of immense power and beauty and of great range, studied with Visetti at the Royal College of Music and with Bouhy and Etelka Gerster. Her many recordings demonstrate this extraordinary voice almost bass-baritonal in the chest register and yet capable of the most delicate nuances and effects. her recording of the Brindisi from Donizetti's *Lucrezia Borgia* is justly famous, as is Handel's 'Rend il sereno'.

Leo Slezak (1873–1946)

Possessor of an outstandingly brilliant tenor voice, this very tall, tenor (he stood six foot two inches tall) had a phenomenally successful career both in opera and on the concert platform as a singer of Lieder. He was a famous Otello (though not eclipsing Giovanni Zenatello as Tamagno's 'successor' in that role) and the leading tenor at the

Vienna State Opera. His recording of 'Magische Tone' from Goldmark's *Königin von Saba* is particularly famous.

Selma Kurz (1874–1933)

A star of the Vienna State Opera from 1899 to 1929. Her 'interminable' trill in 'Saper Vorreste' from *Un Ballo in Maschera* as she perambulated around the stage held up the action much to Caruso's annoyance when they appeared in that opera together. Her recordings of this aria and 'O beau pays' from *Les Huguenots* are truly representative of this fine soprano.

Hermann Jadlowker (1877–1953)

A great favourite in Berlin. This dramatic tenor had a phenomenal coloratura technique, possibly due to his early training as a Cantor. His recording of 'Ecco Ridente' shows this, as does the aria from *Idomeneo*.

Margarete Matzenauer (1881–1963)

A mezzo soprano, she sang with great success both, in the soprano and mezzo soprano repertory. In her prime, she was deemed to be the equal of Lilli Lehmann and Milka Ternina. Her recording of Selika's aria from *L'Africaine* is believed to have captured her vocal quality well.

Sigrid Onegin (1889–1943)

A magnificent contralto with a quite remarkable ability to spin out a long breath on a held note or prolonged trill. She was a famous Fides in *Le Prophète* and recorded two arias from that opera – 'O Prêtres du Baal' and 'O mon fils'. Her versions of the Brindisi from *Lucrezia Borgia*, and a trifle called 'The fairy pipers' display an astounding virtuosity that has to be heard to be believed. She created the role of Dryad in Strauss's *Ariadne auf Naxos*.

The above brief list is a personal one and necessarily very limited, and does not include the many wonderful singers active from 1920 to the present day; nor does it include others whose careers ended before the advent of commercial recording.

A. S. Khambata

Discographical note by Wayne Turner

The best-known makes of Historical Reissue LPs are perhaps Rubini (published by S. J. Gray) and Preiser of Vienna; HMV issue a 'Golden Voice' series and Pearl, too, issue LP transfers from original 78s. Preiser issue the LV series and the CO series; the latter stands for Court Opera, each state capital (eg. Berlin, Munich, Dresden) having its Hofoper or Court Opera, until 1918. Such issues are 'acoustic' or 'pre-electric', i.e. pre-1925. The LV or *Lebendige Vergangenheit* series are of artists of the Inter-War years, though sometimes a pre-electric 78 may have been transferred. During the Second World War, German radio stations, notably *Reichssender-Berlin*, broadcast 'live' opera and studio performances; many were recorded on early tapes and several have been released by the BASF and Acanta record companies. The following is but a selection of extant period recordings.

Adelina Patti Soprano. *Olympus ORL 212* – includes 'Casta Diva', *Norma* (Bellini); 'Ah non credia', *Sonnambula* (Bellini); 'Pur dicesti' (Lotti).
Lilli Lehmann Soprano. *Scala SC 5025* (rec. 1905/07) – includes arias by Mozart, Handel, Bellini, Verdi, Beethoven, Meyerbeer, etc.
Francesco Tamagno Tenor. *Olympus ORL 211* (rec. 1903) – includes a selection of operatic arias.
Pol Plançon Bass. *Olympus ORL 218* – includes a selection of operatic arias. (Complete recordings available on Rubini LP Set).

Voice

Mattia Battistini Bass. *Olympus ORL 218* – includes a selection of operatic arias.

Allesandro Moreschi Castrato. (78s) *Gramophone & Typewriter Co.,* (Rome 1902/03): *54764/54780* – includes songs by Rossini, Laiback, Tosti, Gounod, etc.

Marcella Sembrich Soprano. *Olympus ORL 229* – includes 'Una voce poco fa', *Barbiere di Siviglia* (Rossini).

Nellie Melba Soprano. *Olympus ORL 208* – includes arias from *Hamlet* (Thomas) and *Traviata* (Verdi).

Ernestine Schumann-Heinck Mezzo-Contralto. *RCA Victrola Sovereign* Vic. 1409 (rec. 1906/09) – includes a selection of operatic arias.

Emma Eames Soprano. *Olympus ORL 208* – *Romeo et Juliette* (Gounod)

Allesandro Bonci Tenor. *Preiser CO 343* – includes a selection of operatic arias.

Enrico Caruso Tenor. *Victor LCT 1007* – includes a selection of operatic arias.

Luisa Tetrazzini Soprano. *Olympus ORL 210* – includes arias by Verdi and others.

Clara Butt Contralto. *HMV HLM 7025* – includes arias from *Sosarme* (Handel) and *Lucrezia Borgia* (Donizetti)

Leo Slezak Tenor. *Preiser CO 309* – includes various operatic arias.

Selma Kurz Soprano. *Olympus ORL 227* – includes arias by Meyerbeer and others.

Herman Jadlowker Tenor. *Preiser Co 312* – includes various operatic arias.

Margarethe Matzenauer Mezzo-Soprano. *Preiser CO 313* – includes arias by Meyerbeer and others.

Sigrid Onegin Mezzo-Contralto. *Preiser LV7* – includes arias from Meyerbeer's *Le Prophète*.

Complete recordings of Pol Plançon are available on a 4-record set by Rubini. The same company is preparing a comprehensive issue of songs by Enrico Caruso.

Discography

Wayne Turner
A bass lay-clerk in Chester Cathedral Choir. A member of the B.B.C. Northern Singers and in much demand in opera, oratorio and concerts in the north of England. He owns a vast record collection and has written biographies and discographies for Record Collector magazines and including one of the present editor.

This discography lists a selection of recordings made of many of the pieces mentioned in the text, grouped together with approximate reference to the pages indicated at the head of each section.

pages 2–12 and 42–69

BACH
St. Matthew Passion, No. 40 (Tenor Recit.)
Decca SET 288. Fritz Wunderlich in complete rec., 1964 cond. Karl Munchinger.

BRAHMS
'O wüsst' ich doch'
DGG 25701. Peter Schreier, Tenor in Brahms LP. Recital. *acc.* Peter Rosel.

Feldeinsamkeit
Electrola Da Capo IC 147.01.663/4M. Hans Hotter, Bass-Baritone, 1951. *acc.* Gerald Moore.

DONIZETTI
'O luce di quest' anima' Linda di Chamonix
Decca Jubilee JB 87. Joan Sutherland, Soprano.

FAURÉ
'Pie Jesu' Requiem Mass
complete rec. 76734. Lucia Popp, Soprano 1978. cond. Andrew Davis.

GIBBS
By a Bier Side *('This is a sacred city')*
Saga 5213. Janet Baker, Mezzo-Soprano, 1963 (in recital of English Song). *acc.* Martin Isepp.

HÄNDEL
'O had I Jubal's Lyre' Joshua
Pearl GEMM 217. Isobel Baillie, Soprano, 1929.

'Verdi prati' Alcina
Decca Jubilee JB 98. Teresa Berganza, Mezzo-Soprano.

Voice

'Darkness' Arias *Messiah*
HMV HQM 1238. Sir Keith Falkner, Bass-Baritone 1929, in Columbia 33 CX 1146/48. Norman Walker, Bass, 1954.

'O ruddier than the cherry' (with Recit. 'I rage . . .'), *Acis & Galatea*
Complete rec. (Händel Soc.) HDL 2. Trevor Anthony, Bass, 1947.

HENSCHEL
Young Dietrich
(Sunday Opera) SYO 7. Horace Stevens, Bass-Baritone, 1923.

HOWELLS
King David
Private Record. Kenneth Tudor, Bass-Baritone. *acc*. Paul Hamburger.

Italian 'Arie Antiche' (*Airs by Giordani, Caccini, Scarlatti, etc.*)
Hungaroton SLPX 1289. Sándor Svéd, Baritone, 1966.
USSR D 019475/6. Alexander Vedernikov, Bass, 1968.

LOEWE
Archibald Douglas
DGG 136320. Josef Greindl, Bass, 1956. *acc*. Hertha Klust.

MOZART
'Dove sono' *Figaro*
Electrola IC 187.29225/6M. Maria Cebotari, Soprano.

'Porgi amor', *Figaro*
DGG 2721.058. Gundula Janowitz, Soprano.

'Marten aller Arten' *Entführung*
Electrola IC 063.29082. Edda Moser, Soprano.

Esultate Jubilate
Complete – Phillips 6500.006. Elly Ameling, Soprano.

MUSSORGSKY
Song of the Flea
DGG 19076. Kim Borg, Bass, 1957.

SCHUBERT
'An die Musik'
Electrola IC 147.01.633/4M. Hans Hotter, Bass-Baritone, Oct. 1949. *acc*. Gerald Moore.

'Auf dem Wasser zu singen'
Electrola SHZE 314. Elisabeth Grümmer, Soprano. *acc*. Gerald Moore.
For others, see *Lieder* Section, pp. 139–157

VAUGHAN WILLIAMS
'The Roadside Fire', *'Bright is the ring'* from complete cycle, 'Songs of Travel'
Westminster LP. Richard Standen, Bass, rec. 1957. *acc*. Frederick Stone.

WAGNER
Beckmesser's Scene, Act 1
Die Meistersinger complete set.
Electrola IC 181.01.797/801M. Eugen Fuchs, Baritone, Bayreuth, 1943.

WOLF
'Auf ein altes Bild'
Decca AKF 1-7. Kathleen Ferrier, Contralto. *acc*. John Newmark.

pages 75–80

BRAHMS
'Von ewige Liebe'
Preiser LV 82. Sigrid Onegin, Mezzo-Contralto.

Die Mainacht
Heliodor 2548720. Heinrich Schlusnus, Baritone. *acc*. Sebastian Peschko.

HÄNDEL
'Every valley' *Messiah*
Marble Arch. Wilfred Brown, Tenor, 1961. *dir*. Walter Susskind.
Columbia 33 CX 1146/8. Richard Lewis, Tenor, Jan. 1954. *dir*. Malcolm Sargent.

292

SCHUBERT
'Die junge Nonne'
  Decca AKF 1-7. Kathleen Ferrier, Contralto. *acc*. Phylis Spurr.

'Du bist die Ruh'
  Preiser LV 207. Margarethe Klosc, Contralto. *acc*. Michael Raucheisen.
  HMV ASD 2263. Dietrich Fischer-Dieskau, Baritone. *acc*. Gerald Moore.

'Gretchen am Spinnrade'
  HMV HQS 1261. Elly Ameling, Soprano.

'Erlkönig'
  Preiser LV 257. Gerhard Hüsch, Baritone, 1939.

STRAUSS
'Allerseelen'
  HMV ASD 2431. Janet Baker, Mezzo-Soprano, 1968. *acc*. Gerald Moore.

WARLOCK
Captain Stratton's Fancy
  Westminster LP. Richard Standen, Bass, 1957. *acc*. Frederick Stone.

WOLF
'Verborgenheit'
  Seraphim 60065. Hans Hotter, Bass-Baritone, 1955.

pages 104–116

ARNE
Shakespeare Songs
  HMV CSD 1572. Alexander Young, Tenor, 1964.

BALFE
'Come into the garden, Maud'
  Oiseau lyre DSLO 42. Stuart Burrows, Tenor, 1979.

BUTTERWORTH
A Shropshire Lad
  Columbia. John Cameron, Baritone. *acc*. Gerald Moore.

A Shropshire Lad No. 6. 'Is my team ploughing?'
  Keith Falkner, Bass-Baritone, June 1940. *acc*. Gerald Moore.

DOWLAND
Several songs mentioned in text
  Decca LW5243. Peter Pears, 1956. *acc*. Julian Bream, Lute.

FINZI
'Dies Natalis'
  HMV HQS 1260. Wilfred Brown, Tenor, 1963. *dir*. Finzi (composer's son).

Songs from 'Earth, Air & Rain'
  Complete cycle. SRCS 51. John Carol Case, Baritone, 1970. *acc*. Howard Ferguson.

GIBBS
Silver, Five Eyes
  Private Record. Kenneth Tudor, Bass-Baritone.

GRAINGER
'Six Fishers went a-fishing'
  HMV RLS 748. Peter Pears, Tenor. *acc*. Benjamin Britten.

HÄNDEL
'I know that my Redeemer' Messiah
  HMV HQM. Isobel Baillie, Soprano, 1941.

'He was despised' Messiah
  Decca AKF 1-7. Kathleen Ferrier, Contralto.

'Waft her, Angels' Jephtha
  Decca SKL 4121. Kenneth McKellar, Tenor.
  Pearl GEMM 218. Walter Widdop, Tenor, 1926.

'O ruddier than the cherry' Acis & Galatea
  Händel Soc. HDL 2. Trevor Anthony, Bass, 1947.

HOWELLS
Mally-O
  Private rec. Kenneth Turdor, Bass-Baritone.

Voice

'Come, sing and dance'
Janet Baker, Mezzo-Soprano,
Saga 5213, 1963. *acc*. Martin Isepp.

IRELAND
At Santa Chiara
Saga XID 5207. John Shirley
Quirk, Baritone, 1963.

Lent Lily
In complete cycle, 'Land of Lost
Content'
Argo ZRG 5418. Peter Pears,
Tenor. *acc*. Benjamin Britten.

Sea Fever
Westminster LP. Richard
Standen, Bass, 1957. *acc*. Frederick
Stone.

PARRY
'Love is a bable'
Decca AKF 1-7. Kathleen Ferrier,
Contralto.

PURCELL
'Lord, what is man?'
HMV HQS 1091. Janet Baker,
Mezzo-Soprano, 1967.

The Blessed Virgin's Expostulation
HMV HQM 1015. Isobel Baillie,
Soprano, 1941.

'Mad Bess'
Decca AKF 1-7. Kathleen Ferrier,
Contralto. *acc*. Phylis Spurr.

'Ye twice ten hundred deities' *Indian Queen*
Record Society Set. Richard
Standon, Bass, 1959.

'Sweeter than roses'
Decca SXL 6608. James Bowman,
Alto, 1973. *acc*. Benjamin Britten.

QUILTER
'Now sleeps the crimson petal'
Decca AKF 1-7. Kathleen Ferrier,
Contralto.

'Fair House of Joy'
Decca AKF 1-7. Kathleen Ferrier,
Contralto.

ROSSETER
'When Laura smiles'
CBS 61126. Wilfred Brown,
Tenor, 1969. *acc*. John Williams,
Guitar.
Pavilion SHE 525. Ian Partridge,
Tenor, 1980.

SOMERVELL
'O let the solid ground', 'Birds in the high hall-garden' *Maud*
HMV HQM 1238. Keith Falkner,
Bass-Baritone, June 1940.

'The street sounds' *A Shropshire Lad*
HMV HQM 1238. Keith Falkner,
Bass-Baritone, June 1940. *acc*.
Gerald Moore.

STANFORD
'Soft Day'
Decca AKF 1-7. Kathleen Ferrier,
Contralto.

'Fairy Lough'
Decca AKF 1-7. Kathleen Ferrier,
Contralto.

The Old 'Superb'.
World Record Club SH 135. Peter
Dawson, Bass-Baritone, 1930.
Westminster LP. Richard
Standen, Bass. *acc*. Frederick Stone,
1957.

VAUGHAN WILLIAMS
On Wenlock Edge
HMV HMQ 11. Gervase Elwes,
Tenor, 1909.
HMV HQS 1236. Ian Partridge,
Tenor, 1970.

Silent Noon
Westminster LP. Richard
Standen, Bass, 1957. *acc*. Frederick
Stone.

'Songs of Travel'
Westminster LP. Richard
Standen, Bass, 1957.

Discography

WARLOCK
Piggesnie
Pavilion SHE 525. Ian Partridge, Tenor, 1980.

Sleep
Jupiter JUR 00 A5. Wilfred Brown, Tenor, July 1962. *acc.* Margaret McNamee.

pages 124–138

BERLIOZ
'Voici des Roses' Damnation de *Faust*
Olympus ORL 218. Pol Plançon, Bass, 1904.

BIZET
Cavatina de Leila
Decca SXL 6267. Pilar Lorengar, Soprano, 1966.

Chanson d'Avril
Decca SXL 6577. Marilyn Horne, Mezzo-Soprano, 1974.

Romance de Nadir
HMV ALP 1681. Beniamino Gigli, Tenor, 1931.
RCA ARL 10048. Placido Domingo, Tenor, 1973.
78. HMV C 3409. Heddle Nash, Tenor.

CHAUSSON
Le Charme, Nanny
Decca LW 5201. Gérard Souzay, Baritone, 1959.

Le Colibri, Sérénade Italienne
Electrola IC 063.02375. Elly Ameling, Soprano, 1972.

DEBUSSY
Beau Soir, Romances
SLPM 138758.

DÉLIBES
'Pourquoi dans les bois grands' in 'Highlights from *Lakmé*
Decca SET 488. Joan Sutherland, Soprano.

FAURÉ
Chansons du pêcheur, Lydia, Aprés un rêve, Les Berceaux
WEA C069.11066. Gérard Souzay, Baritone, 1960.

FRANCK
Nocturne
GOUNOD
L'Absent, Serenade
Phonogram SAL 3480 Gérard Souzay, Baritone, 1964.

'Avant de quitter' Faust
Qualiton LPX 11361. György Melis, Baritone, 1969.
RCA Victrola Vic 1340. Lawrence Tibbett, Baritone, 1934.

'Que les songes' Philémon et Baucis
Decca LXT 5269. Gérard Souzay, Baritone, 1962.

LULLY
Air de Charon *Alceste*
Phonogram SAL 3468. Gérard Souzay, Baritone, 1964.

Belle Hermione *Cadmus et Hermione*
SAL 3468. Gérard Souzay, Baritone, 1964.

RAMEAU
Invocation et Hymne *Les Indes Galantes*
Decca LXT 5269. Gérard Souzay, Baritone, 1956.

THOMAS
'Connais tu le pays?' Mignon
Odyssey Y 31738. Risë Stevens, Mezzo-Soprano, 1941.

pages 139–157

BACH
'Bist du bei mir'
HMV ASD 2902. Elly Ameling, Soprano, 1973. *acc.* Dalton Baldwin.

295

Voice

BEETHOVEN
An die ferne Geliebte
Preiser LV 105 Gerhard Hüsch,
Baritone, 1936 (with Schumann's
Dichterliebe)

Geistliche Gedichte – Gellert Lieder
CFP 40025. Hermann Prey,
Baritone, 1962. *acc.* Gerald Moore.

BERG
7 frohe Lieder
Op 2. Nos. 1–4. Concert Hall
CHS. G-12. K. Harvey, Soprano.
dir. Goehr.

BLACHER
13 Ways of Looking at a Blackbird
DGG SLPM 138759. Ernst
Häfliger, Tenor.

BRAHMS
'Der Tod, dass ist die kühle Nacht'
Seraphim 60065. Hans Hotter,
Bass-Baritone, 1953. *acc.* Gerald
Moore.
Preiser LV 48. Josef von
Manowarda, Bass, 1930. *acc.* Árpád
Sándor.
NB HMV SLS 5002 7 Record Set
of Brahms Lieder. Dietrich Fischer-
Dieskau, Baritone, 1974 (various
accompanists).

'Die schöne Magelone'
HMV SAN 291. Dietrich Fischer-
Dieskau, Baritone, 1971 (various
accompanists).

'Die schöne Magelone'
Vox TV 341765. Jakob Stämpfli,
Baritone, 1967.

Vier ernste Gesänge
Electrola IC 147 01 633/4M. Hans
Hotter, Bass-Baritone, Nov. 1951.
acc. Gerald Moore.

Vier ernste Gesänge
HMV HQM 1101. Alexander
Kipnis, Bass, 1931. *acc.* Gerald
Moore.

Ver ernste Gesänge
Columbia CMS 6734. George
London, Bass-Baritone, 1961.

Zigeunerlieder Nos. 1–7, plus No. 11
Electrola IC 063 00826. Christa
Ludwig, Mezzo-Soprano. *acc.*
Gerald Moore.

Liebesliederwalzer
Vox TV 342775. Gachinger
Chorale. *dir.* Rilling, 1970.

'Verrat'
Seraphim 60065. Hans Hotter,
Bass-Baritone, 1955. *acc.* Gerald
Moore.

CORNELIUS
Weihnachtslieder
DGG 2530 108. Hermann Prey,
Baritone, 1973.

'Trauer und Trost' (with 2 others)
Electrola IC 065 01 251. Dietrich
Fischer-Dieskau, Baritone.

FRANZ
'Stille Sicherheit'
Electrola IC 063 29077. Wolfgang
Anheisser, Baritone, 1972.

'Aus meinen grossen Schmerzen'
Preiser SPR 9951. Hans Hotter,
Bass-Baritone.

HAAS
'Die bewiglischte Musiker', Op. 49.
DGG 253019. Dietrich Fischer-
Dieskau, Baritone. *acc.* Jörg Demus.

HAYDN
'She never told her love'
HSLP 2051. Jennie Tourel,
Mezzo-Soprano, 1950. *acc.* Ralph
Kirkpatrick, 18th-century piano.

HINDEMITH
Marienleben
Musicaphon BM 30 SL 15. 14/15.
Gerda Lammers, Soprano.

LOEWE
9 Loewe Ballads (incl. Tom der
Reimer, Edward and Archibald
Douglas)

DGG 136 320. Josef Greindl,
Bass, 1957.
13 Loewe Ballads (incl. Erlkönig,
Meeresleuchten)
   Heliodor 2548 063. Josef Greindl,
Bass. *acc*. Hertha Klust.
12 Loewe Ballads (incl. Edward,
Erlkönig, Tom der Reimer)
   Preiser LV 19. Paul Bender, Bass,
1919/1933.
5 Loewe Ballads (with Brahms,
Wolf and Schubert)
   Preiser LV 48. Josef von
Manowarda, Bass, 1930. *acc*. Árpád
Sándor.

MAHLER
'Um Mitternacht'
   Decca AKF 1–7. Kathleen
Ferrier, Contralto, 1951. VPO. *dir*.
Buno Walter.
'Ich atme einen Linden Duft'
   Decca AKF 1–7. Kathleen
Ferrier, Contralto, 1951. VPO. *dir*.
Bruno Walter.
Kindertotenlieder
   HMV ASD 2338. Janet Baker,
Mezzo-Soprano, 1967. Halle, *dir*.
John Barbirolli.
Des Knaben Wunderhorn Nos. 1/10,
plus 13 and 14
   SDD R.326. Janet Baker, Mezzo-
Soprano, 1966. LPO. *dir*. W. Morris.
5 Ruckert-Lieder
   DGG 2707.082. Christa Ludwig,
Mezzo-Soprano, 1976. Berlin PO.
dir. von Karajan.
   SLS 785. Janet Baker, Mezzo-
Soprano, 1969. New Philharm.
Barbirolli.

MARX
'Japanisches Regenlied'
   Preiser LV 104. Luise Willer,
Mezzo-Soprano.
See also *Caprice 61*
   7 Marx Lieder sung by D. Irving,
Soprano. *acc*. Erik Werba.

MENDELSSOHN
'Auf Flügeln des Gesanges'
   Electrola IC 063 29077. Wolfgang
Anheisser, Baritone, 1972.

MOZART
'Das Veilchen', *'Abendempfindung'*,
and others
   Electrola IC 063 29024. Elly
Ameling, Soprano.
   NB. BASF. Merian 2222637–9.
includes these two Mozart songs and
his 'Warnung', also, Songs by
Wagner, Strauss mentioned in text.

PETERSEN
9 Lieder – settings of Goethe and
Des Knaben Wunderhorn
   DaCamera 90003. Frederick
Dalberg, Bass, 1967.

PFITZNER
'Der Einsame', *'Zum Abschied
meiner Töchter'*, *'Der Gärtner'*,
'Nachts'
   Preiser LV 208. Gerhard Hüsch,
Baritone, 1939. *acc*. composer.
   BASF 2021087–1. (Recital of
Pfitzner Songs) Wolfgang Anheisser,
Baritone, 1973.
'Der Einsame', *'Zum Abschied
meine Töchter'*, *'Nachts'*
   Urania 7053. Margarethe Klose,
Contralto, 1944. *acc*. Michael
Raucheisen.

REGER
3 of Reger's Songs mentioned in
text, plus 29 others
   Electrola IC 065 30143. Wolfgang
Anheisser, Baritone, 1973.
Recital of 20 Reger Songs
   DGG SLPM 139127. Dietrich
Fischer-Dieskau, Baritone, 1973.
acc. Günther Weissenborn.

REICHARDT/ZELTER
Recital of Reichardt Songs and
Zelter Songs
   DGG 2533 149. Dietrich Fischer-
Dieskau, Baritone.

Voice

REIMANN
Engführung
Wergo 60072. Ernst Hafliger, Tenor, 1976 *acc.* Composer.

REUTTER
'Weihnachtskantilene'
DGG 2530219. Dietrich Fischer-Dieskau, Baritone.

3 Hölderlin Lieder
Da Camera 90020. Bernd Weikl, Baritone. *acc.* Jörg Demus.

SCHOECK
'Mit einem gemalten Bande',
'Peregrina'
Disco Jecklin DJ 504. Ernst Häfliger, Tenor. *acc.* Karl Grenacher.

SCHÖNBERG
Buch der hängenden Gärten
Hungaroton SLPX. Erika Sziklay, Soprano, 1980. *acc.* Jenö Jando.

15 Gedichte aus dem Buch der hängenden Gärten
Musicaphon BM 30 SL 1523. Clara Heinius, Soprano. *acc.* Aribert Reimann.

SCHUBERT
Die schöne Müllerin
HMV ASD 381.059. Dietrich Fischer-Dieskau, Baritone, 1962. *acc.* Gerald Moore.
CFP 40043. Ian Partridge, Tenor, 1973. *acc.* Jennifer Partridge.
Decca SXL 2200. Peter Pears, Tenor, 1960. *acc.* Benjamin Britten.

Die Winterreise
Seraphim IC 6051. Hans Hotter, Bass-Baritone, 1955 (also on Electrola 147.01.274/5M). *acc.* Gerald Moore.

Schwanengesang (a Collection).
Seraphim IC 6051. Hans Hotter, Bass-Baritone, 1955. *acc.* Gerald Moore.

'Gretchen am Spinnrade'
HMV HQS 1261. Elly Ameling, Soprano, 1972. *acc.* Jörg Demus.

'An der Mond I', 'An der Mond II'
DGG 2530 229. Dietrich Fischer-Dieskau, Baritone. *acc.* Gerald Moore.

'Grenzen der Menschheit'
Columbia 33 CX 1162. Hans Hotter, Bass-Baritone, 1953. *acc.* Gerald Moore.

'Prometheus'
Seraphim IC 6051. Hans Hotter, Bass-Baritone, 1953. *acc.* Gerald Moore.

'Totengräbers Heimweh'
Decca LW 5235. Heinz Rehfuss, Bass-Baritone, 1955. *acc.* Frank Martin.

SCHUMANN
Liederkreis
HMV ASD 3037. Elisabeth Schwarzkopf, Soprano, 1974. *acc.* Geoffrey Parsons.

Frauenliebe und Leben
HMV ASD 3037. Elisabeth Schwarzkopf, Soprano, 1974. *acc.* Geoffrey Parsons.

Frauenliebe und Leben
Ace of Clubs ACL 307 and Decca AKF 1–7. Kathleen Ferrier, Contralto, 1951. *acc.* Phylis Spurr.

Dichterliebe
Preiser LV 105. Gerhard Hüsch, Baritone, 1936. *acc.* Hans-Udo Müller.
Preiser PR 3145. Hans Hotter, Bass-Baritone, 1955. *acc.* Hans Altmann.

SPOHR
Deutsche Lieder
Electrola IC 063 29072. Anneliese Rothenberger, Soprano, 1972, with Clar. and Pno. accomp.

STRAUSS
'Freundliche Vision'
HMV ASD 2888. Elisabeth Schwarzkopf, Soprano, 1966. Berlin RSO Szell.

'Freundliche Vision', 'Traum durch die Dämmerung'
Heliodor 2548 729. Heinrich Schlusnus, Baritone, 1950. Orch. *acc.*

'Morgen'
HMV ASD 2493. Elisabeth Schwarzkopf, Soprano, 1965.
NB These two songs with *'Zueignung', 'Morgen', 'Ständchen',* etc., 18 in all, Phillips SAL 3483. Gerard Souzay, Baritone, 1963. *acc.* Dalton Baldwin.

'Heimliche Aufforderung', 'Zueignung'
Electrola IC 063 29077. Wolfgang Anheisser, Baritone, 1973. *acc.* Günther Weissenborn
These are included on Phillips SAL 3483 above.

TELEMANN
Frauenzimmer
Pye Vanguard HM 2021005–7. Edith Mathis, Soprano, 1972.

WAGNER
Wesendonck Lieder: Fünf Gedichte von Mathilde von Wesendonck
EMI SDD. Kirsten Flagstad, Soprano, VPO. Boult, 1955.

WEBERN
Einheit: Fünf Stefan Georglieder
Musicaphon BM 30 SL 1523. Clara Heinius, Soprano. *acc.* Aribert Reimann.

WOLF
Excerpts from *Goethe Lieder, Spanische Liederbuch*, with complete Mörike and Eichendorff settings
Electrola IC 181.01.470/6. Dietrich Fischer-Dieskau, Baritone.

'Gesang Weylas'
Preiser LV 48. Josef von Manowarda, Bass, 1930. *acc.* Árpád Sándor.

'Verborgenheit'
Seraphim 60065. Hans Hotter, Bass-Baritone, 1955. *acc.* Gerald Moore.

'Fussreise'
Seraphim 60065. Hans Hotter, Bass-Baritone, 1955. *acc.* Gerald Moore.

'Heimweh'
Decca SXL 6207. Hermann Prey, Baritone, 1965. *acc.* Gerald Moore.

'Der Feuerreiter'
Preiser LV 60. Heinrich Rehkemper, Baritone.

'Der Freund'
Preiser LV 58. Hans-Hermann Nissen, Bass-Baritone.

Michaelangelo Lieder
Electrola IC 147.01.633/4M. Hans Hotter, Bass-Baritone, May 1953. *acc.* Gerald Moore.

Italienische Liederbuch
Phonogram 6700.041. Elly Ameling, Soprano, 1968. *acc.* Dalton Baldwin.

Spanische Liederbuch
DGG 2707035. Dietrich Fischer-Dieskau, Baritone, 1967. *acc.* Gerald Moore.

ZELTER
See under **REICHARDT**

ZILLIG
'Lieder des Abschieds' (with 6 other Zillig Songs)
Musicaphon BM 30 SL 1534. Clara Heinius, Soprano. *acc.* Aribert Reimann.

pages 158–169

DENZA
'Luna fidel', 'Non t'amo più'
Electrola COO 47.00657. Enrico Caruso, Tenor.

GOBBI OPERATIC SELECTION
DONIZETTI
'Una furtiva lagrima' L'Elisir
d'Amore
RCA SER 5613. Placido
Domingo, Tenor, 1971.
LEONCAVALLO
Prologue *Pagliacci*
Decca SXL 6083. Robert Merrill,
Baritone, 1963.
PUCCINI
'Che gelida manina' La Bohème
Pearl GEMM 192. Tito Schipa,
Tenor, 1925.
Pye Ember GVC 13. Enrico
Caruso, Tenor.
'Quando m'en vo' La Bohéme
Conifer SH 289. Ljuba Welitsch,
Soprano.
ROSSINI
'Largo al factotum' Il Barbiere di
Siviglia
Qualiton LPX 11361. György
Melis, Baritone, 1969.
'Senza mamma' Suor Angelica
Decca SXL 6548. Maria Chiara,
Soprano, 1971.
VERDI
'La Donna è mobile' Rigoletto
RCA SER 5613. Placido
Domingo, Tenor, 1971.

ITALIAN ARIAS OF **SEVENTEENTH AND**
EIGHTEENTH CENTURIES
1. Hungaroton SLPX 1289:
Sándor Svéd, Baritone, 1966.
2. USSR D.019475-6: Alexander
Vedernikov, Bass, 1968.

TOSTI
Recital of Songs
9500 743. José Carreras, Tenor,
1980.
'Parted'
Decca SLO 43. Stuart Burrows,
Tenor, 1979.
'Addio'
Telefunken SHZ EL 92. Rudolf
Schock, Tenor.

Malia (with 3 others by Tosti)
Decca SXL 6650. Luciano
Pavarotti, Tenor, 1974.

pages 170–180

FALLA
El Amor Brujo
SDD 134. Marina de Gabarain,
Mezzo-Soprano, 1960. Orch. S.
Rom. *dir*. Ansermet.
HMV SXLP 30140. Victoria de
los Angeles, Soprano, 1965. Philhar.
dir. Giulini.
Victor LM 1054. Nan Merriman,
Mezzo-Soprano, 1950. Hollywood
Bowl Orch., Stokowski.

Nos. 3, 4, 5 from *7 Canciones*
Populares Españolas
SDD 324. Teresa Berganza,
Mezzo-Soprano, 1959.
SXL 6577. Marilyn Horne,
Mezzo-Soprano, 1973.

3 Mélodies (Gautier). Saga 5409. Jill
Gomez, Soprano, 1975, *acc*. John
Constable.

GRANADOS
Tonadillas al Estilo Antiguo (Nos.
1–6 only).
Saga 5409. Jill Gomez, Soprano,
1975.
SXL 6866. Pilar Lorengar,
Soprano, 1978.
Canciones Amatorias (7 Songs).
SXL 6866. Pilar Lorengar,
Soprano, 1978.
HMV ASD 2957. Victoria de los
Angeles, Soprano, 1961.
La Maja Dolorosa (3 Songs).
HMV ASD 2260. Victoria de los
Angeles, Soprano, 1961.

GURIDI
'Como quieras que divine',
'Mananita de San Juan', *Seis*
Canciones Castellanas
SDD 206. Teresa Berganza,
Mezzo-Soprano, 1962.

MOMPOU
Combal del Somni (4 Songs).
HMV ASD 2517. Victoria de los
Angeles, Soprano, 1969.

MONTSALVATGE
Canciones Negras (5 Songs).
Decca SXLP 30147. Victoria de
los Angeles, Soprano, 1972.

NIN
'Asturiana', 'Pano Murciano'
HMV ASD 3656. Victoria de los
Angeles, Soprano, 1979.

RODRIGO
Cuatro Madrigales Amatorias
WEA K 53563. Sandra Browne,
Mezzo-Soprano, 1978.

Note: Recital Records of Spanish
Songs.
HMV ASD 3656. Nin,
Montsalvatge, de Falla. Victoria de
los Angeles, Soprano, 1979.
HMV SXLP 30147. Granados,
Guridi, Rodrigo, Montsalvatge,
Mompou. Victoria de Los Angeles,
Soprano, 1961/72.
Saga 5409. de Falla (10), Turina,
Granados. Jill Gomez, Soprano,
1975.
Decca SXL 6866. Granados (18
Songs). Pilar Lorengar, Soprano,
1978.

pages 181–198
*Many of the following American
songs do not appear in UK
catalogues. It has not been possible to
hear some of these but they are listed
nevertheless, for the sake of interest.*

ANTES
'Go, Congregation, go!'
LM 57. Margaret Turner,
Soprano.

BACON
Songs from Emily Dickinson
Cambridge CRS 1707. Helen
Boatwright, Soprano.

See also 'Songs by American
Composers' (with Songs by Beeson
and Rorem).
Desto 7411/2. Eleanor Steber,
Soprano.

CARPENTER
Gitanjali
Set of songs to Joyce's poems, 2-
record set. Duke Univ. Press DWR
6417/8.

COPLAND
12 Poems of Emily Dickenson, Old
American Songs.
Argo ZRG 862. Robert Tear,
Tenor, 1976.

12 Poems of Emily Dickenson,
'Hermit Songs' (Barber)
Enigma K 53541. Sandra Browne,
Mezzo-Soprano, 1977.

'Zion's Walls', 'At the River'
RCA LSB 4091. Shirley Verrett,
Mezzo-Soprano, Carnegie Hall, 30
Jan. 1965.

FOSTER
*'Beautiful dreamer', 'Jeanie',
'Camptown Races', 'O Susanna',
'My old Kentucky home', 'Old folks
at home', Old Black Joe',* plus 7
others
RCALP 6035. Robert White
Tenor, 1981.

GRIFFES
'By a lonely forest pathway'
Victor LP. Eleanor Steber,
Soprano, 1946.
Also in Duke Univ. Press DWR
6417/8. John Hanks, Tenor.

HAGEMANN
'Do not go, my love'
2-record set. Duke Univ. Press
DWR 6417/8.

HOPKINSON
*'My days have been so wondrous
free', 'My generous heart disdains'*
Only on LM57. Margaret Truman,
Soprano.

Voice

IVES
100th Anniv. Issue.
Columbia M4 32504 Set – 25
Songs. Helen Boatwright, Soprano,
1974.
Overtone 7
24 Songs. Helen Boatwright,
Soprano, 1974.
Columbia M 30229. 'American
Scenes, American Ports', Evelyn
Lear, Soprano and Thomas Stewart,
Baritone.
18 Songs.
DGG 2530696. Dietrich Fischer-
Dieskau, Baritone, 1976.

ROREM
War Scenes
Desto 7101. Donald Gramm,
Baritone.
'Songs by Rorem'
Desto 6480. Beverley Wolff,
Soprano.
'Songs by Rorem'
Odyssey 32160274. Phylis Curtin,
Soprano.
Note: See also American Anthology
(Gershwin, Copland, Cage,
Thomson and Carter).
Unicorn RHS 353. Meriel
Dickinson, Mezzo-Soprano, 1977.

BOULEZ
*normally listed as French but
included in this section.*
Le Marteau sans maître
CBS 73213. Yvonne Minton,
Mezzo-Soprano, 1973 (directed by
the Composer).

SCHÖNBERG
*normally listed as an Austrian
composer but included in Miss
Boatwright's contribution.*
Pierrot Lunaire (Cycle):
Hungaroton SLPX 11385. Erika
Sziklay, Soprano, 1970.
CBS 76720. Yvonne Minton,
Mezzo-Soprano, 1978.

pages 199–216
NB. *There is only one Soviet record
company; it trades outside the Soviet
Union on the* Melodiya *label. In Russian pressings, each side is numbered,
therefore* D 012 115–6 *is simply one
double-sided LP.*

BALAKIREV
Songs of Balakirev, incl. The Song
of the Golden Fish
D 014799–80. Zara Dolukhanova,
Mezzo-Soprano; Sergei Lemeshev,
Tenor; Alexei Ivanov, Baritone;
Alexander Pirogov, Bass.

BORODIN
4 solos from *Knyaz Igor*
Yaroslavna's Aria, Vladimir's
Aria, Igor's Aria, Galitzky's Aria,
with other items from a complete
recording on a 'Highlights' disc,
Eurodisc K86722 R
M. Tugarinova, Soprano; Elena
Obratsova, Mezzo-Soprano;
Vladimir Atlantov, Tenor; Ivan
Petrov, Artur Eizen, Alexander
Vedernikov, Basses.

DARGOMIZHKY
The Miller's Song. Act 1 *Russalka*
In 4-record set D 035105/12.
Mark Reizen, Bass.

GLINKA
*'I remember the wonderful moment',
'Midnight Review'*
In HMV ASD 547. Boris
Christoff, Bass, 1963.
Farewell to St. Petersburg (Cycle)
D 04530–1. Georgi Nelepp,
Tenor.
'Midnight Review'
See D 011859–60. With Songs by
Borodin, Cui, Sviridov and others of
Glinka – Boris Gmyria, Bass.
See D 021567–8. With Songs by
Borodin, Tchaikovsky, Rimsky,
Mussorgsky, etc. Alexander
Vedernikov, Bass.

Pearl GEMM 173. Norman Allin, Bass, 1927. in English.
Sunday Opera SYO 12. Robert Easton, Bass, 1928.

'A Life for the Tsar' (now called 'Ivan Sussanin' in USSR)
Sussanin's Aria. *They guess the truth*
D 023183–4. Maxim Mikhailov, Bass.
Delta TQD 3010. Fedor Chalyapin, Bass-Baritone, 1910.

'Russlan i Ludmilla'
Farlaf's Patter-Rondo. CM 02929 30. Yevgeni Nesterenko, Bass, 1973.
Columbia COLH 100. Fedor Chalyapin, Bass-Baritone, 1927.

GRETCHANINOV
'Over the Steppe', 'The Captive'
Victor 1434. Alexander Kipnis, Bass, Nov. 1939.

KABALEVSKY
Shakespeare Settings. D 06943–4. Pavel Lisitsian, Baritone.

MEDTNER
See HMV DB 6718/24 and 6900/6. (78s), Medtner Soc. Vols. II/III. Margaret Ritchie, Soprano and Oda Slobodskaya, Soprano.

'Arion'
See MS M10–35697/700. 2 record set of Pushkin Settings. Irina Arkhipova, Mezzo-Soprano.

MUSSORGSKY
Songs and Dances of Death (with other Mussorgsky Songs)
HMV ALP 2310. Boris Christoff, Bass, 1958
ND 03378–9. Boris Gmyria, Bass.
Supraphon SUA. ST 50038. Kim Borg, Bass, 1963.
Columbia CMS 6734. George London, Bass-Baritone, 1961 (with Brahms Serious Songs).

Sunless
HMV ASD 3700. Yevgeni Nesterenko, Bass.

Opera, *Boris Godunov*
Act II Monologue. HMV ALP 1323. Boris Christoff, Bass, 1962. ('Highlights' record from complete rec.)
Columbia COLH 100. Fedor Chalyapin, Bass-Baritone, 1925.
D 035105/12. Mark Reizen, Bass.
Death Scene – in HMV ALP 1323 – 'Highlights' recording above. Boris Christoff, Bass.
Varlaam's Song (with Act II Monologue)
Decca LW 5607. Rafaël Arié, Bass, 1951.
Pimen's Monologue. D 023183–4. Maxim Mikhailov, Bass.
Private Rec. Norman Lumsden, Bass.

Opera, *Khovanchina*
Martha's Song. Melodiya ASD 2475. Irina Arkhipova, Mezzo-Soprano.
Dosifey's Aria – DGG 135090. Kim Borg, Bass.
(with other excerpts from Russian Opera: Borodin, Tchaikovsky, etc.), 1963.

RACHMANINOFF
'Before my window', 'Vocalise', 'How fair this spot' (plus 3 others).
C10-05075-6. Bella Rudenko, Soprano, 1975.

'Lilacs'
Supraphon 10499. Kim Borg, Bass, 1963.
(with Songs by Tchaikovsky, Borodin, Rimsky, etc.)

'How fair this spot', 'Lilacs', 'Before my window', 'To the Children'
HMV ASD 2928. Nikolai Gedda, Tenor, 1974.

Voice

'Before my window', 'How fair this spot', 'The Dream'
D 013755-6. Ivan Kozlovsky, Tenor.

Opera, Aleko, 'Cavatina'.
D 011845-6. Ivan Petrov, Bass.
CM 02929-30. Yevgeni Nesterenko, Bass, 1973.

RIMSKY-KORSAKOV
Opera, Sadko
Song of the Hindu Guest.
Electrola IC 147 28963–4. Rudolf Schock, Tenor, 1948.
Song of the Viking Guest.
D 035105/12. Mark Reizen, Bass.
(with operatic arias by Mussorgsky, Rubenstein, Dargomizhky, plus songs by Borodin, Tanaiev, Glinka, etc. 4-record set.)
CM 02929-30. Yevgeni Nesterenko, Bass, 1973.

'On the Hills of Georgia'
D 013331–2. Boris Gmyria, Bass. (see below).

'The prophet'
in Reizen Set above, D 035105/12 (see under Boris Godunov).

'What is my name for thee', 'Hebrew Song'
D 013331–2. Irina Arkhipova, Mezzo-Soprano (recital of Rimsky Songs with other artists).

SHOSTAKOVITCH
Preface to the Complete Collection of my Works and Brief Recollections, 5 Romances to words from 'Krokodil' Magazine.
HMV ASD 3700. Yevgeni Nesterenko, Bass. 1979.

TCHAIKOVSKY
NB. Complete Tchaikovsky Songs (but not '16 Children's Songs' Op. 54) on 6-record set, D 02611/22 with Tomara Milashkina, Soprano; Irina Arkhipova, Mezzo-Soprano; Georgi

Nelepp, Tenor; Yuri Mazurok, Baritone; Boris Gmyria, Bass, etc, etc.

'At the Ball', 'To the Forest', 'None but the lonely heart', 'Don Juan's Serenade'
Supraphon 10499. Kim Borg, Bass, 1963. acc. Alfred Holeček.
D 011997-8. Boris Gmyria, Bass.
D 08355-6. Ivan Petrov, Bass.

'To forget so soon', 'Why did I dream of you?', 'None but the lonely heart'
CM 02099-100. Alexander Ognivtsev, Bass.

Opera, Yevgeni Onyegin
Tatyana's Letter Scene
– EMI. World Record SH 289. Ljuba Welitsch, Soprano.
Lenski's Aria – Electrola IC 147 2893/4M. Rudolf Schock, Tenor.
Prince Gremin's Aria – DGG 135090. Kim Borg, Bass, 1963.

Other Tchaikovsky Song Recitals
10 Songs. D 028449-50. Georg Ots, Baritone.
D 015301-2. Ivan Petrov, Bass.
Melodiya LDX 78453. Yuri Mazurok, Baritone.
CM 02143-4. Valentina Levko, Mezzo-Soprano.
D 016337-8. Mark Reizen, Bass.
Note: Supraphon 50499, rec. 1963, includes 4 Tchaikovsky Songs (above), 2 by Rubenstein, 2 by Rachmaninoff, 2 by Rimsky, 2 by Mussorgsky, 2 Tanaiev and others by Gretchaninov, etc.
Kim Borg, Bass, acc. Alfred Holeček.

pages 216–217

DVOŘÁK
Biblical Songs
Supraphon SUAST 50898. Věra Soukupová, Mezzo-Soprano, 1972.

Gipsy Songs
  Pinnacle Supraphon 1121349.
Jindřich Jindřàk, Baritone, 1975
(with 8 Love Songs, op. 83).
11 Love Songs
  Private Rec. Norman Lumsden,
Bass, 1958.

JANÁČEK
*Diary of a Young Man who
Disappeared* (Cycle).
  Supraphon SUA 10288. Stepanká
Stepanová, Mezzo-Soprano and
Beno Blachut, Tenor, 1958.

page 217

CHOPIN
Songs, Op. 74.
  ARGO ZRG 814. Robert Tear,
Tenor, 1975.

MONIUSZKO
*'Nadzieja', 'Dwie Zorze', 'Aniele
Moj', 'O wladco swiata'*
  Polonia London EP 1030. Marjan
Nowakowski, Bass, 1963.

pages 218-230

ALNAES
4 Songs
  Ace of Diamonds SDD 209.
Kirsten Flagstad, Soprano.

BERWALD
2 Songs, plus others by Thrane,
Grieg, Wolf, Strauss and Liszt.
  Conifer BELL III. Elisabeth
Söderstrom, Soprano, 1980.

GRIEG
'Autumn Storm'
  Ace of Diamonds SDD 209.
Kirsten Flagstad, Soprano.

'A Dream', 'I love thee' (with 14
other Grieg Songs).
  Decca Eclipse ECS 622. Kirsten
Flagstad, Soprano. *acc*. Edwin
MacArthur.

KILPINEN
*'Laullule', 'Tunturille',
'Kirkkorannassa', 'Suvilaulu'*
  Decca SXL 6522. Martti Talvela,
Bass, 1971. *acc*. Irving Gage.
20 Songs, *acc*. composer's daughter
and under composer's personal
supervision.
  Preiser LV 80. Gerhard Hüsch,
Baritone, 1938.
Tunturilauluja (plus others by
Kilpinen).
  Decca, Kim Borg, Bass, 1961.

SIBELIUS
Miscellaneous Songs.
  Decca 9983. Kim Borg, Bass,
1958.
  Decca SDD 248. Kirsten Flagstad,
Soprano, 1959. LSO, *dir*. Olvin
Fjelstad.
  Decca SXL 6046. Tom Krause,
Baritone, 1963.

pages 231-239
*(State Record Company is Qualiton-
Hungaroton)*

BALASSA
Antinomia
  LPX 11494. Erika Sziklay,
Soprano.

BARTÓK
Opera, *A Kékszakállú Herceg Vára*
(Duke Bluebeard's Castle)
  Hungaroton LPX 11001. Klára
Palankay, Mezzo and Mihály
Székély, Bass, 1956. Budapest PO.,
dir. Ferencsík.
  Hungaroton LPX 11486. Katolin
Kasza, Soprano and György Melis,
Baritone. Budapest PO., *dir*.
Ferencsík.

BOZAY
'Paper slips', 'Two Landscapes'
  LPX 11412. Erika Sziklay,
Soprano, 1968, with Clar. and
Cello. accomp.

Voice

FARKAS
Fruit Basket (12 Songs), *Naptar*
(Calendar – 12 Songs)
LPX 12054. Klára Takács, Mezzo-
Soprano, 1977.

FOLK SONGS
(1). arr. *Bartók* – 'Szekély Friss'
Hungaroton LPX 1253. Erzsébet
Török, Mezzo-Soprano.

(2). arr. *Kodály* – 'Dudanóta' (Vol.V).
Hungaroton LPX 11722. Erzsébet
Török, Mezzo-Soprano.

KADOSA
7 Poems of József, 3 Poems of
Radnoti.
LPX 1235. Erika Sziklay,
Soprano.

4 Poems of Nelly Sachs.
LPX 11713. Erika Sziklay,
Soprano.

KODÁLY
'Mónár Anna', *'Kádár Kata'*, *'A
Közelitö tél'* (Approaching Winter),
'Sirni, sirni' (Cry, cry).
LPX 11450. György Melis,
Baritone and Márta Szirmay,
Mezzo-Soprano, 1969.

'Tiszán innen', *'Toborzó'*, in opera,
Háry János
Decca SET 399/400. György
Melis, Baritone and Erzsébet
Komlóssy, Mezzo-Soprano, 1969.
LSO Kértesz.

'Kit kéne elvenni?' (Which one
should I marry?) in opera
Szekélyfóñо
LPX 11504-5. Sándor Pálcso,
Tenor, 1970.

7 Songs, Op. 6, 5 Songs, Op. 9 and
others.
SLPX 11766/7. Éva Andor, Ilona
Tokody, Sylvia Sass, Sopranos;
Attila Fülöp, Tenor; István Gati,
György Melis, Sándor Solyom-Nagy,
Baritones; József Gregor, Kolos
Kováts, Basses.

LISZT
Songs, Vols. I/II
LPX 1224/5.
Vol. III
LPX 1272.
Both discs: Erika Sziklay, Margit
Laszlo, Maria Werner, Judit Sándor,
Sopranos; Marta Szirmay, Mezzo;
Alfons Bartha, József Simandy,
József Réti, Tenors; György Melis,
Zsolt Bende, Baritones.

'O quand je dors'
BASF 22226948. Paul Schöffler,
Bass-Baritone, 1951 (with songs by
Loewe, Schubert, etc.)

pages 270–276

BRAHMS
'Feldeinsamkeit'
Electro IC 147 01 633/4M. Hans
Hotter, Bass-Baritone, May 1951.
acc. Gerald Moore.

'Von ewige Liebe'
Preiser LV 82. Sigrid Onegin,
Mezzo-Contralto.

DUPARC
'Exstase'
HQS 1258. Gérard Souzay,
Baritone. *acc.* Dalton Baldwin.

FAURÉ
'Clair de Lune'
HMV, SXLP 30147. Victoria de
los Angeles, Soprano, 1961. *acc.*
Gerald Moore.

SCHUBERT
'Du bist die Ruh'
Preiser LV 207. Margarethe
Klose, Contralto. *acc.* Michael
Raucheisen.
HMV ASD 2263. Dietrich
Fischer-Dieskau, Baritone, 1965.
acc. Gerald Moore.

'Litanei', 'Nacht und Träume'
Fontana 6747 059. Hermann Prey,
Baritone.

'Erlkönig'
Preiser LV 257. Gerhard Hüsch,
Baritone, 1939. *acc.* Hans-Udo
Müller.

'Der Musensohn'
Preiser LV 257. Gerhard Hüsch,
Baritone, 1939. *acc.* Hans-Udo
Müller.

'Ave Maria'
SLS 812. Janet Baker, Mezzo-
Soprano, 1971. *acc.* Gerald Moore.

SCHUMANN
'Ich grolle nicht', 'Am Rhein'
See *Dichterliebe*

Bibliography

Armhold, Adelheid *Singing*
  Tafelburg-Uitgewers, Cape Town (1963)

Cranmer, Arthur *The Art of Singing*
  Dennis Dobson (1957)

Dossert, Deane *Sound Sense for Singers*
  J. Fischer & Bro. Press (1932)

Duey, Philip A. *Bel Canto in its golden age*
  Kings Crown (1951)

Franca, Ida *Manual of Bel Canto*
  Coward McCann (1959)

Garcia, Manuel *Hints on Singing*
  Ascherberg (1894)

Gardiner, Julian *A guide to good singing and speech*
  Cassell (1968)

Grout, Donald Jay *A history of Western Music*
  W. W. Norton (1960)

Grout, Donald Jay *A short history of Opera*
  Columbia University Press (1947)

Grove Dictionary of Music (3rd edition)
  Macmillan (1928)

Kagen, Sergius *On studying singing*
  Rinehart & Co. Inc. (1950)

Kennedy-Scott, Charles H. *Madrigal Singing*
  O.U.P. (1931)

Mancini, C. B. (1716–1800) *Practical reflections on the figurative art of singing*
  P. Buzzi, Gorham Press (1912)

Bibliography

Plunket-Greene, H.   *Interpretation in Song*
  Macmillan and Stainer and Bell (1912)

Richards, Anthony N. G.   *Farinelli in Spain*
  (1951)

Scholes, Percy A.   *Concise Oxford Dictionary of Music*
  O.U.P. (1952)

Stevens, Denis   *A history of Song*
  Hutchinson (1960)

Warlock, Peter   *The English Ayre*
  O.U.P. (1926)

Wood, Sir Henry J.   *The gentle art of Singing*
  O.U.P. (1927)